Harrap's Dictionary of
Business & Finance

ACKNOWLEDGEMENTS

Clark Robinson Limited wish to acknowledge the help of all those who have contributed to the creation of this dictionary. In particular, we would like to thank the following: Peter Bently, Martin D H Bloom, Michael Dash, Stephen Hobbiss, David Pierce, William Saville, Nick Thomson, Damien Timmer, John Walford.

Harrap's Dictionary of

Business & Finance

HARRAP'S *REFERENCE*

First published in Great Britain 1988
by Harrap Ltd
19 – 23 Ludgate Hill, London EC4M 7PD

© Clark Robinson Limited, 1988

ISBN 0 245 – 54571 – 9 (cased edition)
ISBN 0 245 – 54660 – x (plastic edition)

Copy preparation: Clark Robinson Limited, London
Typesetting: Action Typesetting Limited, Gloucester
Printed in Great Britain by Richard Clay Ltd, Bungay, Suffolk

Preface

The world of business and finance is ever-changing, and as it changes, its language changes too. New trading regulations, the introduction of more sophisticated electronic communications and information equipment, and the upsurge of new markets, have all been catalysts for growth in the language of every form of business activity. As the world is transformed ever more rapidly into a "global village", words from other languages begin to filter through into English. In a fast-moving environment such as this, shorthand terms and acronyms become standard speech, and even words coined in moments of levity may acquire currency, at least for a while.

Harrap's Dictionary of Business and Finance has been created to facilitate access to this mercurial and potentially confusing world. It concentrates on words and phrases in everyday business usage, and endeavours to make clear not only their meaning, but also, where appropriate, the way in which they are used. Many words have come into currency while this Dictionary was being compiled and special care has been taken to include these with definitions that are as accurate as possible at the time. However, many new words evolve and change their meanings subtely. Some disappear as fast as they appeared, and we can be certain that yet other new words will emerge even as the Dictionary runs on press. Because a dictionary, like the language it seeks to represent, is a living thing, the editors will always be glad to hear about alternative definitions or usages, and indeed, any new words.

It is the purpose of this Dictionary to assist learning. Therefore, single-word entries are listed alphabetically, with any variations and abbreviations. Terms with two or more words are listed under the noun so that a comparison may be drawn. Furthermore, entries are cross-referenced to related entries. Many of the entries include sentences to give the reader a clear idea of the way in which terms are used. Optional words or phrases, in brackets, are ignored for the purposes of alphabetization.

L. B. — Clark Robinson Limited, London 1988

A

A1 The best. The term originates in shipping, where A1 denotes a vessel that is in perfect condition, the letter refering to the condition of the hull and the number to the condition of the ship's trappings.
"The ship was registered A1 at Lloyd's."
More generally,
"The food at that restaurant is always A1."
See also **Lloyd's**.

AAA = triple A

AAR Abbreviation of **against all risks**.

abandonment Act of passing ownership of insured property to the insurer in the event of a total **loss**. This takes place in certain circumstances, if the loss is unavoidable, or if the cost of repair exceeds the value of the property. Abandonment occurs most often in marine insurance when a vessel is declared dangerous or unseaworthy.
"The ship was stranded on a reef and could not be salvaged, so the owners declared a constructive total loss and gave the underwriters notice of abandonment."
See also **insurance, marine; loss, constructive total; underwriter**.

abatement Reduction.
"They expected an abatement in the number of companies making staff redundant within the next two months."
The term should not be confused with **rebate**.

ABC code = code, commercial

ability-to-pay taxation = taxation, ability-to-pay

above-the-line Term in accounting that distinguishes between extraordinary and exceptional **costs**. *See also* **advertising, above-the-line**.

above par Normally used of a **share** that has a market value above its denomination or par value. *See* **value, par**.
"The shares of G & B Electronics were traded above par for the first time today."

absenteeism Absence from work for no valid reason.
"The high rate of absenteeism contributed to the authorities' decision to make New Year's Day a public holiday."

absolute advantage Argument in favour of international trade, put forward by **Adam Smith** (1723-90). Absolute advantage applies where, for example, two countries can both produce two commodities they need, but country A is more efficient at producing commodity X and country B is more efficient at producing commodity Y, so they would both profit by concentrating on the particular commodity each produces best and trading them.

abusive shelter *(US)* = **shelter, abusive**

a/c Abbreviation of **account**.

acc Abbreviation of **account**.

acceleration Term that can be applied to an increase in the rate of a price trend.

accelerator principle Theory that growth in production is directly related to the level of investment.

acceptance Broadly, the act of agreeing to do something. In business and finance, it can be taken in four ways.
First, acceptance is one of the two stages in negotiating a **contract: offer** and acceptance. A contract is complete only when the offer has been formally accepted by the **acceptor**.
Second, it is the act of writing on a **bill of exchange**, by which the acceptor accepts the bill and agrees to pay the **drawer**.
Third, it is used to denote a bill that has been endorsed in the above way and has thereby been accepted.
Fourth, in **insurance**, acceptance is notice given by the insuror that specified cover will be given.

acceptance for honour supra protest Situation that occurs when a bill of exchange is turned down (or protested) and is then accepted by another party, thereby saving the honour of the **drawer**.

accepting (acceptance *US*) house Financial institution whose business is concerned mainly with the negotiation of **bills of exchange**, by either guaranteeing or accepting them. Accepting houses usually operate in much the same way as merchant banks. *See* **bank, merchant**.

acceptor Person who accepts either the terms of a **contract**, or a **bill of exchange**. When a bill of exchange is accepted, the **drawee** becomes the acceptor.

accommodation Money that is lent to someone for a brief period. *See also* **bill, accommodation**.

accord Frequently used in the USA to mean any form of agreement, especially between companies, the business communities of different countries or the governments of two countries.
"The tie-up accord between the country's two leading biotechnology companies will mean some swift and important advances in the field."

accord and satisfaction When one party has discharged its obligations under a **contract**, it may elect to release the other party from its obligations. When this is done in return for a new **consideration**, the release is known as accord and satisfaction.

account Very generally, a note kept of any financial transaction. It is abbreviated to a/c, acc or acct. The term has three broad meanings.
  First, it is used in banking to designate an arrangement made to deposit money with a **bank, building society** or a number of other financial institutions. An account may be of many different types, usually indicated by a qualifying word, depending on the conditions of withdrawal, level of interest, minimum amount of money in the account, or other factors.
  Second, on the London Stock Exchange it is a period of two weeks (when Bank Holidays occur, this period usually extends to three weeks) in which trading is carried out. Broadly, transactions are made in the two weeks of the account and the relevant paperwork is carried out during the following week, followed by payments (settlements), made on

the sixth business day after the end of the account. This method of
working means that transactions may be made with deferred payment,
enabling **speculation** to take place.
"Prices fell sharply at the end of the last account."
  Third, it is a record of financial transactions, and in this sense, often
termed **accounts**.
" He spent three days preparing his accounts for the Inland Revenue"

account day The Monday ten days or six business days after the end of
  each stock exchange account, on which all settlements must be made.
  Also known as settlement day.

accounts payable Accounts on which a company owes money.

accounts receivable Accounts on which there is a **debt** owed to a
  company. *See also* **factoring**.

annual accounts Report submitted annually, showing the current
  financial state of a company and the results of its operations for that
  year. *See also* **report, annual**.

appropriation account One of the elements of a profit and loss account, in
  which the division of profit is detailed. *See* **account, profit and loss**.

bank (banking US) account Arrangement to deposit money with a bank.
  See **account, current; account, deposit**.

below-the-line accounts Those items included in company accounts that
  refer to the distribution of profits. Details of *e.g.* **dividends** would thus
  be included in the below-the-line accounts.

blocked account Bank account that becomes subject to restrictions,
  especially those imposed by governments.
"After the coup, the new military government blocked the accounts of
all foreign nationals."
See also **account, frozen**.

budget account Form of current account on which an agreement is made
  that the holder pays into the account a fixed amount each month and is
  then guaranteed **overdraft** facilities to cover periods of high
  expenditure.

capital account Part of the **balance of payments**, which refers to
  international movements of **capital**, including intergovernmental loans.

charge account Alternative term for credit account. *See* **account, credit**.

consolidated accounts If a company has subsidiary companies, each subsidiary has its own set of profit and loss accounts, but these must also be consolidated to form accounts for the whole group. These are known as consolidated accounts. *See* **account, profit and loss**.

credit account Account offered by **retail** stores and chains, which allows a customer to buy goods on the spot (usually by means of a plastic card) and to pay for them at the end of the accounting period or in **instalments**. Some current accounts also pay **interest**. *See* **account, current**.

current account Term with two meanings.

First, it is the most common type of bank account for personal use, which pays no interest but funds may be accessed immediately by writing a **cheque**. In this sense it is also known as a cheque account, or in the USA, a checking account.

Second, it is part of the balance of payments, which refers to national **income** and **expenditure**, including visible and invisible trade. *See* **trade, invisible; trade, visible**.

deposit account Account that pays **interest**, but sometimes notice has to be given before funds may be withdrawn.

discretionary account Account into which discretionary funds are placed. *See* **fund, discretionary**.

drawing account Bank account from which funds may be withdrawn at will.

expense account Money that is allowed to an executive for the purposes of travel and entertainment of clients.

external account Account held with a UK bank, by a non- resident.

final accounts Normally, the annual accounts. However, the term may also refer to the final report submitted by a liquidator at the end of a **liquidation**. *See* **accounts, annual**.

frozen account Account that is affected by a court order, with the consequence that no money may be deposited or withdrawn.

group accounts Alternative term for consolidated accounts. *See* **accounts, consolidated**.

impersonal accounts On a **book-keeping** ledger, accounts that deal with **capital** and **assets** (the real accounts) or income and expenditure (the nominal accounts) or a combination of the two. The only element of the ledger the impersonal accounts do not cover is the record of debtors and creditors (the personal accounts). *See* **accounts, personal; accounts, real; accounts, nominal**.

imprest accounts System of accounting that must balance against a specified figure. *E.g.* a petty cash account may be balanced against a figure of £250. At any time, the cash present plus the total of vouchers should add up to this figure. *See* **cash, petty**.

income and expenditure account Similar in form to a profit and loss account, an income and expenditure account is a record of all cash transactions over a given period. *See* **account, profit and loss**.

interim accounts Short financial statement produced by a company (often unaudited) in the middle of the year, halfway between publication of the annual accounts. *See* **accounts, annual**.

nominal accounts One of the three parts into which a book-keeping **ledger** is divided. The nominal accounts are the records of **income** and **expenditure**. *See also* **accounts, impersonal; accounts, personal; accounts, real.**

numbered account Bank account that is identified by a number only, in order to keep the identity of the account holder confidential. Bank accounts administered by banks in Switzerland are most often numbered.

personal account Term with two meanings.
First, on the stock market, it is an account maintained by a dealer on his or her own behalf and at personal risk, independent of the company for which he or she works.
Second, in **book-keeping**, it is an account that lists **creditors** and **debtors**.

profit and loss account Annual summary of a company's financial operations, required by law to be submitted by every trading company. The profit and loss account has three sections: the trading account, the profit and loss account and the appropriation account. The profit and loss section of the account takes the profit or loss figure from the trading account, and after accounting for income not concerned with trading, and expenses such as those incurred in administration, deducts **tax** from the final profit or loss figure. *See also* **account,**

appropriation; account, income and expenditure; account, trading.

real accounts On a book-keeping **ledger**, the record of **assets** and **capital**. *See also* **accounts, impersonal; accounts, nominal; accounts personal**.

realization account When a company is being wound up and its assets are being realized in order to pay creditors, a bank account may be opened in which to deposit receipts and upon which to draw payments to creditors. This is known as a realization account.

sales account Document presented to a consignor when goods are sent to a foreign country for sale through an **agent**. The agent submits to the consignor an account of sales made, along with details of the agent's **commission**, expenses and the final net **profit** on the sale.

stated account Account that shows how much one party owes another. The stated account is agreed upon by both parties and is legally binding unless it can be shown to be false.

statement of account Not to be confused with stated account, a document sent from a creditor to a debtor, detailing recent transactions and amounts owing, sometimes with terms for payment. *See also* **account, stated**.

trading account first section of a profit and loss account, in which income and expenditure concerned in a company's trading activities are detailed. The final figure on this account is the company's **gross profit**. *See* **account, profit and loss**.

zero-balance account US Cheque account operated by a company by which cheques are drawn against the account balance, which at the start of the day is always zero. At the end of the day the value of all cheques drawn is totalled and the amount is transferred into the account, so that the account balance reverts from a **debit** to zero.

See also **executive, account**.

accountancy Body of knowledge relating to financial matters. Also the work done by an **accountant**, involving knowledge of the law as it affects financial matters (*e.g.* the **tax** laws), **book-keeping**, and the preparation of annual accounts. *See* **accounts, annual**.

accountant Any person practising accountancy, whether qualified or not. The term may be prefixed with various other terms, denoting the specialism of the accountant (*e.g.* **cost accountant**, **management accountant),** that accountant's position within a business (*e.g.* **chief accountant**), or his or her professional qualification (*e.g.* **certified accountant**, **certified public accountant**, **chartered accountant**).

certified accountant Accountant who has passed the examinations of the Association of Certified (and Corporate) Accountants, and is either an associate or fellow of the Association.

certified public accountant US Accountant who has passed professional accounting examinations.

chartered accountant In England and Wales, an accountant who has passed the examinations of the Institute of Chartered Accountants and is either an associate or a fellow of the Institute. In Ireland and Scotland, a chartered accountant is a fellow or associate of the Institute of Chartered Accountants in Ireland, and Scotland, respectively. The main difference between a chartered and a certified accountant is that the training of the former normally involves a period of time working with a firm of accountants and that of the latter does not.

chief accountant Accountant within a business who deals with all company accounting and the provision of financial information to managers and **directors,** in particular the financial director.

cost accountant Accountant who specializes in reckoning the **cost** of manufacturing a unit of a product, taking into account such variables as cost of raw materials and **labour**, and thereby making a **projection** of probable cost at the planning stage of a project. This in turn enables the manufacturer to **tender** a price to a prospective buyer.

financial accountant Accountant who is concerned with the movement of cash, rather than with money that is involved in production (*see* **accountant, cost**). The financial accountant is responsible for overseeing the level of cash available for paying debts and for investment, and for managing and recording all financial transactions.

management accountant Accountant who is involved in the day-to-day running of a business, providing **management** information upon which managers are able to make decisions. The distinction between cost and management accountancy is now becoming increasingly blurred.

See also **auditor.**

accounting Very broadly, the activity of recording and verifying all monies borrowed, owed, paid or received.

accounting concepts Basic concepts by which sets of accounts are made up. The four generally accepted accounting concepts are the **accruals concept**, **consistency concept**, going concern concept and **prudence concept**.

accounting principles Another term for **accounting concepts.**

accounting standards Standards by which annual accounts are made up, set by professional bodies such as the Accounting Standards Steering Committee (ASSC) in the UK. *See* **accounts, annual**.

cost accounting Work undertaken by a cost accountant. *See* **accountant, cost**.

current cost accounting (CCA) Also known as inflation accounting, a method of accounting that takes changes in prices due to **inflation** into account, adjusting values of assets, costs, etc.

current purchasing power accounting (CPP) Method of accounting that has been advocated since the 1970s, and which involves stating all accounts in terms of a unit of purchasing power, calculated from a price **index**. Current purchasing power accounting has not yet become a common method.

historical cost accounting Method of assigning value to *e.g.* assets for accounting purposes. In historical cost accounting, the original cost of an asset is taken into account, rather than its replacement cost. *See* **accounting, current cost**.

inflation accounting Alternative term for current cost accounting. *See* **accounting, current cost**.

See also **cost, accounting; ratio, accounting**.

accredited Describes someone who is authorized to act on behalf of a company or individual.

accrual Gradual increase by addition over a period of time.

accruals concept Principle used in **accounting** by which **income** and **expenditure** are taken into the profit and loss account for the period in which they occur. This method of accounting is useful in that it

9

pulls together **receipts** and the **costs** incurred in generating them, avoiding the time lag between the time **income** is received and the time **liabilities** become due. *See* **accounting concepts; account, profit and loss; consistency concept; prudence concept**.

See also **benefits, accrued; charges, accrued; dividend, accrued; interest, accrued**.

acct Abbreviation of **account**.

acid-test = ratio, acid-test

acquisition The takeover of control of one company by another or by an individual is known as an acquisition of the target company. The purchase of an **equity** stake in the target company is the usual method of acquisition.

acquisition trail Course embarked upon when a company becomes **acquisitive**.
  "A & C Electonics reported improving finances after its takeover of B D Small Electronics, indicating a possible return to the acquisition trail."

acquisitive Company that is always on the look out to grow by taking over other companies. *See also* **takeover**.

ACT Abbreviation of advance corporation tax. *See* **tax, advance corporation**.

act of God Event caused by nature which is so unpredictable as to be unavoidable, *e.g.* the timing and location of earthquakes or floods. Acts of God are normally insured against as a matter of course.

action Equity stake.
"The company seemed to have a great deal of potential and so she bought herself a piece of the action."

actionnaires French term, referring to the holders of shares in a French public company (*société anonyme*). *See* **company, public limited**.

active Busy, constantly changing. *See* **partner, active; stock, active**.

actuals Physical commodities that may be purchased on the commodities market and delivered immediately. Also known as spot goods. *See also* **futures**.

actuary Someone who assesses probabilities on the basis of reliable statistical information. Most often employed in **insurance**, an actuary works out the likelihood of an event happening, information that determines the level of **premiums**.

additional personal relief For **taxation** purposes, the additional amount allowed against a married woman's earned **income** over and above the marriage personal **allowance** which the couple receive jointly. *See also* **relief, tax**.

adjudication Act of giving judgement. Adjudication may be the act of resolving a legal problem, industrial dispute or of declaring **bankruptcy**. *See also* **bankruptcy, adjudication of; order, adjudication**.

adjuster (**adjustor** *US*) In **insurance**, someone who calculates **losses**.

average adjuster Someone who calculates how much money is to be paid on an insurance claim.

loss adjuster Someone who arranges payment of an insurance claim between the policy holder and the insurance company.

administration Broadly, the sum of actions involved in the organization or management of a company. *See* **expenses, administration**.
  In law, however, administration is either the winding-up of the estate of a deceased person in the absence of an executor or in the event of intestacy, or it is the winding-up of a company. Both cases involve the court appointment of someone to act as administrator.

letters of administration Court order that appoints someone to act as administrator in either of the two above cases.

ad Abbreviation for advertisement or a Latin prefix to various terms.

ad referendum When referring to a contract, ad referendum indicates that while the contract has been agreed and signed, there are still some matters to be discussed.

ad valorem In **taxation**, ad valorem (literally, according to the value) indicates that tax is calculated as a percentage of the value of the transaction, rather than charged at a fixed rate. *E.g.* value-added tax is paid as a percentage of the value of the goods or services sold, whereas car road tax in the UK is paid at a fixed rate. *See* **tax, value-added**.

ADR Abbreviation of American depositary receipts, which are issued by American banks declaring that a certain number of a company's shares have been deposited with them. ADRs are denominated in dollars and although they usually refer to non-American companies, they are traded on the American markets as US **securities**.

advance Part-payment for work contracted made ahead of total payment, before the goods or services contracted for have been rendered. Sometimes, if payment depends upon sales, the advance is set against those sales.
" It is usual to pay rent in advance."
" The author received a £1000 advance against royalties."

ways and means advance Advance paid by the Bank of England to the consolidated fund. *See* **fund, consolidated**.

See also **arrears**.

adverse Bad or, at the very least, unhelpful. *See* **balance of trade, adverse**.

advertising Range of activities that surround the practice of informing the public of the existence and desirability of a product. The main purpose of advertising is to boost sales, or, in the case of charities and national bodies, to provide information or solicit contributions.

above-the-line advertising Advertising that uses the traditional media of television, radio, cinema, newspapers and magazines and posters.

advertising agency Company that specializes in planning and executing advertising campaigns.

aerial advertising There are several methods of aerial advertising: banners trailed from aircraft; writing in smoke in the sky; writing on the sides of hot air balloons and airships. Aerial advertising is now restricted, mainly to airshows.

below-the-line advertising Advertising by direct mail and merchandising etc.

consumer advertising Advertising directed at the consumer. This form of advertising may be either informative or persuasive. *See* **advertising, informative; advertising, persuasive**.

informative advertising Advertising that concentrates on providing the target with information about the product, thereby helping consumers to choose between products.

persuasive advertising Advertising that concentrates on the characteristics of the product, often intimating that use of the product will enhance the consumer's personal status in some way.

prestige advertising Form of advertising in which the company sponsors prestigious sporting or cultural events, *e.g.* in 1987-1988, the national football league was sponsored by Littlewoods and therefore known as the Littlewoods Cup.

trade advertising Advertising that is restricted to one section of the public, *i.e.* those people (such as retailers) who operate within the advertiser's own industry.

advertorial Form of advertising, usually found in newspapers and magazines. The advertorial is printed in such a way that it looks like an editorial or article, in an effort to add the authority of the publication as a recommendation of the product.

advise fate Request from a collecting **banker** to a paying banker to confirm that the **cheque** to which it refers will be honoured. This confirmation cannot be given until the paying banker receives the cheque, because the **account** to which the cheque refers may have had other **debits** made to it, or the **payer** may stop the cheque. It is a speedy method of confirmation, and it circumvents the use of a **bankers' clearing house**.

AE Abbreviation of account executive. *See* **executive, account**.

AFBD Abbreviation of Association of Futures Brokers and Dealers, an **SRO**. *See* **Financial Services Act**.

affidavit Statement or declaration made in writing and witnessed by a commissioner for oaths (such as a **solicitor**), often for use in legal proceedings.

affirmative action program *US* Scheme to avoid or discourage discrimination in employment, equivalent to equal opportunities employment in the UK.

affreightment Carriage of goods by sea.

after date Written on a **bill of exchange**, after date indicates that the bill will become due a certain (specified) period after the date on the bill. Hence, the bill might read, "60 days after date, we promise to pay..." *See also* **after sight; at sight**

aftermarket Trading in **stocks** and **shares** after they have made their initial debut on the **market**. The aftermarket may also be the market in components and services arising after a product has been sold. This is also known as the add-on market.

"The flourishing computer aftermarket is created by enthusiasts who soup up old models in preference to buying new ones."

after-sales service Acts performed by a manufacturer or supplier after the goods have been sold, such as repair, maintenance work or perhaps training (in the case of computers, etc.). After-sales service packages are frequently put together as inducements to buy, especially in the sale of branded capital goods.

after sight Written on a **bill of exchange**, term that indicates that the period for which the bill is drawn is to be calculated from the date upon which the **acceptor** first saw (or accepted) it. This date is normally written on the bill by the acceptor. *See also,* **after date; at sight**.

AG *Ger* Abbreviation of the German *Aktiengesellschaft*, denoting the equivalent of a public limited company (plc) in the UK. *See* **company, public limited**.

against all risks (AAR) Term used in marine **insurance**, indicating that a vessel and its cargo have been insured against all insurable eventualities. Roughly equivalent to fully comprehensive insurance of road vehicles.

agency Term with two meanings.

First, it is a person or **company** that represents another in a particular field.

Second, it is a contractual **agreement**, by which one party agrees to represent another, the agent's word becoming as binding in the affairs of the other as if the latter had acted on his/her own behalf.

agency of necessity Situation that arises when an **agent** acts to safeguard the principal's interests, without the principal's permission. This situation can arise only when (a) the principal cannot be reached, (b) there is a **contract** of agency already in existence between the two parties and, (c) immediate action is absolutely necessary. If these conditions exist, then the agent's actions are legally binding on the principal.

advertising agency Company that plans and implements **advertising** campaigns on behalf of other companies.

credit agency (credit bureau US) Company that gathers information on the credit-worthiness of individuals and companies, and distributes this information to those providing credit facilities.

sole agency Agreement by which only one party represents a principal either in a certain capacity or in a particular geographical area.

agenda List of matters to be discussed at a meeting. An agenda can constitute a legal document.

agent Person or **company** that has entered into a **contract** of **agency** with another party, and acts as its representative.

commission agent Agent who is paid a **commission**, calculated as a percentage of sales.

general agent Agent with authority to represent the principal in all matters concerning a particular activity.
"The sales representative acted as general agent for the company."

manufacturer's agent Agent who agrees to market a company's products, usually in a specific geographical area, on a **commission** basis. Such agents are often employed overseas to enhance a manufacturer's **export** trade.

mercantile agent Person or company that takes part in **factoring**.

special agent Agent with authority to perform one particular action on behalf of another.

universal agent Agent with unlimited authority to close contracts on behalf of the principal.

See also **attorney, power of; warranty of authority**.

aggregate Sum total.

agio **Commission** or **charge** made by a **bank** or **bureau de change** in return for converting cash from one **currency** to another.

AGM Abbreviation of annual general meeting, a **shareholders'** meeting, required by law to be held yearly by every public company. An AGM is normally used to discuss the annual **report** and **accounts**, to announce **dividends** and to elect **auditors** and **directors**. This is often the only opportunity shareholders have to air their views. *See* **company, public limited**. *See also* **EGM; gadfly**.

agreement Verbal or written contract between two or more parties to explain the way they intend to act in respect of each other.

blanket agreement Agreement that covers many, if not all, items concerning one party's relationship with another.

exclusive agreement Agreement whereby an agent is authorized to act as sole agent in representing a particular company or product.

gentleman's agreement Verbal agreement between two parties who trust each other and have a strong sense of honour.

knock-for-knock agreement In motor **insurance**, agreement between a group of insurers who agree that no question of responsibility will be discussed and that each company will pay for damage to its own clients' vehicles, so long as the client is covered for such damage by his or her **policy**.

listing agreement Agreement to abide by the rules of the London Stock Exchange when applying for listing.

See also **Official List**.

recourse agreement In **hire purchase** transactions, agreement that enables the seller to repossess the goods in the event of the purchaser being unable to make the payments required.

standstill agreement When bidding for shares in a **target** company, agreement that no more bids will be made for the time being.

threshold agreement Agreement between an employer and employees (or the representative union) that wages will increase only if the rate of **inflation** reaches or exceeds a certain level, the threshold.

trade agreement Agreement between two or more countries or two groups of countries (*e.g.* the **EEC** or **COMECON**) regarding general terms of trade.

unlocking agreement Agreement, often attached to a contract, by which one party may, under certain conditions, require the other to buy him out, thereby ending or unlocking the agreement between them.

agribusiness Industry that encompasses and includes farming and all commercial aspects of agriculture.

agricultural bank = bank, land

agricultural disarmament Reduction in protectionist practices, such as price subsidizing, in agriculture.

all-in Including everything, most often used to describe a **price**. "She bought the lot at auction for £25 all-in."

allocatur **Certificate** of approval of **costs** incurred in an action (*e.g.* **liquidation**) for **taxation** purposes.

allonge Slip attached to a **bill of exchange** that provides extra space for the noting of **endorsements**. Allonges were most useful when bills of exchange moved freely from one holder to another, but are now less common.

allotment Broadly, the sharing out of something, usually funds, among a group of people.

allotment of shares When a company issues **shares** by publishing a
prospectus and inviting applications, allotment is the assignment of
shares to each applicant. In cases where the issue is oversubscribed,
shares are allotted in proportion to the quantity requested and so
applicants do not always receive the number of shares they originally
requested. *See also* **oversubscription; application and allotment**.

letter of allotment Means by which shares are allotted, a letter of
allotment may be used as proof of ownership and entitles the holder to
certificate for the number of shares stated in the letter. Not to be
confused with an **allotment note**. *See* **note, allotment**.

all-out Complete, very serious.
"The nurses' union decided against all-out strike action."

allowance Term with two meanings.
First, it is money that is allotted (allowed) to individuals for a specific
reason, or a provision made for unusual or uncertain events.
Second, it is the amount deducted for one of various reasons before
income is calculated for **tax** purposes.

age allowance Tax allowance made to an individual over the age of 65 or
a married couple where one partner is over that age.

capital allowances Amounts deducted from a company's **profits** before
tax is calculated, to take into account **depreciation** of capital **assets**
(such as vehicles, plant and machinery, and industrial buildings).

child allowance Payment made in cash by the Department of Health and
Social Security in the UK, to parents for each child they are supporting.
There is an additional allowance payable to one-parent families.

entertainment allowance Amount an executive is allowed to spend on the
entertainment of clients or prospective clients during the course of his
or her business.

initial allowance Amount deducted from a company's profits for the
purposes of calculating tax in the first year after **acquisition**.

investment allowance Alternative term for capital allowance. *See*
allowance, capital.

marriage personal allowance Amount a married couple in the UK may
earn before they are obliged to pay income tax. *See* **tax, income**.

personal allowance Amount a person may earn before he or she is obliged to pay income tax. This amount varies from year to year. *See* **tax, income**.

travel allowance Amount added to a person's **salary** to cover the cost of travelling to work, or journeys undertaken in the course of work.

See also, **relief, tax; insurance, national**.

allowed time = **time, allowed**

all risks policy = **policy, all risks**

alphanumerics In computing, alphanumerics are the letters, numbers and punctuation marks that appear on a keyboard, screen or printout.

alpha Stock Exchange categorization of the top 100 most actively traded shares with a large capitalization value. *See also* **beta**; **delta**; **gamma**.

amalgamation The coming together or unification of two or more companies. *See also* **merger; takeover**.

ambulance stock = **stock, ambulance**

American Express (AMEX) International **credit** company based in the United States. *See also* **card, credit**.

American Plan Also known as the white plan or the Bretton Woods Agreement, a proposal to encourage international **trade** by fixing international currency **conversion** rates and enabling those currencies to be freely converted. *See also* **Bretton Woods Conference**.

AMEX Abbreviation of **American Express** or American Stock Exchange.

AMH Abbreviation of automatic (or automated) materials handling, a computerized system designed to move materials and components from one location to another in a factory or warehouse.

amortize To pay off a **debt** by means of payments over a period of time.

More specifically, in **accounting**, the cost of a fixed **asset** is written in to the profit and loss account over a period of years, rather than being taken into account when it is first bought. The cost of the asset has been amortized when this period is over. *See* **account, profit and loss**. "The capital cost of the packaging equipment will be amortized over 5 years."
See also **depreciation**.

analysis Determination of the composition or significance of something. In business and finance, an analysis can be a detailed study or investigation of a particular subject, often culminating in a report, upon which executives may base their decisions.

analysis-paralysis What happens when managers spend their time having endless meetings and writing interminable reports, but never making any decisions.

cost analysis Examination of the **cost** of producing a particular product, normally undertaken before the project is begun.

fundamental analysis Analysis of the **value** of a company's **stock**, in order to predict movements in its share prices.

technical analysis Analysis of the changes in price of a company's **stock**, based on past movements in the value of its shares; also called chartism.

analyst Person who undertakes **analysis**.

technical market analyst US Someone who studies the stock market and predicts changes on the basis of market trends and the state of the market as a whole.

fundamental market analyst US In contrast to the modus operandi of the technical market analyst, the fundamentalist takes the performance of the company in question as the basis for prediction of share-price movements.

annual Once a year. It is used to qualify many terms. *E.g.* annual **charges**, annual general meeting (*see* **AGM),** annual **report**, annual **return**, annual **value**.

annualized percentage rate (APR) Rate of **interest** charged on a monthly basis (*e.g.* on a **hire purchase** transaction) shown as a yearly **compound** rate.

annuitant Somebody who takes out an **annuity**.

annuity Personal investment plan whereby a person pays a certain amount of money to an institution such as an **assurance** company, either as a lump sum or in instalments, and is repaid that money plus the investment income it accrues during the annuitant's lifetime as a **pension** or guaranteed **income**. There are many different types of annuity.

annuity certain Annuity that is payable over an agreed period, such as 10 or 15 years, rather than over the lifetime of the annuitant.

contingent annuity Annuity that is paid to the annuitant only in the event of a certain set of circumstances arising. *E.g.* a wife may take out a contingent annuity for her husband which becomes payable only in the event of her death.

deferred annuity Annuity that requires payment of the premium some time before the payments are due to start.

Hancock annuity Annuity taken out by a company to provide an employee with income during retirement. The capital used by the company in this way is deductible as an **allowance** against corporation tax.

immediate annuity Annuity that provides the annuitant with payments immediately the assurance company has received the investment.

self-employed annuity Annuity restricted to self-employed people, proprietors of and partners in businesses, and employed people who are not eligible to join a **pension** scheme. This kind of annuity provides for a retirement pension out of gross income, there being tax relief on this kind of contribution up to a certain ceiling. *See* **relief, tax**.

annul To make void in law, to cancel.
"The contract was annulled by the court."

antedate To put on a document, *e.g.* an **invoice** or a **cheque**, a date which is already past.
"The invoice was antedated to 1 December of last year."
See also **postdate**.

anti-trust laws *US* Legislation in the United States, enacted to prevent the formation of **monopolies**. Similar to the Monopolies and Mergers Act in the UK.

AOB Abbreviation of any other business. AOB normally appears at the end of an **agenda** and provides an opportunity for discussion of any matters not already dealt with or arising too late for inclusion on the formal agenda.

application and allotment System whereby a company may issue **shares**. This is done by publishing a **prospectus**, inviting applications from institutions and individuals to buy shares, and then allotting shares to those who take up the offer. *See also* **allotment; stag**.

apportion To share out. The term is normally applied to **costs**.
"They decided to apportion start-up costs equally between the members of the co-venture."

appreciation Increase in value. In **accounting**, appreciation is an increase in value of (fixed) **assets**.
"Over the years the company directors were pleased to see their office-block appreciate."
See also **depreciation**.

apprentice Traditionally, a (young) person who agrees to work for a period of years under a skilled worker, in order that the apprentice may learn the worker's skills. Nowadays appprenticeships often cover a wide variety of skills and may also contain an element of college study.

appro Abbreviation of **approval**.

appropriation Act of putting aside (funds) for a special reason.
"They decided to appropriate funds from the production budget to set up a marketing department."
There are three specialist meanings of the term.
First, in company accounting, it is the division of pre-tax **profits** between corporation **tax**, company **reserves** and **dividends** to shareholders. The term works in the same sense in a **partnership** situation.
Second, in the shipping of produce, the appropriation is the document

by which the seller identifies to the buyer the relevant unit in the shipment.

Third, if a **debtor** makes a payment to a **creditor** and does not specify which debt the payment is in settlement of, the creditor may appropriate it to any of the debts outstanding on the debtor's account. This is often known as appropriation of payments. *See also* **account, appropriation**.

APR Abbreviation of **annualized percentage rate**.

arb *US* Shortened form of **arbitrage**.

arbitrage Practice of dealing on two markets almost simultaneously in order to profit from differing exchange **rates**. Arbitrage may take place when dealing in **commodities, bills of exchange** or **currencies**. It only occurs in situations where prices and returns are fixed and in this sense arbitrage may be contrasted with **speculation** in that there is little risk involved. In the USA, often shortened to arb.

index arbitrage US Process of selling stocks at the same time as buying stock-index futures, or vice versa. A form of program trading.

risk arbitrage US Practice of buying in to a takeover bid in the expectation that share prices will rise.

arbitrager (*or* **arbitrageur**) Person who practises **arbitrage**.

arbitration In disputes arising out of a **contract**, the parties involved may either go to court or appoint someone (an arbitrator) to settle the dispute. The agreement to go to arbitration does not preclude either of the parties taking legal proceedings if they desire. *See also* **umpirage**.

Ariel Name of a computerized system that makes possible share dealing between subscribers (all of whom are institutions) without having to deal through the London Stock Exchange.

ARM Abbreviation of adjustable rate mortgage. The **interest** payable on this type of **mortgage** rises and falls along with interest rates in general.

arrangement Generally, the settlement of any financial matter. More specifically, a deed of arrangement is an agreement between a **debtor** and some or all of his **creditors**, reached in order to avoid the debtor's **bankruptcy**. Arrangement may be encountered in various forms: as a letter of licence, deed of inspectorship, **assignment** of property or a deed of composition. It may take place either before or after a bankruptcy petition has been presented to the courts.

arrears Money owed but not yet paid.
" Having been out of work for several months, she found that her rent was in arrears."
See also **advance**.

arrestment Scottish term for **attachment**.

articles of association = **association, memorandum of**

ASAP Informal abbreviation of as soon as possible.

as per advice Term normally found as a note on a **bill of exchange**, indicating that the **drawee** has already been notified that the bill has been drawn on him.

assay Testing of a metal or ore to determine the proportion of precious metal it contains. Assay most often applies to metals used in coinage, and to gold and silver. Metals assayed are stamped with a hallmark and an **assay mark**.

assay master Official who is responsible for the testing and grading of metals in the above way.

ASSC Abbreviation of Accounting Standards Steering Committee. *See* **accounting standards**.

assented In a situation where a company is threatened with a **takeover**, assented stocks or shares are those whose owner is in agreement with the takeover. In these circumstances, there may arise separate markets in assented and non-assented stock. Assented stock may also be stock whose owner is in agreement with a proposed change in the conditions of issue.

assessment Act of calculating **value**.
"Her income was assessed for tax."

"The insurance company made an accurate assessment of the value of his possessions."

asset Something which belongs to an individual or a company and which has a **value**, *e.g.* buildings, plant, stock, but also **accounts receivable** and stock. There are several types of assets for business purposes, and they are usually classified in terms of their availability for **exchange**.

asset backed Term that refers to investments which are related to tangible assets, *e.g.* property, so that the investment participates in **growth** which can be easily determined. *See* **assets, tangible**.

asset-based financing Loans secured on a company's assets, especially its accounts receivable or its stock.

asset play US Company, the major part of whose value is based on its assets rather than its operations.

asset stripping Practice, normally frowned upon, whereby a company is bought so that the buyer may simply sell off its assets for immediate gain.

capital assets Another term for fixed assets. *See* **assets, fixed**.

current asset Asset that is used by a company in its day-to- day operations, *e.g.* raw materials, etc.

fictitious assets Assets that do not exist but are entered onto a company's **balance sheet** to balance the books. *E.g.* a trading **loss** may be one example of a fictitious asset for tax purposes.

fixed assets Sometimes also known as **capital assets**, assets used in the furtherance of a company's business, *e.g.* machinery or property.

floating asset Alternative term for current asset. *See* **asset, current**.

frozen assets In contrast with liquid assets, frozen assets are those that may not be converted into ready money without incurring a **loss** of some kind, or which may not be converted because someone has a claim on them.

invisible asset Alternative term for intangible asset. *See* **asset, tangible**.

liquid assets Assets which may be readily converted into money. The most liquid of all assets is **cash**.

non-performing asset US That part of a company's **capital** that is currently yielding no **return**, and on which none is expected. fixed assets are generally classified as non-performing. *See* **asset, fixed**.

quick assets Another name for liquid assets. *See* **assets, liquid**.

tangible assets Literally, assets that may be touched, such as buildings or stock. Tangible assets may be contrasted with intangible (or invisible) assets, which are those that are not visible, such as a company's goodwill or the expertise of its staff.

working assets All the assets of a company except its capital assets. Working assets include outstanding debts, stocks of raw materials, stocks of finished product and cash in hand. Also known as current assets.

See also **management, asset; value, asset**.

assignment Legal transfer of a property, right or obligation from one party to another. Assignment takes place most commonly where a **contract** is involved.

associate Term prefixed adjectivally to indicate a company or individual linked in some way to another. *See* **company, associate; operations, associated**.

association Group of people or companies with a common interest. *E.g.* a **trade association** is a group of companies operating in the same business, who come together to provide information and services to each other. Association is also what happens when a company is formed.

memorandum of association Document that has to be registered and filed at Companies House in the UK, giving details of a company's particulars and aims. It is accompanied by the **articles of association**, which sets up the internal regulations for the company's operation, and states, among other things, the powers of the directors.

assurance Personal investment plan which provides for an event that will certainly happen, as opposed to an event that may happen (*see* **insurance**). There are many forms of assurance policy.

endowment assurance Similar to life assurance, but money is paid out after a certain stated date, rather than upon death. *See also* **endowment**.

life assurance Probably the most common form, life assurance is a plan whereby the policy holder pays a **premium** over a period of time and when the person whose life is assured dies, payment is made to the **beneficiary**.

term assurance Insurance policy whereby a premium is paid to cover a certain sum of money over a certain period (term). If the person insured dies during this period, then the sum is paid. If he or she survives this period, then nothing is paid on the policy. Term assurance is often used to cover loans.

unit-linked assurance policy Policy whereby the profits from the life assurance policy are invested in a **portfolio** in units, thus potentially providing additional **revenue**.

See also **unit trust**.

at and from In marine insurance, at and from refers to a policy which covers the vessel and its cargo both in port and at sea. *See* **insurance, marine**.

at best Instruction to a **broker** to buy or sell **shares** or **commodities** at the best possible price. *See also* **at limit**.

at call Money at call has been borrowed but must be repaid on demand. *See also* **at short notice**.

at limit Instruction to a **broker** to buy or sell **shares** or **commodities** with a limit on the upper and lower prices.

ATM Abbreviation of automatic telling (*US* teller) machine. An ATM is a computer-linked machine, usually mounted on the wall of a bank or other financial institution, which dispenses cash, statements and balances on production of a card and the provision of the correct **PIN number**.

at par = **parity**

at short notice Describing money that is borrowed for a very short period of time, say twenty-four or forty-eight hours, usually at a low **interest** rate. *See also* **at call**.

at sight Note on a **bill of exchange** indicating that payment is due on presentation of the bill. *See also* **after sight**.

at-the-money option = **option, at-the-money**

attaché Junior diplomat.

commercial attaché Diplomat who specializes in representing the commercial interests of his or her country.

attachment Act of court whereby the court is able to recover money owed by a debtor in order that the creditor may in turn pay the court. **Arrestment** is the equivalent of attachment in Scottish law.

attorney In the UK, someone who is legally authorized to act for another, or a person practising at the bar. In the US, however, the term is more often used to denote a **lawyer**.

power of attorney Legal agreement giving one person the authority to act in legal matters on behalf of another.

attractive stock = **stock, attractive**

at warehouse **Goods** or **commodities** that are waiting at a warehouse either to be bought or delivered to a customer. A price at warehouse (or ex warehouse) does not normally include delivery costs. *See also* **goods, spot; futures**.

auction Method of selling goods in public. The auctioneer acts as an agent for the seller, offers the goods and normally sells to the highest bidder (for which service the auctioneer charges a **commission).**

Dutch auction Form of auction in which the seller begins by proposing a high price and gradually lowers the price until someone agrees to buy.

mock auction Auction that is in some way illegal. This may occur in several cases: when goods are sold for a price lower than the highest bid; when some goods are given away in order to attract bidders; when those who have not already bought lots are excluded from bidding; when part or all of the agreed price is privately returned to the bidder.

audit Examination of the **accounts** of a company. It is a legal requirement in the UK that all company accounts be scrutinized annually by a qualified **auditor**.

audit trail US System whereby each stage of a transaction is formally recorded.

internal audit Audit of a company's books that takes place virtually continuously and is undertaken by internal staff, rather than by an external auditor. Internal auditing is carried out in order to monitor company profitability and guard against fraud.

sales audit US Method of calculating the state of the **retail** trade, by comparing the throughput of money against stock.

auditor Person appointed by a company or other organization to perform an **audit**.

autarky (autarchy) Country that is economically self-sufficient, consuming only and all of what it produces. The concept of an autarky is normally used as a model in analyses of international trade.

authenticate To state that something is true. *E.g.* an **auditor** signs a company's **accounts**, thereby authenticating them.

authority Broadly, authority is the given power to act in a certain way. Hence, a **banker** receives an authority from a client to operate the account in a certain way, or an **agent** receives authority to act in such a way on behalf of his or her principal.

automatic (automated) materials handling = AMH

automatic telling machine = ATM

AVC Abbreviation of additional voluntary contribution. *See* **contribution**.

average Single number or value that indicates the general tendency of a collection of numbers or values. The average of *n* values is the sum of the values divided by *n*. *See* **adjuster, average; date, average due; earnings, average available; pricing, average cost; revenue, average**.

avoirdupois System of weights used in the UK and USA, now being gradually replaced by the metric system.

axe Used as a verb, the term means to stop abruptly or to cut back (normally for financial reasons).
"The R & D department was the first to be axed when the company found it was in financial trouble."

B

back Term with two meanings.
First, it is used adjectivally to refer to the past.
Second, to back is to lend money to a project to enable it to start or continue operating.
"He finally found a bank to back his idea. It is lending him £50,000."
See also **date, back; duty, back; interest, back; tax, back**.

backing away *US* Failure of a securities dealer to carry through a deal at the price he or she has quoted. Backing away is usually frowned upon in all markets.

back-to-back Form of **credit** by which a finance house acts as an intermediary between a foreign seller and a foreign buyer, concealing the identity of the seller. The seller passes to the finance house the documents relevant to the sale and the house will re-issue them to the buyer in its own name. *See* **house, finance**.

back door Method by which the Bank of England may assist discount houses when they are short of funds. It does this by buying treasury bills at the market rate. *See also* **bill, treasury; front door; house, discount**.

backer Person or institution that backs projects or operations.
"She found it relatively easy to find a backer for such an interesting business proposition."

backfreight **Freight** for the return of cargo paid by the **consignor** when goods are not delivered through the consignor's own fault, or are refused by the **consignee**.

backhander Bribe or unofficial payment in cash for work done.
"You won't get any orders from that company's purchasing manager unless you give him a backhander."

back-in **Poison pill** tactic sometimes used by the shareholders of a company threatened by **takeover**, whereby the shareholders sell their holdings back to the company at a price agreed with the board.

backing Financial support given by a **backer**.

back month On financial **futures** markets, those contracts that are being traded for the month that is furthest in the future.

back office Alternative term for **backroom**.

backroom *US* Informal name given to the department in a stockbroking firm that deals with matters other than the buying and selling of shares, *e.g.* share **dividends**, shareholder registration, payments.

backroom backlog US Delay in processing stockbroking transactions, caused by a large volume of business.
"A huge backroom backlog followed the deregulation of the London market."

backwardation Two meanings are possible.
   In a commodity market, it is the situation in which a future price is lower than the spot price, because of excessive present demand, which is expected to fall as time passes. Opposite, in commodity terms, to contango.
   In stock markets, the situation in which the highest bid price is higher than the lowest offer price, making it theoretically possible to buy from one market maker and sell to another immediately, at a profit. *See also* **price, choice**; **price, touch**.

bagging the Street *US* Concealment of information about the sale of **stock** from dealers and specialists by institutional investors or **brokers**. Such information may include reasons why the stock is being sold off, and the number and price of the shares in question.

bailment Act of placing goods into the care (but not possession) of someone else. The person who places the goods is the **bailor** and must be the rightful owner. The **bailee** is the person who receives the goods.

bail out To go to the rescue of a company that is experiencing financial difficulties by providing it with **capital**.

bailout *US* Government intervention in the affairs of a public company to prevent it going bankrupt, providing loans at low interest, or tax concessions.

Bailout also means the withdrawal of capital from a public company by its founders before the public has a chance to do so.

balance Quite apart from its general applications, the term is used, primarily in double-entry book-keeping to refer to the sum owed or owing when an **account** has been reckoned. Hence, the phrase to **balance the books** means to add in this sum to the relevant side of the account so that both columns show the same total.

adverse balance In general, an account balance that shows a **loss** or **liability**. More especially, it is shorthand for adverse **balance of trade**.

balance of payments Account of all recorded financial exchanges made between the residents of a country and those of other countries. The balance of payments is divided into current and capital accounts. The current account takes stock of all **invisible** and **visible trade** (the **balance of trade** is part of the balance of payments current account) and the capital account includes all movements of **capital** in or out of the country.

balance of trade Also known as the visible balance, the difference between the value of a country's visible imports and exports. When the value of visible imports total more than the value of visible exports, it is known as an adverse balance of trade. *See* **balance of payments; exports, visible; imports, visible**.

balance sheet Statement that shows the financial position of a company in respect of its assets and liabilities at a certain time.

balance ticket Alternative term for certification of transfer. *See* **transfer, certification of**.

bank balance Statement relating to an account with a bank, showing only the level of funds in the account and not details of recent transactions.

credit balance In accounting, balance showing that more money has been received than is owed and so the account is in **credit**.

debit balance In accounting, balance that shows a **debit**.

passive balance **Balance of payments** that shows a **deficit**.

trial balance In accounting, test that the books of account are accurate, by extracting each balance and checking that the debits equal the credits. This may take place monthly, but must be carried out at least annually, during an **audit**.

trade balance Alternative term for **balance of trade**.

visible balance Alternative term for **balance of trade**.

See also **account, zero-balance**.

ballot While in general terms a ballot is a method of voting by marking a paper, it more specifically refers to a method of alloting **shares** to applicants in the event of a share issue being **oversubscribed**. All applications are entered for the ballot and those drawn at random receive some or all of the shares applied for. *See* **application and allotment; oversubscription**.

secret ballot Vote conducted by having voters mark their papers in secret, as opposed to a public show of hands or other form of ballot.

weighted ballot Ballot (for shares) that is in some way biased towards a certain type of investor.
"The issuing house was instructed to weight the ballot for shares in favour of small investors."

bank There are three main types of bank.
First, and most commonly known, a bank is a business that handles a person's money and financial matters. This type of bank is generally known as a public bank.
Second, a bank is an institution that deals in **finance** and international trade.
On a third level there are government-controlled **central banks**.

agricultural bank Bank specializing in granting loans for agricultural development. Also known as a land bank.

Bank of England The central bank of the UK. *See* **bank, central**.

central bank Bank that often carries out government economic policy, influences interest and exchange rates and monitors the activities of commercial and merchant banks. In this way it functions as the government's banker and is the **lender of the last resort** to the banking system.

clearing bank Bank that is a member of a clearing house (*e.g.* in the UK, the **Banker's Clearing House**) to facilitate the passing and clearing of cheques. *See* **house, clearing**.

commercial bank Bank that concentrates on cash deposit and transfer services to the general public, often to be found on the High Street. It may be a joint-stock bank or a **private bank**. *See also* **Big Four**.

correspondent bank When a transaction is initiated at a foreign branch of a bank, the home branch to which the instructions are sent is known as the correspondent bank. *See also* **bank, originating**.

discounting bank Bank that specializes in discounting **bills of exchange**.

Federal Reserve Banks Central banks of the USA, each of which is controlled by a state government. *See* **bank, central**.

industrial bank One of a group of smaller finance houses, which operate rather like a merchant bank, receiving investment from the general public. *See* **house, finance**.

issuing bank Financial institution that administrates a new issue of shares.

joint-stock bank Alternative term for a commercial bank that is constituted as a joint stock company. *See* **bank, commercial**.

land bank Alternative term for agricultural bank. *See* **bank, agricultural**.

merchant bank Institution that specializes in raising capital, particularly for use in business or industry. *See also* **capital, venture**.

originating bank In international trade, transactions involving a foreign branch of a bank (with head office, say, in London), the originating bank is the foreign branch at which the transaction originated. *See also* **bank, correspondent**.

private bank Commercial bank that is not owned by a joint-stock company. Such banks are now almost non-existent in the UK, but are still to be found in the USA. A private bank may also be a bank that is not a member of a clearing house, using a member bank as an agent for this purpose. *See* **house, clearing**.

public bank Alternative term for a commercial or joint-stock bank. *See* **bank, commercial**.

savings bank Bank in which money may be deposited and interest received.

trading bank AUS Australian term for a commercial bank. *See* **bank, commercial**.

World Bank Central bank of the United Nations. *See* **bank, central**.

See also **account, bank; bill, bank; book, bank; charges, bank; draft, bank; giro, bank; note, bank; overdraft, bank; rate, bank; reconciliation, bank**.

banker Person involved in the business of banks and banking. *Or* an institution that performs the same task for other institutions.

collecting banker Bank through which a cheque is presented for payment, and where the payee's account may be held.

paying banker Bank on which a cheque is drawn, *i.e.* the banker being asked to honour the cheque.

See also **card, banker's; cheque, banker's; Banker's Clearing House; draft, banker's; order, banker's**.

Banker's Clearing House The best-known of the clearing houses in the UK, which facilitates the passing of cheques that are presented at the many branches of each member bank, by making an account of each bank's indebtedness to the others at the end of each banking day.

banking Business undertaken by **banks**.

branch banking Banking system whereby a small number of commercial banks have many branches and serve a large number of customers. The UK's **Big Four** banks are examples of this type of banking. *See also* **banking, unit**.

consumer banking Alternative term for retail banking. *See* **banking, retail**.

high-tech banking Banking that uses electronic methods, such as **ATMs** and electronic mail, rather than personal or paper-based transactions.

investment banking Practice of providing finance for businesses.

retail banking Banking activities where the main emphasis is on services for individuals rather than institutions. Also known as consumer banking.

unit banking Banking system that operates in the USA, whereby banks are not permitted to open branches. *See* **banking, branch**.

bankruptcy State of being unable to pay debts.

act of bankruptcy There are three specific acts of bankruptcy: attempting to leave the country to avoid creditors; giving away property in order to defraud creditors; failing to comply with a bankruptcy notice filed by a **creditor**. By acting in any of these ways, a person may make himself or herself liable to bankruptcy charges.

adjudication of bankruptcy Court order declaring a person or company bankrupt.

bankruptcy petition Application to the court to be declared bankrupt or to have someone else declared bankrupt.

discharge in bankruptcy Occurs when the bankrupt is released after his or her debts have been paid, or it has been seen that all reasonable efforts have been made to do so.

undischarged bankruptcy Occurs when the debts of the bankrupt have not been paid. In this case the individual has no property that may be called his or her own and is barred from public office, and from holding management positions or directorships.

bar Term with three meanings.
  First, it is the profession of a **barrister**.
  "In 1976 she was called to the bar."
  Second, it is an obstacle that prevents something happening.
  "His inadequate knowledge of accounting acted as a bar to his career progress."
  Third, it is an informal term meaning one million.

bare, going *US* In **insurance**, going bare is operating a company without the cover of property or casualty insurance.

bargain In Stock Exchange jargon, any deal struck involving the buying and selling of **shares**.

early bargain Deal struck on the stock exchange after the exchange has closed and considered to be among the first transactions of the following day. Early bargains are also known as after-hours dealings.

matched bargain Deals made by finding clients who wish to sell particular stocks and ones who wish to buy those same stocks.

time bargain Deal struck on the understanding that settlement will be postponed until the next settlement day.

unconscionable bargain Bargain that turns out to be unfair because one party has not had the time to consult an expert. Unconscionable bargains may be made void in law.

bargaining Act of negotiating a price or other terms.

bargaining theory Theory whereby wage levels are seen as the result of talks between management and the labour-force rather than of supply and demand in the labour market.

(free) collective bargaining Negotiation of wages, hours and conditions between the labour-force, represented by a trade union, and management. The concept of collective bargaining is the crux of the trade union movement.

barker card Card placed on a shelf in a retail outlet to advertise a product. Also known as a shelf-talker.

barrier Obstacle that prevents entry or makes it difficult.

barrier to entry Set of economic and other conditions that make it difficult to set up a business, *i.e.* to enter the market.

customs barrier High level of customs duty that makes trade difficult. Also known as tariff barrier.

nontariff barrier US Barrier to trade that takes a form other than a financial imposition or **tax**. *E.g.* quantity or quality controls imposed on imports.

tariff barrier Alternative term for customs barrier. *See* **barrier, customs**.

trade barrier Something that restricts or discourages trade, such as high levels of import **duty** or low import **quotas**. "The leaders of the car industry in the UK called for trade barriers to be set up to restrict foreign competition."

base Lowest or starting point from which calculations are made, especially calculations of relative stock price movements.

base stock (method) Method of stock valuation whereby stock levels are assumed to be constant and the goods are valued at their original cost. *See also* **first in last out**.

See also **date, base; period, base; rate, base; year, base**.

basis *US* Value of an **asset** for **tax** purposes.

bear Stock Exchange dealer or analyst who believes that prices or investment values will go down.

bear closing Situation that occurs when a dealer has sold shares or commodities he does not yet own and then buys them back, at a lower price, thus making a profit. *See also* **short selling**.

bear raid Vigorous selling in concert in order to force down the price of a particular commodity or share. *See also* **concert party**. "After the 1929 crash, massive bear raids on stocks were recognized as an activity that must be stopped."

bear slide What happens when stock and share prices move towards a bear market situation.

bear squeeze Situation in which bears who have been **short selling** are faced with a price rise rather than a fall.

covered bear Dealer who sells **shares** or **commodities** he owns, hoping to buy them back later at a lower price (*i.e.* he or she is not taking the risk of **short selling**). Also known as a protected bear.

protected bear Alternative term for covered bear. *See* **bear, covered**.

See also **bull; market, bear; position, bear**.

bear hug In **corporate finance**, an informal term for notice given to the board of a **target** company that a **takeover** bid is imminent.

strong bear hug During a **takeover**, a situation in which there is a high level of publicity surrounding the bid, putting pressure on the **target** company.

teddy bear hug Situation in which the target company approves of a takeover bid in principle but requires a higher price.

bearer Someone who holds a **bill**, **cheque** or certificate. If the cheque is uncrossed and is made payable to the bearer, then it may be cashed over the counter of a bank by the bearer, without liability devolving onto the bank in the event that the cheque has been stolen. *See also* **bond, bearer; securities, bearer; stocks, bearer**.

bearish Someone or something (*e.g.* a market) with the qualities of a **bear**.
"Some market analysts believe that reaction to this week's money-supply figures will not be so bearish after all."

bed and breakfast deal Transaction used to minimize the impact of capital gains tax. A **shareholder** sells his or her holding at a **loss** after trading closes for the day, and registers the loss for tax purposes. Next day, the shareholder buys his or her holding back. The US term for a bed and breakfast deal is swap. *See also* **tax, capital gains**.

benchmark Point on an **index** that has a significance and is used as a reference point.

beneficiary Person who gains money or property from something; *e.g.* from a financial transaction such as a life assurance policy or a will.
"She was surprised to find herself the principal beneficiary of the will."

benefit Two meanings are possible.
First, it is a payment made under an **insurance** or social security scheme.
Second, it is a payment to a worker, either in kind or in cash, apart from his or her wages.

accrued benefits Under a company **pension** scheme, accrued benefits are those to which a person is entitled up to a certain point in time, regardless of whether or not he or she stays in the job.

fringe benefit Items given to employees as part of their payment but apart from their wages or salary, *e.g.* a company car, health insurance, goods at a discount.

supplementary benefit Payment made in the UK to someone who is either out of work but does not qualify for unemployment benefit, or who is on a low wage.

unemployment benefit Commonly known as the dole, unemployment benefit is a payment made in the UK to someone who is out of work and has previously paid a certain number of national insurance contributions.

See also **insurance, national; taxation, benefit**.

beta (factor or **coefficient)** Measurement of the volatility of a company's shares, *i.e.* how sensitive the stock is to market fluctuations. The beta is denoted in figures, *e.g.* 1.5, which means that this share will rise 15% in a market that has risen 10%. Shares that under-perform the market are rated below 1.

high-beta Denotes shares that are volatile.

low-beta Denotes shares that are relatively stable
"Some analysts expect the current trend to continue and so believe that low-betas are good buys."

*beta shares (***stocks** *US)* Second-line shares, as opposed to the less numerous highly-capitalized alpha (first-line) or more numerous gamma (third-line).

better, to go When share prices go better, they rise or improve.
"When the news of the last quarter's increased trading is confirmed, the shares are expected to go better on their current level."

bet the ranch *US* To take a substantial risk in stock exchange dealing or other financial transactions.

bi- Prefix meaning twice or double.

biannual Twice a year.

biennial Every two years.

bimonthly Twice a month or once in two months.

bid Offer to buy something (*e.g.* shares) at a certain price. A seller may make an offer and a prospective buyer may make a bid. The bid cancels out the offer.

More especially, a bid is an offer by one company to buy the shares of another, a **takeover bid**.

bidder Someone who makes a bid for something.
"At the auction, many of the bidders remained anonymous."

bidding ring Group of stock market or antique dealers acting in concert in order to drive prices up or down. This practice is illegal. *See also* **concert party**.

closing bid Last bid at an **auction**, or more generally, the bid that is successful.

opening bid First bid at an auction.

skinny bid Alternative term for **thin bid**. *See* **bid, thin**.

takeover bid Offer by one company to buy all the shares of another, thereby gaining control of the target company. Often shortened to 'bid'.

thin bid Takeover bid backed by an aggressor who holds only a small number of shares. Also known as a skinny bid.

See also **price, bid; spread, bid-offer**.

Big Bang Popular term for the deregulation of the London Stock Exchange on 27 October 1986. Among the changes implemented were the admission of foreign institutions as members of the Exchange, the abandonment of rigid distinctions between **stockbrokers**, **jobbers** and **bankers**, and the abolition of fixed **commissions**. *See also* **single capacity**.

Big Blue *US* Nickname for IBM (International Business Machines).

Big Board *US* Nickname for the New York Stock Exchange.

big four Nickname for the four main commercial banks in the UK: Barclays, Lloyds, Midland and National Westminster. They are also known as High Street banks. *See* **bank, commercial**.

bigger fool theory *US* Justification for buying shares that are over-priced, which runs that there is always a bigger fool somewhere on the market who will buy them from you at an even higher price.

bill Three main meanings are possible.

First, it is a list of charges to be paid on goods or services. "The supplier presented an exorbitant bill which we refused to pay."

Second, it is a document promising to pay someone a certain amount of money. It is in this sense that the US meaning of the term is a bank note.

Third, it is a document describing goods, most often used in dealings with customs.

absolute bill of sale **Bill of sale** by which goods are transferred to the possession of another.

accommodation bill **Bill of exchange** signed by one person in order to help another to raise a loan. The signatory (or accommodation party) is acting as a guarantor, and normally does not expect to pay the bill when it falls due. Accommodation bills are also known as kites, windbills or windmills.

bank bill Instruction to a bank to pay someone a certain sum of money. Usually used in transactions involving foreign currencies. In the USA the term refers to a banknote.

bill of exchange Document indicating that one party (the drawee) agrees to pay a certain sum of money on demand or on a specified date, to the drawer. Two very familiar bills of exchange are cheques and bank notes. Another form of bill of exchange is used by the government to regulate the **money supply**.

bill of lading Document detailing the transfer of goods from a (foreign) supplier to a buyer. It may be used as a document of **title**.

bill of quantities Document produced by a quantity surveyor detailing materials and labour required for construction or alteration of a building. *See* **surveyor, quantity**.

bill of sale Document certifying the transfer of goods (but not real estate) to another person. Goods transferred in this way may not become the property of the receiving party and may be redeemed when the bill is paid.

bill of sight Document passed to a customs inspector by an importer who is unable to describe in detail the imported goods. When the goods are landed a full description must be given, known as perfecting the sight.

bills in a set Foreign **bills of exchange** are normally made out in triplicate and sent to the drawee separately to prevent loss. These copies are known as bills in a set.

bills payable In accounting, **bills of exchange** that are held and must be paid at some future date. These are effectively liabilities. *See also* **bills receivable**.

bills receivable In accounting, **bills of exchange** that are held and are due to be paid at some future date. These are effectively assets. *See also* **bills payable**.

blank bill **Bill of exchange** on which the payee is not specified.

conditional bill of sale **Bill of sale** by which the owner of the goods transferred retains the right to repossess them.

demand bill **Bill of exchange** to be paid on demand.

fine bill **Bill of exchange** where the backer is extremely creditworthy and so there is little or no risk.

foreign bill **Bill of exchange** that is drawn in a foreign country. *See also* **bill, inland**.

inland bill **Bill of exchange** that is drawn and payable within the British Isles. *See also* **bill, foreign**.

long bill **Bill of exchange** with more than ten years to maturity.

period bill Fixed-term **bill of exchange** payable on a specified date, and not on demand.

T-bill Abbreviation of **treasury bill**.

trade bill **Bill of exchange** between traders. The value and acceptability of the trade bill depends upon the standing of the accepting trader.

treasury bill *US* Often abbreviated to T-bill, short-term **bill of exchange** issued by the US Treasury in $10,000 denominations.

See also **broker, bill; discounting; rate, bill**.

billion Term with two meanings.

In the USA, it is one thousand million (*i.e.* 1,000,000,000). In the UK, it has normally been used to mean one million million (*i.e.* 1,000,000,000,000). However, now the term is more frequently used in the American sense. *See also* **yard**.

billfold biopsy *US* First test given to an emergency patient on entering a hospital, to determine whether the patient is able to pay for the medical services he or she requires.

bin card In **warehousing**, a note of stock held in a particular location or container. A note is made on the card each time a unit of stock is removed.

BIS Abbreviation of Bank for International Settlements.

black To forbid or boycott trade in certain goods or with certain trading partners.
"Many people have now voluntarily blacked goods from South Africa."

black, in the An **account** that is in the black is in **credit**. *See also* **red**.

blackleg Person who continues to work during a strike; also known as a scab.

blacklist List of companies, products or people that are undesirable.
In the USA the term means more specifically the denial of work to certain people on the grounds of their past beliefs or actions.
"John Smith believes he has been blacklisted by management because of his prominence during the 1981 strike."

black magic *US* What a computer wizard performs when he makes a computer accomplish a task that nobody else has been able to make it do.

Black Monday Monday 19 October 1987. The phrase was coined shortly after the huge losses sustained on the equities markets on that day.

Black Tuesday *US* 18 October 1983, the day IBM announced the launch of two new micro-computers, causing extreme concern on the part of market analysts over competition in the computer industry and fears that there would be a market **shakeout**. During the day share prices of competing firms fell considerably.

blank In general, any form that has not been filled in. *See* **bill, blank; cheque, blank; credit, blank; endorsement, blank; transfer, blank**.

blanket Something that covers all eventualities. *See* **agreement, blanket; policy, blanket; rate, blanket**.

bliss point In **marketing** theory, the point at which the consumer is most satisfied with the goods or a combination of goods, so that any change in combination or quantity brings about less consumer satisfaction.

block Group of something (*e.g.* shares); or an obstruction or prevention of entry or exit. *See also* **account, blocked; currency, blocked**.

blowout *US* Informal term referring to unexpectedly strong sales of something, *e.g.* goods sold at retail.
"Traders regarded the Eurobond issue as a blowout because it sold quickly and sparked real excitement on launch."

blue button Button worn by an employee of a stockbroking firm who is allowed to enter the floor of the London Stock Exchange but is not authorized to trade. Such employees are known as blue buttons.

blue chip Investment that is regarded as extremely safe, without being **gilt-edged**.
"Analysts believe that blue-chip stocks will continue strong, but that other shares will continue to drift."

blue-collar worker Alternative term for a manual worker.

blue-sky Security that is either worthless or highly speculative, or something with no specific aim.
"Along with its research and development programme, the company invested in a certain amount of blue-sky research."

blue-sky laws US State laws intended to protect investors from potentially worthless share issues.

blurb Short piece of advertising copy, especially publisher's copy on the jacket or cover of a book.

board Group of people who run a company, society or trust.
A second meaning refers to goods loaded onto a ship or aircraft.

advisory board Group of specialists who advise others.

board of directors In the UK, a group of directors of a company, in a public company elected by the shareholders to run it. In the USA the board of directors draws up company policy and appoints executives to run the company. Sometimes also known simply as the board.
"The board were unanimous in recommending to shareholders the terms of the takeover bid."

board of inquiry Group of people brought together to inquire into the circumstances of an event or situation.
"After the death of two children in fairground accidents, the government set up a board of inquiry to investigate safety standards at fairgrounds."

board meeting Meeting of the board of directors.

See also **free on board**.

bogus Fake or counterfeit.
"The police are investigating reports of a con man posing as a salesman, carrying a bogus identity card."

boilerplate language *US* Overly detailed or obscure language found mainly in standard contracts.
"A special contract takes time to draft, whereas a boilerplate contract can be used almost immediately."

bomb Something that happens suddenly with disastrous results.

debt bomb Financial repercussions envisaged if a major international debtor were to default.
"There was general concern on the money markets as the economy of two of the debt bomb nations showed a marked deterioration."

bona fide Latin for in good faith. Usually appears with reference to contracts, especially contracts of **insurance**. All parties to a contract are expected to reveal all information relevant to the contract in hand. That is, they are expected to contract in good faith. Also used simply to mean honest or trustworthy. *See also* **mala fide**.

"After completing an in-depth investigation, the authorities decided that the company was bona fide after all."

bona vacantia Property such as real estate or shares that have no owner and no obvious claimant, *e.g.* property that remains in the hands of a liquidator after the creditors have been paid.

bond Term with three meanings.

First, it is a security issued at a fixed interest rate by central government, local authorities or occasionally by private companies. It is essentially a contract to repay money borrowed, and as such represents a debt. Normally, bonds are issued in series with the same conditions of repayment and denominations. Also known as a fixed-interest security.

Second, it refers to the importing of goods from abroad. If goods are imported and import duty is not paid immediately, the goods are placed in a bonded warehouse (*i.e.* they are held in bond) until all customs formalities are completed.

Third, it is a firm tie or agreement between individuals. "My word is my bond" is the motto of the London Stock Exchange.

bearer bond Bond payable to the bearer rather than to a specific, named individual. *See also* **bond, registered**.

bond-washing Practice of buying bonds cum dividend and selling them ex dividend, to reduce the rate of tax payable on the transaction. The dividend on the bond becomes a capital gain, on which a lower rate of tax is payable than if tax were paid on the proceeds as dividend income. Because of recent changes in the tax laws in the UK, there is no longer scope for this kind of manoeuvring, although it still happens in the USA. *See* **dividend, cum; dividend, ex**.

bulldog bond Sterling denominated bond issued by foreign governments for sale on the UK market.

callable bond Bond that may be called for payment before **maturity**.

contract bond Alternative term for performance bond. *See* **bond, performance**.

convertible bond Also known as convertible loan stock or convertible, bond that is offered at a fixed, low rate of interest with an option to convert the bond into an equity share.

corporate bond Bond issued by a company, which most frequently happens in the USA.

coupon bond Alternative term for bearer bond. *See* **bond, bearer**.

defence bond Bond issued by the UK government to cover spending during and immediately after World War II. Defence bonds were issued in 1939 and discontinued in 1964.

government bond Fixed-interest security issued by a government agent such as the treasury. Also known as a treasury bond.

income bond Investment in a unit trust that produces a good annual income as opposed to capital growth realizable at the end of a certain period of time.

junk bond Bond, especially common in the USA, issued by a company with a low credit rating. It is often used to raise funds for leveraged buyouts, secured against the assets of the target company. *See* **buyout, leveraged**.
"The bond-rating agencies regard the junk bonds issued by the subsidiary as below investment grade."

local authority bond Bond issued by a local government authority. Also known as a municipal bond.

long bond Bond with more than fifteen years to maturity. *See also* **bond, medium; bond, short**.

medium bond Bond with between five to fifteen years to maturity. *See also* **bond, long; bond, short**.

mortgage bond Certificate stating that a mortgage has been taken out and that a property is security against default.

municipal bond Equivalent to a local authority bond. *See* **bond, local authority**.

performance bond Bond delivered by a contractor to a public authority for a sum in excess of the value of a contract, and which is to be paid in the event of breach of contract. It is therefore a form of **guarantee**. Also known as a contract bond.

premium savings bond Stake in a form of lottery run by the British government since 1956. The bonds purchased carry no interest, but each week and month tax-free prizes are awarded to the holders of bonds selected by a random number generator out of the interest accumulated on all premium bonds. They are not transferable, but may be redeemed at any time at their face value.

registered bond Bond that is registered in the name of the holder. It may be transferred to another holder only with the consent of the registered holder. *See also* **bond, bearer**.

short bond Bond with less than five years to maturity. *See also* **bond, long; bond, medium**.

straight bond Also known as straight fixed-interest stock, a bond issued by a company.

treasury bond Alternative term for a government bond. *See* **bond, government**.

yankee bond Bond that is issued in dollar denominations to attract US investors.

yearling bond UK fixed-interest security that has a life of under five years; issued through banks and stockbrokers on a weekly basis.

zero coupon bond US Bearer bond that pays no **dividend**, but is issued at a substantial discount. A capital gain is made by the bearer when the bond matures, and so tax on the proceeds is paid at a lower rate than if the proceeds were in the form of dividends. Zero coupon bonds are not issued in the UK. *See also* **bond, bearer; bond-washing**.

See also **Eurobond; note, bond**.

bonded Held in **bond**.

bonus Additional payment.

incentive bonus Also known as a **productivity bonus**, a payment offered to a worker to encourage him or her to work harder.

no-claims bonus In motor and household insurance, a payment (normally rendered in terms of a discount on the **premium**) made if the insuree has made no previous claim against the policy.

"The driver responsible for the car accident decided to pay for the damage out of his own pocket instead of claiming from his insurance company, because he did not wish to lose his no-claims bonus."

productivity bonus Alternative term for incentive bonus. *See* **bonus, incentive**.

reversionary bonus In life assurance, a bonus paid to holders of with profits life assurance policies, related to the profitability of the assurance company.

terminal bonus Money paid to an insuree as a lump sum at the termination of some insurance policies.

See also **issue, bonus**.

boodle Informal term for money obtained through illegal dealings, often in the form of a **bribe**.

book In business, the books most frequently referred to are the **books of account** in which business transactions are recorded. Books of account are normally held to be legal documents.

bank book Book showing credits and debits made to a bank account.

black book Company's pre-planned strategy to be put into action in the event of a hostile **takeover** bid.

Blue Book Popular term for a UK government publication entitled *National Income and Expenditure*, best described as the national annual **report** and **accounts**.

book of prime entry Account book in which transactions are recorded from day to day before being transferred to the main **ledger**.

book of original entry Alternative term for **book of prime entry**.

jobber's book Before the **Big Bang**, a book showing the **position** a jobber holds in the market: whether he holds stock for which he has yet to find a buyer, or whether he is short on stock that he has already sold.

Yellow book Popular term for a publication entitled *Admission and Securities Listing*, issued by the London Stock Exchange Council, setting out regulations of admission to the Official List and the obligations of securities admitted.

See also **debt, book**.

book-keeping Business of keeping records of financial transactions.

double-entry book-keeping Process of recording financial transactions under two parallel headings; **debits** and **credits**. *See* **balance**.

boom Popular term for a period when employment, prices and general business activity are at a high level and resources are being used to the full. Booms have a nasty habit of turning into **slumps**. *See also* **recession**.

baby boom Period during which a larger than usual number of children are born. 1957 was the peak baby boom year in many Western countries, after which the number of births decreased. People born during these affluent times are often known as baby boomers, or simply boomers.

boomer Alternative term for baby boomer. *See* **boom, baby**.

bootstrap Mostly used in the USA where **takeover** activity is most prevalent, to describe a cash offer for a controlling interest in a company which, if accepted, is followed by another offer (usually at a lower price) for the remainder of the shares.
"The tycoon found bootstrapping a very cost-effective method of taking over other companies."

borrowing Most widely used in the sense of accepting money that is not one's own on the understanding that it will be repaid, usually with interest, at a later date.
On the London Metal Exchange, borrowing is the process of buying a metals contract due to be completed on a near date, and at the same time selling forward a contract for a date further in the future.
See also **carry; lending**.

bottom Generally refers to the lowest point of something. In shipping, however, the term refers to a ship, and bottomry is anything to do with shipping.

bottom line Last line of an **account**, showing either **profit** or **loss**. In this sense the phrase has come to mean the 'brutal truth' in general usage.

bottoming out Informal term for a very sudden and serious fall in market prices.

bought Something that comes into one's possession through some kind of exchange is said to have been bought. *See* **deal, bought**.

bounce When a **cheque** is not honoured by the paying **banker**, it is said to bounce, because it is passed back to the collecting banker. This may happen for several reasons, but the most common is that there are not enough funds in the account to cover the cheque. A cheque that bounces may be popularly called a rubber cheque.

bounty In a modern business context, a government **subsidy** given to aid particular industries. It may be in the form of **tax** concessions or a cash handout.

Bourse French term for the French Stock Exchange in Paris, but also used to refer to other European exchanges (in this sense written 'bourse').

boutique Relatively new form of financial services company, operating in much the same way as a high street shop, into which customers may walk to seek investment advice and services. Also known as a financial supermarket.

boycott Refusal to trade with a certain company or nation or in certain goods.

bracket Broadly, a group of people or things that are in some way similar to each other.

bracket creep What happens when **inflation** forces groups of people into the next tax or income bracket. Normally brackets are fixed annually to account for inflation but bracket creep can occur if inflation runs at a higher level than anticipated. *See* **bracket, income; bracket, tax**.

income bracket Range of income (wages, salaries), normally rated from a specific minimum to a specific maximum. Also applied to people in that range.
"She is in the middle income bracket."

tax bracket Range of (usually income) tax. Also applied to people in that bracket.
"She is in a higher tax bracket than he is."

brain-drain Popular term describing the migration of specialists (usually scientists or technologists) from their home country to another country, often lured by higher salaries and more sympathetic research grants.

brand To put a name (the brand name) on something or to design and package a product so that it is easily recognizable by a consumer. A brand name can be protected by law against misuse by competitors hoping to benefit from the reputation associated with a particular branded product.

branded goods Goods that are packaged by the manufacturer with the brand name clearly visible. Branded goods may often be sold at a higher price than others, because of the selling power of the name.

brand leader Brand of a certain type of goods that has the largest share of the market. A brand leader may often be seen as a company's most valuable **asset**.

brand loyalty Marketing concept by which consumers continually purchase certain goods which they identify by brand name (and associate with quality or value for money).

brand manager Person, usually employed by a large supplier of consumer goods, who co-ordinates the activities of developing and marketing a group of branded products.

break When prices have been rising steadily over a period, the break is a sudden and substantial drop in prices.

break even To cover one's costs, making neither a **profit** nor a **loss**.

break-even chart Graph showing the relationship between total fixed costs, variable costs and revenues for various volumes of output.

break-even point Point at which fixed and variable costs are exactly covered by sales revenue. At greater volumes of output an operation would normally be expected to make a **profit**.

See also **amortize**.

breakout What happens when a share or commodity price breaks a previously fixed, or at least, stable pattern.

break-up Term with two meanings.

In real estate, a tenanted property is worth less on the property market than a vacant one. A property with some tenanted and some vacant apartments may be bought and then broken up, so that the tenanted flats may be sold to the tenants and the vacant flats may be sold to outsiders at a much higher rate.

In corporate terms, break-up occurs when several or all of the operating arms of a company are sold off, usually after a **takeover**.

See also **asset stripping; value, break-up**.

Bretton Woods Conference Held in 1944 in Bretton Woods, New Hampshire, this conference between the USA, Canada and the UK formed a new system of international monetary control and resulted in the setting up of the International Monetary Fund (IMF) and the International Bank for Reconstruction and Development. *See also* **American Plan**.

bribe Illicit payment made by one person to another in order to gain rights or privileges that the payee would not normally be entitled to. Offering or accepting a bribe is often a criminal offence.

bricks and mortar *US* Informal term for the fixed assets of a company. *See* **asset, fixed**.

bridge financing Any form of short-term funding in anticipated arrival of funds, whether for a venture company on the verge of raising new capital, or a bridging loan for a home buyer who needs to pay for a house before receiving the proceeds on the sale of the former property.

broad money = **money supply**

broadside *US* Informal term for a publicity leaflet or handout.

broker Broadly, an intermediary between a buyer and a seller. There are several forms of broker, the job title referring to what it is that this particular broker deals in. *E.g.* a **stockbroker** deals in stocks and shares.

bill broker Person or company that buys and sells bills of exchange, either on their own account, or as an intermediary.

broker-dealer Firm that acts in the dual capacity of share broker for its clients and as dealer for its own account.

broker-trader On the London International Financial Futures Exchange, a firm that acts as both broker and trader for its own account. Similar to a **broker-dealer**.

government broker Firm of brokers used by the UK government to transact its business in **gilt-edged securities** and to provide the Treasury with advice.

insurance broker Someone who arranges and sells **insurance**.

loading broker Someone who acts for a ship owner, obtaining cargos for the vessel to transport.

money broker Money market dealer in short-term loans and securities. On the London stock exchange, six firms act as money brokers, channelling borrowed **stocks** from institutions onto the market, thereby enhancing the **liquidity** of the **gilt-edged** and **equity** markets in particular.

outside broker Dealer in stocks and shares who is not a member of any exchange.

running broker Someone who acts as an intermediary between those who issue **bills** and the **discount houses.**

share broker Broker who charges commission on each share, rather than on a total transaction. *See also* **broker, value**.

value broker US Broker who charges a commission on a total transaction, rather than per share. *See also* **broker, share**.

brokerage Payment made to a **broker** for services rendered. Also known as a broker's **commission**.

bubble Industry or trend with no substance to it. A bubble usually bursts with more-or-less disastrous consequences for those financially involved. Probably the most famous bubble was the South Sea Bubble which exploded in 1720.

bubble company Company formed with no real business to undertake, often as a vehicle to defraud the public.

bucket shop Popular phrase describing brokers of stocks, shares and commodities who are not recognized as members of any **exchange**.

budget Plan that details expected future income and outgoings, normally over a time span of a year. Also the sum of money set aside for a given activity or project.

The Budget is a government's financial plan for the forthcoming financial year, announced as a statement by the Chancellor of the Exchequer, and concerned principally with the raising of revenue by **taxation**.

capital budget Forward planning of corporate capital movement, involving larger sums of money and longer timescales than a cash budget. *See* **budget, cash**.

cash budget Forward plan of day-to-day income and expenditure.

operating budget Alternative term for cash budget.

See also **account, budget; deficit, budget**.

buffer stock In manufacturing industries, a stock of raw materials held as an insurance against shortages or sudden price rises.

On the commodity markets, buffer stocks are held for release at certain strategic times in order to stabilize prices and markets.

building and loan association *US* Roughly equivalent to a **building society** in the UK and also known as a savings and loan association.

building society Institution in the UK that accepts **deposits** upon which it pays varying rates of **interest** and lends money, originally only in the form of a **mortgage** to enable people to purchase property. Some building societies now issue cheque books and cash cards, and so operate in much the same way as a **bank**. *See also* **building and loan association**.

built-in Something that is planned or accounted for at the outset. *See* **obsolescence, built-in**.

bull Stock exchange dealer or analyst who believes that prices or investment values will increase. On this conviction, the dealer buys now and profits by selling later at a higher price.

stale bull Dealer who has bought in the expectation that prices will rise but cannot then sell at a profit, either because prices have remained static or fallen, or because nobody is buying.

bullish Describes a market or person with the qualities of a **bull**.

See also **bear; market, bull; position, bull**.

bullet loan *US* = **loan, bullet**

bumping *US* Occurs when a senior person takes the place of a junior.

burden of debt When a **debt** is passed on to successive generations, the burden of debt is the **interest** payments on the accumulated debt.

bureau Office that specializes in a certain form of business, *e.g.* an employment bureau specializes in supplying temporary or permanent staff to employers for a commission.

bureau de change Office at which currencies may be exchanged on payment of a commission.

Bureau of the Mint US Equivalent to the **Royal Mint** in the UK.

burn-out turnaround Strategy to prevent a badly-performing company going into **liquidation**, involving a total restructuring of the company and a large injection of capital which dilutes the percentage shareholding of existing holders.

burn rate = **rate, burn**

business cycle = **cycle, business**

bust Informal term meaning bankrupt.
" After as bad a year as this one has been, I would not be surprised if a large number of small companies went bust."

busted convert = convert, busted

buy To gain title to something in exchange for money.

buy back A company that is originally financed by venture capital may pay back the capital invested either by seeking a **quotation** or by being taken over. In either case, it will be buying itself back from the venture capitalist. *See* **capital, venture**.

buy earnings To buy earnings is to invest in shares that have a low yield but a good earnings growth record.

buy forward Act of buying shares, commodities etc. for delivery at a later date. In essence, buying forward is a gamble on the current price, *i.e.* that it will rise in the future and the buyer will then be able to sell at a profit. *See also* **selling short**.

buy in Refers to a situation where a seller of shares etc. fails to deliver on the agreed date, which sometimes happens if the seller is **selling short**. In this case the buyer is entitled to buy shares from another source and to charge the seller with any expenses incurred. This process is known as buying in.

buy on close Buying contracts on a financial **futures** market at a price within the **closing range**. *See also* **buy on opening**.

buy on opening Buying contracts on a financial futures market at a price within the **opening range**. *See also* **buy on close**.

buy side US Expression that refers to **institutional investors** on the New York Stock Exchange.

buyer Someone who buys.

buyer's market Market in which there are too many sellers and not enough buyers, so that buyers are in a position to influence prices or conditions of purchase. The opposite is a seller's market.

buyers over On the Stock Exchange, a situation in which there are more buyers than sellers. The opposite is **sellers over**.

buyout Purchase of an entire company.

leveraged buyout Buyout of a large company by a smaller one, the capital for which has been borrowed from a friendly source, secured on the assets of the company being bought. *See also* **leverage**.

management buyout Purchase of a company by its managers, one of the most common forms of buyout.

See also **policy, buyout**.

C

CA Abbreviation of chartered accountant. *See* **accountant, chartered**.

call Act of demanding payment for shares or stocks, or repayment of a **debt**.

call provision Condition attached to a **bond** by which the issuer is entitled to redeem the bond at a fixed price after a specified period of time.

call money Type of loan made by a bank, which must be repaid upon demand. Also known as money at call.

call over Method of trading on a stock exchange whereby the securities listed are called out in order, and dealers make bids or offers for each **security** according to their instructions.

call up Alternative term for **call**, especially with respect to partly-paid shares. *See* **shares, partly-paid**.

margin call In futures trading, if an adverse price movement more than eradicates a party's **margin**, the balance of the deficit is called upon, often cancelling the **bargain**.

See also **option, call**.

C & F Abbreviation of **cost and freight**.

CAP Abbreviation of **Common Agricultural Policy**, a **European Economic Community** agreement on farming that aims to protect the farmers of member countries by *e.g.* subsidizing their produce and setting minimum prices.

cap Interest rate **option** that enables the investor to hedge against the possibility of **interest** rates rising to the investor's disadvantage. *See* **hedging**.

capacity Measurement of the ability of a company to produce goods or services.

excess capacity Capacity to produce goods over and above the current rate. Excess capacity is more strictly used to denote the increase in production necessary to bring the average cost to a minimum.

See also **dual capacity; single capacity**.

capital Vague term that most often requires a qualification. Unqualified, it usually refers to the resources of an organization or person (*e.g.* equipment, skill, cash).

authorized capital Amount of capital that a company is authorized to raise through the issue of shares, as set down in the company's articles of association. *See* **association, articles of**.

called-up capital Sum of money that has been paid to a company by its shareholders. *See also* **capital, uncalled; shares, partly-paid**.

capital employed Capital that a company uses to finance its assets. It is taken to be the sum of shareholders' funds, loans and deferred taxation.

capital-intensive Describing an industry that uses a higher proportion of fixed capital than labour. *See* **capital, fixed**.

circulating capital Money used by a company to invest in **assets** for resale. When such assets have been sold, the capital raised returns to the company.

debenture capital That part of a company's capital that is issued in the form of **debentures**.

equity capital Capital of a company that belongs to the owners of the company (in many cases, holders of ordinary shares), rather than capital provided by owners of fixed-interest securities. *See* **equity; security, fixed interest**.

fixed capital Alternative term for fixed assets. *See* **assets, fixed**.

flight capital Capital removed from a country that seems to be politically (or economically) unstable, and taken to a more stable environment.

human capital Value of a company's employees.

issued capital That part of a company's capital that comes from a share issue. Also known as subscribed capital.

loan capital That part of a company's capital that is lent over a fixed period of time.

medium-term capital Loan capital lent in the medium-term, *i.e.* for between 5 and 15 years.

paid-up capital Capital obtained by a share issue in which the shares are fully paid. *See* **shares, fully-paid**. *See also* **capital, called-up; capital, uncalled**.

primary capital Capital that is used in the start-up of a business. See also **capital, venture**.

risk capital Capital invested in a company, or security that presents a risk (*i.e.* the possibility of loss or, indeed, gain). Also used as an alternative term for venture capital. *See* **capital, venture**.

seed capital Capital used to determine whether a proposed project is viable.

share capital Capital raised by a company through an issue of shares. *See also* **capital, authorized; capital issued; capital uncalled**.

short-term capital Loan capital lent in the short-term, *i.e.* for less than five years. *See also* **capital, medium-term**.

subscribed capital Alternative term for issued capital. *See* **capital, issued**.

uncalled capital Money owing to a company on partly-paid shares. Uncalled capital exists as a reserve to be called upon at any time by the directors of the company. *See* **shares, partly-paid**.

venture capital Also known as risk capital, capital invested in a venture (usually a young company in high-technology areas) that presents a risk. *See also* **vulture capital**.

working capital Capital available for the day-to-day running of a company, used to pay such expenses as salaries, purchases, etc.

See also **account, capital; allowances, capital; assets, capital; budget, capital; clause, capital; expenditure, capital; gain, capital; goods, capital; market, capital; outlay, capital; profit, capital; ratio, capital-labour; reserves, capital; saturation, capital; stock, capital; tax, capital gains; tax, capital transfer; units, capital**.

capitalism Economic and political system in which people are entitled to trade for profit on their own account. Also known as free or private enterprise. *See also* **communism**.

popular capitalism Capitalism that has reached a large number of a country's population, through increased personal investment, growth in small businesses, proliferation of profit-sharing schemes, etc.

capitalization Term with two meanings.

First, it is the conversion of a company's reserves into share capital by issuing more shares.

Second, it is the total amount of capital available to a company in the long term.

over-capitalization Situation in which a company has more capital than it can employ to its profit. *See also* **gearing**.

under-capitalization Situation in which a company begins trading without enough capital to take it through the initial (and usually very expensive) stages.

market capitalization Value of all the securities of a company at current market prices.

See also **issue, capitalization**.

CAR Abbreviation of compound annual **return**, the total return on a sum insured or lent over a period of a year, including the return on **interest** previously accrued.

car Alternative term for a **futures** contract.

card Plastic card embossed with account details and provided with a magnetic strip, used in (usually personal) financial transactions.

banker's card Plastic card issued by a bank to its creditworthy customers, which guarantees the payment of a cheque up to a certain sum (usually £50-£100).

charge card Plastic card similar to a credit card. However, most charge cards may only be used at specific retail outlets or chains.

credit card Plastic card that enables the user to buy goods on **credit**, paying outstanding sums on his or her account in monthly instalments.

smart card Plastic card that is provided with an integrated circuit, that enables it to carry out financial transactions (debits and credits) without the aid of a central computer.

carryforward *US* Tax **rebate** that is paid because a company has gone into the **red** for a period of time.

carry Money borrowed or lent in order to finance trading in **futures**. The process of borrowing and lending in this way is known as carrying.

carry over To postpone payment on a bargain traded on a stock exchange from one settlement day to the next. *See* **day, settlement**.

cartel Group of companies that come together to monopolize a market, agreeing between them which company presides over which area of operation. Cartels are illegal in the UK and the USA.

case of need Endorsement made on a **bill of exchange**. It is followed by the name of a person or company to whom the holder of the bill may apply in the event that the bill is not paid.

cash Ready money – coins and notes – or to turn into ready money.

"He realized that he would not have enough cash to pay the bill and so he went to the bank to cash a cheque."

cash against document (CAD) Method of payment for goods for export, whereby the documentation for a shipment is sent to an agent or bank at the destination. These are passed to the consignee, who makes the payment. Then the consignee is free to take delivery of the shipment when it arrives. Cash against document is a process of payment that is also used by large UK investment houses.

cash and carry Popular term for a wholesale warehouse, from which retailers buy their goods and transport them away. More and more frequently, cash and carries are used by members of the general public.

cash and new On a stock exchange, a method of postponing payment on a **bargain** until the next settlement day. The investor begins with a bargain for which he or she would like to postpone payment. Towards the end of that **account**, a deal is made that is opposite to the first (*i.e.* the investor either buys or sells a similar **instrument**). The original position is then restored by yet another purchase or sale, to be settled on the next settlement day. In effect, the investor negates the original position and then returns to it in the next account.

cash book In **book-keeping**, book in which all receipts and payments are recorded in the first instance.

cash cow Product that continues to provide a healthy **revenue** after its initial launch, with relatively little extra investment.

cash dealings Stock exchange deals that must be settled on the following day. Such bargains are said to be for cash settlement rather than account settlement.

cash flow Movement of money through a company from the time it is received as income (or borrowing), to the time it leaves the company as payments (*e.g.* for raw materials, salaries, etc.). A negative cash flow is the situation in which there is too little money coming in to pay for outgoings. Conversely, a positive cash flow occurs when a company receives income before it is due to pay outgoings. *See also* **discounted cash flow**.

cash on delivery (COD) Distribution system whereby the person in receipt of goods makes payment for them on the spot to the deliverer. Such a system is operated by the UK Post Office, where it is the postman who takes receipt of payment.

cash management Type of bank account available to business clients, which offers services such as debt collection and cash flow services.

cash settlement Payment for **cash dealings**.

petty cash Money in notes and coins kept for payment of small bills and day-to-day expenses.

See also **budget, cash; discount, cash; price, cash; ratio, cash**.

cashpoint Alternative term for automatic telling machine (**ATM**).

CATS *US* Acronym for certificates of accrual on treasury securities, a form of zero coupon bond. *See* **bond, zero-coupon**.

caveat emptor Latin for 'buyer beware'. In legal terms this maxim means that a buyer of goods should use his or her own common sense, and that the law is not prepared to aid someone who buys goods foolishly.

caveat subscriptor Latin for 'signer beware', meaning that anyone who signs a document is bound by its contents, regardless of whether or not he or she has read it, or understood its legal implications.

CBD Abbreviation of cash before delivery.

CBOT Abbreviation of Chicago Board of Trade.

CCA Abbreviation of current cost accounting. *See* **accounting, current cost**.

census National survey that provides information on population, economics and social matters. In the UK the national census is taken every ten years.

Census of Distribution Survey taken every five years of wholesale and retail distribution services.

Census of Production Survey taken annually of industrial production and public utility services.

central unit UK Treasury department that co-ordinates economic information from the other departments, and manages the government's economic strategy.

CEO Abbreviation of chief executive officer.

certificate Document that proves something, *e.g.* right of ownership or that certain actions have taken place.

certificate of incorporation Document issued to a company when it has completed legal incorporation procedures and satisfied the terms of the Companies Acts.

certificate of origin Import-export document that declares the country of origin of goods.

certificates of deposit Essentially, certificates (originally issued by merchant banks) declaring that a certain sum had been deposited with a bank. Sterling certificates of deposit refer to long-term fixed deposits of sums over £10,000 and therefore offer high interest rates.

share certificate Document that proves a person's ownership of a company's **shares**.

certificated Something that has documentary evidence to prove that it is genuine.

cesser Legal term meaning to stop.

cesser of action One court may have proceedings taking place in another court halted. This is known as cesser of action.

CET Abbreviation of common external tariff. *See* **tariff, common external.**

ceteris paribus Latin for 'other things remaining equal'. Used in economic analysis to study the effects of economic variants while assuming that other factors remain the same.

CGT Abbreviation of capital gains tax. *See* **tax, capital gains**.

CH Abbreviation of **corporate hospitality.**

chairman Term with two meanings, depending on the context. A now frequent substitute for chairman is chairperson.
First, he or she is the person who takes charge and directs a meeting.
Second, he or she is the most senior person in a company, public or private, with specific responsibility for running meetings of the **board of directors**. In most cases, the chairman's role includes safeguarding the interests of shareholders, and overseeing the conduct of the company's relations with external institutions, particularly the financial community.

chamber of commerce Organization that promotes and represents the interests of those involved in commerce in a particular geographical area.

champerty Illegal practice of paying the **costs** of a court case in which one is not involved, in return for a proportion of the **damages**.

Chapter 11 *US* Clause in American company law, that enables a company to continue to operate after it has been declared bankrupt (under the direction of the court), so that it may find a way to pay its creditors. The rough equivalent in Britain is **administration**.

charge Sum of money that must be paid on goods or services or the act of requesting that sum.

"The price for our services is £20 per hour, which we must charge for in advance."

accrued charges Charges that have not yet been accounted for or paid. *E.g.* if a demand for **rent** is made in arrears, it must appear on the accounts as an accrued charge, because the service has already been used, but not paid for.

annual charges For **taxation** purposes, that part of a person's or company's income that has been paid after tax has been deducted. *E.g.* a **covenant** to a person is deemed by the Inland Revenue to have been paid net of tax.

bank charges Charges made by a bank on many types of account. Typically, charges are made each time a cheque is drawn or a facility used, although many banks are now advertising no charges on accounts that remain in credit.

charges forward When goods are delivered, notice that all charges must be paid at the time the goods are delivered.

charge off US Alternative term for **write off**.

charges register Part of the certificate issued by the UK Land Register that details all mortgages and charges in respect of a certain piece of land.

fixed charge Asset against which a **mortgage** is secured. Also used as an alternative term for fixed costs. *See* **costs, fixed**.

See also **account, charge; card, charge; order, charging**.

chargeable Something that may be charged for, most usually a sum of money on which **tax** is liable to be paid.

chargeable asset Asset that is liable to give rise to a charge for capital gains tax. *See* **tax, capital gains**.

chargeable gain Gain, or more specifically capital profit, on which tax is payable.

charter Term with two meanings.

First, it is the granting in writing of a title, right or privilege. *E.g.* a bank may be established by the granting of a bank charter.

Second, it is the practice of hiring out a ship or aeroplane for commercial or private use.

chartered Person or institution that has been granted a **charter**. *See* **accountant, chartered; company, chartered**.

chartist Stock market or economic analyst who believes that trends (*e.g.* in price movements, etc.) follow recognizable patterns and so predicts future trends with the aid of charts. *See also* **fundamentalist**.

chattels Moveable property, as opposed to **fixtures**, property that cannot be removed.

cheap jack Person who buys goods at very low prices (*e.g.* from bankrupt companies or goods that are of poor quality) and sells them at below the normal price, sometimes in the street or on a market. *See also* **auction, mock; caveat emptor**.

cheap money Alternative term for easy money. *See* **money, easy**

check *US* Alternative spelling of **cheque**.

checking Computer process that takes place on the London Stock Exchange between trading sessions, by which the records of brokers and market makers are reconciled. *See also* **reconciliation**.

checkless society US spelling of **chequeless society**.

checkoff *US* System whereby union payments are deducted automatically from a worker's wages or salary.

cheque The most familiar form of bill of exchange. A cheque is used to transfer funds from a bank to someone else and is the usual way of withdrawing money from a current account. *See* **account, current**.

banker's cheque Cheque that is drawn on one bank by another bank, usually in order to transfer a customer's funds.

blank cheque Cheque that has been signed by the drawee, but that does not specify the sum to be drawn.

crossed cheque Cheque that is scored across with two parallel lines. This indicates that the cheque must be paid into a bank account. *See also* **cheque, uncrossed**.

gift cheque Cheque printed with additional decoration (*e.g.* a picture), supplied by banks to customers who are willing to pay for their aesthetic value.

open cheque Alternative term for uncrossed cheque. *See* **cheque, uncrossed**.

rubber cheque Cheque that is drawn on an account that has insufficient funds to make the payment. In this event the cheque is 'bounced' back to the drawer.

stale cheque Cheque that was drawn over three months before it was presented. Stale cheques are often refused by banks.

uncrossed cheque Cheque that is not crossed, indicating that it may be exchanged for cash. Also known as an open cheque. *See also* **cheque, crossed**.

See also **account, cheque**.

chequeless (checkless *US)* **society** Future society in which the use of cheques has been superseded. The imminence of the chequeless society may be seen in the more widespread use of credit cards and smart cards.

Chinese fire drill *US* Popular term for total confusion.

Chinese wall Artificial barrier erected between the underwriting and broking departments of a stockbroking company. The Chinese Wall has become necessary since the **Big Bang** changed the London Stock Exchange to a **dual capacity** system in 1986. The purpose of the Chinese Wall is to prevent **insider dealing**. *See* **underwriter**.

Chinese water-torture tactic *US* Popular term for the gradual **takeover** of a company by building up a majority shareholding from shares bought on the open market.

choses-in-action Legal term for the right to assets such as property and money. Hence a **debt** may be termed choses-in-action until the sum is repaid and then becomes **choses-in-possession**.

choses-in-possession Legal term for property owned by a person. *See also* **choses-in-action**.

churning Informal term for the practice of buying and selling stocks and shares solely in order to generate higher **commission** income.

CIF Abbreviation of **cost, insurance and freight**.

City Name given to the financial district of London, situated in the City of London. It covers an area of roughly one square mile and for this reason is also known as the Square Mile.

clause Condition of an agreement, most often used in reference to a **contract**.

capital clause In the memorandum of association of a company, that section setting out the details of the company's **capital**. *See* **association, memorandum of**.

escalator clause Also known as an escalation clause, condition of a long-term contract, that sets out the agreement concerning rising costs *e.g.* of raw materials or labour.

escape clause In a contract, clause that allows one or other party to withdraw from the contract should certain events take place. *E.g.* in a **lease**, it is possible to have a clause that allows the leasee to withdraw should the leasor increase the **rent**.

most-favoured-nation clause In bilateral international trade agreements, clause stating that each country agrees to look upon the other as its 'most-favoured' trading partner, thus offering each other the best tariffs, first refusal, etc.

penalty clause Clause in a **contract** stating that if one party breaks the contract (*e.g.* by late delivery of goods) it will be liable to pay a penalty, usually in money.

claw back Practice of demanding that a person or company return money paid by the Inland Revenue in the form of a tax **rebate**. A claw back most often occurs because of the changed status of the person or company involved. *See* **Revenue, Inland**.

clear Term with three broad meanings.

First, to clear is to have something authorized.

"The goods cleared customs with no problems."

"It took five days to clear the cheque with the bank."

Second, it is to sell goods in order to make room for new **stock**.

"They are having a sale; everything is reduced to clear."

Third, it is a period of so many days, or a sum of money on which there is nothing to be paid.

"He was told that it would take three clear days before the sum was paid into his account."

"This year the company made a clear profit."

clearing Practice of authorizing the payment of financial instruments such as cheques. In the UK, commercial banks are usually members of the **Banker's Clearing House**, which settles their daily balances.

general clearing Clearing of cheques outside London. General clearing takes place in one daily stage.

town clearing Clearing of cheques in London. Town clearing takes place in two stages. The first, in the morning, deals with cheques of less than £500, received the previous day. The second, deals with cheques over £500.

See also **bank, clearing; house, clearing**.

clerk In the UK, person who deals with records of some kind. In the USA, the term is used in the more general sense of anyone dealing with customers, *e.g.* a salesperson in a retail store.

articled clerk Kind of **apprentice**, generally working in one of the professions, such as law or accounting.

authorized clerk Employee of a **stockbroker**, who is authorized to make transactions on his or her behalf.

close Term with three meanings.

First, on a financial **futures** market, it is the thirty seconds before trading closes for the day.

Second, it is also sometimes used to refer to the closing price. *See* **price, closing**.

Third, to close a **position** is to cover an open position on a futures or options market by making a further transaction.

closed Something that is not open to such things as **risk** or the general public. *See also* **company, closed; economy, closed; indent, closed; fund, closed end**.

closing Action that ends something, *e.g.* a day's trading or an auction.

closing range On a financial futures market the highest and lowest prices recorded during the close. *See* **futures, financial**.

See also **bid, closing; price, closing; purchase, closing; sale, closing**.

CME Abbreviation of Chicago Metals Exchange.

CMEA Abbreviation of **Council for Mutual Economic Assistance**.

CNAR Abbreviation of compound net annual rate.

Co Abbreviation of **company**.

COD Abbreviation of **cash on delivery**.

code System of symbols, letters or numbers.

bar code Code printed onto goods in the form of black bars of different widths on a white background. The bar code is capable of being read and deciphered by computer. Most commonly used at checkout points in retailing, the system is capable of reading price and product details, of charging the customer and updating stock records. *See also* **electronic point of sale**.

commercial code Code that is used by international traders in order to reduce the cost of sending telexes and cables.

See also **zip code**.

coemption Legal term for **cornering the market**.

co-insurance Practice of insuring one thing so that the **risk** is divided between several insurers.

cold call Sales practice of approaching a potential customer, either by telephone or in person, without any prior introduction.

collateral Informal term for **security** put up against a loan.

collective Group of people working together towards a common aim.

(free) collective bargaining Practice of workers in trade unions electing representatives to bargain on their behalf with management on such issues as wage levels and working conditions.

collective ownership Ownership of *e.g.* a business or property, with all gains being equally divided among the members of the collective.

collectivism Economic system in which all factors of production are owned by the community and controlled largely by the state. *See also* **communism**.

combat pay *US* Alternative term for danger money. *See* **money, danger**.

come to market *US* Alternative term for a new issue. *See* **issue, new**.

COMECON Acronym for **Council for Mutual Economic Assistance**.

COMEX Acronym for Commodity Exchange of New York.

commercial Thing or person associated with business or commerce. The term has also recently come to mean a product that will sell well. *See* **bank, commercial; code, commercial**.

commission Money paid to an intermediary, usually calculated as a percentage of the sum involved in the transaction.
"The salesman recieved 5% commission on each sale he made."

address commission In shipping, commission paid to a shipping **agent** in return for seeing that the cargo is loaded onto the vessel.

over-riding commission Commission paid to a broker in return for finding underwriters to an issue of shares. *See* **issue, share; underwriter**.

See also **agent, commission; house, commission**.

commitment window *US* The amount of time an employee is prepared to spend in the service of one company.

committee of inspection Committee made up of a bankrupt company's creditors to direct the company's **winding-up**, either in the hands of a receiver or a liquidator. *See* **liquidation; receivership**.

commodity Term with two meanings.
First, in economics, it is any tangible good that is traded.
Second, it is raw materials and foods, especially such goods as cocoa, coffee, corn, jute, potatoes, tea, etc.

primary commodity Commodities that are essential to a nation, *e.g.* food and raw materials for industry.

staple commodity Alternative term for primary commodity. *See* **commodity, primary**.

See also **exchange, commodity; futures, commodity**.

common Something that happens very frequently, or that applies equally to a number of people, without exclusion or differentiation. *See* **tariff, common external**.

communism Political and economic system whereby all factors of production are owned and controlled by the state. *See also* **capitalism**.

company Group of people that has been legally incorporated to produce certain goods or services, or to transact any other type of business.

associate company Company that is partly owned by another.

company doctor Person who is brought into a company that is on the brink of liquidation, usually at board level. The company doctor often has powers to administer very strong medicine in order to put the company back on its feet.

chartered company Company that is incorporated by Royal Charter. The main difference between a chartered and an ordinary company, is that the former is treated as an individual person in law.

close company Company whose shares are held privately, by a few individuals (usually not more than five people), and not traded on a stock exchange. The US alternative is closed company or closely-held company.

closed company US Alternative term for close company. *See* **company, close**.

closely-held company US Alternative term for close company. *See* **company, close**.

company spy US Employee who keeps an eye on union activities and reports them to management.

family company Company founded by and owned almost exclusively by members of one family.

holding company Company that exists to own shares in other companies, that are (depending on the level of shareholding) its subsidiaries. An immediate holding company is one that holds a controlling interest in another company, but in turn, the immediate holding company itself may be owned by a holding company.

independent company Company that operates entirely under its own authority, and is not owned or controlled (in part or in whole) by any other company.

joint-stock company Alternative term for limited company. *See* **company, limited (liability)**.

limited (liability) company Company formed from a group of people, whose **liability** is limited to the extent of the investment they have made.

listed company Company whose shares are listed on a stock exchange.

management company Company that practices management consultancy.

parent company Company that owns or part-owns, but more importantly, controls several subsidiary companies.

private (limited) company Company whose shares are not available to the general public through the medium of a stock exchange, and whose members do not exceed 50 in number.

public limited company (plc) Company whose shares are available to the general public through a stock exchange.

quoted company Company that has received listing on a stock exchange. The shares of such a company may thus be traded on the open market. *See* **Official List.**

shell company Company that does not produce anything in the usual sense, but exists only in name. Shell companies may be set up and sold to people who are unfamiliar with the procedure for doing this, or may be the remnants of a defunct company that has been sold on to someone else. They may also be set up for use at some future time, or to operate as the holder of shares.

statutory company Company set up by Act of Parliament to produce essential services such as the provision of power and water.

subsidiary company Company that is owned or partly-owned by another, called the parent company. *See* **company, parent**.

threshold company US Company that has moved out of the **start-up** stage and is moving towards becoming secure and more profitable.

unlimited company Company that consists of members who are all liable for the total of the company's debts.

unquoted company Company that does not have its shares quoted on a stock exchange.

See also **finance company; secretary, company**.

comparative advantage State of being more efficient in one activity than in another, relative to a different country. *E.g.* a country is able to produce cars twice as efficiently as another, but produces aeroplanes ten times more efficiently. In a free market, this country would export aeroplanes and import cars and it is said that, in the production of aeroplanes, it has a comparative advantage over the other.

compensation Usually a sum of money paid in lieu of something lost. "She received substantial compensation for the injuries she sustained in a road accident which prevented her from working for a full year." *See also* **damages**.

competition Effort directed towards doing better than someone else, especially that among rival companies in the same market. "When they entered the market, Honeybone Productions found themselves in direct competition with several much larger companies."

competition analysis US The process of gathering and assessing information about one's corporate competition.

free competition Situation in which rival companies are allowed to compete freely with each other for a share of the market. In a free competition or free market economy, the laws of supply and demand regulate prices. *See also* **competition, perfect**.

imperfect competition Situation of competition in which the goods are not homogenous, i.e. they are not perfect substitutes for each other. This dissimilarity gives the producer a small amount of control over price. Also known as monopolistic competition. *See also* **competition, perfect**.

monopolistic competition Alternative term for imperfect competition. *See* **competition, imperfect**.

perfect competition Situation of competition in which the product is perfectly similar so that the consumer has no preference, and there are a large number of producers and consumers, so that any producer who tries to raise the price of the product above market price is undercut by competitors and consumers only buy at the lowest price. This model is frequently used by economists.

pure competition Alternative term for perfect competition. *See* **competition, perfect**.

complements Two goods that are related in such a way that when **demand** for one increases, demand for the other rises at the same time. *E.g.* cameras and photographic film are complements, as are cars and petrol.

completion The finish of something, such as a job or contract.

compound Term with two meanings.
First, it is to agree with creditors to settle a debt by paying only part of it.
"He compounded his debts with his creditors."
Second, it is to add something to a thing that is already there. *E.g.* compound interest is calculated by adding each interest payment to the capital sum and taking this new total as the basis for the next reckoning. *See also* **interest, compound**.

79

con Popular abbreviation of **confidence trick**.

concern Alternative term for a business or company.
"When he left the company, it was still a going concern."

concert party Group of people who come together secretly to 'act in concert', that is, to orchestrate a market in the group's favour. *E.g.* Two or more people may form a concert party to buy shares in a company in order to effect a takeover. Such action is illegal.

concession Term with two broad meanings.
First, it is the right to use someone else's property as part of a business. Second, it is an allowance made to someone who would otherwise be charged.

in-store concession In order to maintain their own profits, some large stores allow smaller retailing operations to set up and staff areas of the store for the sale of their own goods. The store then takes a percentage of the concession's takings in payment.

mining concession Land that is conceded to a mining concern for a certain period of time, so that the company is able to mine it.

tax concession Allowance made by the Inland Revenue to taxpayers in certain categories, which means that these people or companies pay less tax than they would otherwise be liable for. *E.g.* tax concessions are often used by the government to induce companies to relocate in areas high in unemployment.

conditional Something that is not certain but depends upon an event or situation. *See also* **bill of sale, conditional**.

conference line Term with two meanings.
First, it is a service available to corporate telephone users, which allows several callers in different locations to talk to each other at the same time.
Second, it is a group of shipping companies that have agreed on freight rates and passenger fares. Conference line shippers usually charge lower rates than non-conference lines.

confidence Feeling of certainty or security. *E.g.* confidence in a company's ability to produce the goods is extremely important if it is to find **investment**.

confidence trick Business deal (or any form of agreement) in which one person gains another's confidence and proceeds to do the unexpected, *i.e.* to trick him or her.

conglomerate Very large public company that is extremely diverse and probably international in its operations.

conman Informal term for someone who plays *confidence tricks* – a confidence trickster.

consideration In some forms of **contract**, the agreement is made binding by the payment of a sum of money from one party to the other. Such a payment is known as a consideration.

consignment Shipment of goods sent to someone (*e.g.* an agent), usually so that he or she may sell them for the consignor.

consistency concept In **accounting**, a concept whereby accounts for one period are constructed on the same principles as for another.

consolidation Term with three meanings.
  In shipping, it is the practice of putting together goods for shipping to the same destination.
  In **accounting**, it is the practice of putting together the accounts of the **subsidiary** companies of a group, to calculate overall results for the group as a whole.
  In share dealings, it is the practice of combining a number of low-priced shares, to produce a realistically marketable **lot**. *See also* **split**.

consolidated tape US Ticker tape that brings information regarding transactions that are listed on the New York Stock Exchange, but transacted on any of the regional US exchanges.

See also **accounts, consolidated; fund, consolidated**.

CONSOL Abbreviation of Consolidated Stock or Consolidated Loan, a form of fixed-interest government security.

consortium Group of companies that come together to bid for a certain project. It is usually dissolved after that one project is complete. Similar to a **syndicate**, only more short-term.

constitution Set of rules and details of aims, laid down by a society or club.

consumable Something that is used up (*e.g.* welding rods, typewriter ribbons, computer printing paper) in a business or industry, as opposed to things (*e.g.* raw materials) that are incorporated into a product.

consumables Goods that are **consumable**.

consumer Person who buys goods for consumption. *See* **durable, consumer; goods, consumer; banking, consumer**.

consumption Act of consuming, *i.e.* using goods or services that are thereby damaged or destroyed and cannot therefore be re-sold.

conspicuous consumption Consumer trend that involves the consumer buying goods (usually status symbols, such as sports cars, etc.), deriving satisfaction, not from consumption of the goods themselves, but from being seen by other people to own them.

contango Stock exchange term for a delayed settlement of a bargain from one account to the next. A **premium** is payable. Also used more frequently in futures trading to mean the opposite of **backwardation**.

contingency Something that is liable, but not certain to happen at some time in the future. *See also* **contingent**.

contingent Something that depends upon an uncertain event taking place.
"The bank's willingness to lend the company money is contingent upon our breaking even at the end of this financial year."
See also **annuity, contingent**.

continuation Alternative term for **contango**.

contra Latin for on the opposite side. *See* **per contra**.

contract Term with two meanings.
First, it is a legally binding agreement between two or more parties.
Second, it is to form such an agreement.

contract out In general, to make an agreement to forego some activity (and its possible benefits). In particular, with term refers to a company that believes it can provide sufficient **pension** cover for its employees more economically using a private scheme than using the state pension system. In this case, the company is required by law to provide at least the minimum payments of a state pension. *See also* **contract in**.

contract in In general, to make an agreement to join some scheme (and participate in its benefits). In particular, it is the decision of a company to make contributions towards the state **pension** scheme for its employees. If a company does contract in in this way, it is also able to provide extra pensions by using private schemes. *See also* **contract out**.

contract size Size (*i.e.* weight) of a futures contract, so as to ascertain its value. Contract sizes are all fixed, *e.g.* COMEX gold is 100 oz.

free contract Alternative term for **rendu**.

hell or high water contract US Informal term for a guarantee that a municipal bond will be paid, come hell or high water. *See* **bond, municipal**.

infant's contract In general terms no contract may be enforceable if it is made against a person under the age of 18.

open contract Contract that has been bought or sold on a financial futures market, but has not been closed by making an offsetting transaction or taking delivery of the financial instrument involved. *See also* **position, open**.

parole contract Simple, unwritten (*i.e.* verbal) contract.

quasi-contract Contract that is either verbal or partly voidable, which a court decides is enforceable in part.

under contract To be bound by the terms of a contract.

voidable contract Contract that may be avoided by one or other of the parties to it. *E.g.* if one party fails to make known all information relevant to the contract, it may be deemed voidable.

void contract Contract that was drawn up on the basis of what turns out to be misunderstandings on both sides. Such a contract is deemed in law never to have existed. *See also* **contract, voidable**.

contra proferentem rule Nickname for the following Latin maxim: *verba chartarum fortuis accipiuntur contra proferentem* - the words of the contract are construed more strictly against the person proclaiming them. In effect, the contra proferentem rule means that if a contract is ambiguous, it will be construed in a way that is the least advantageous to the party that drew up the contract.

contrarian *US* Informal term for a speculator in stocks and shares who goes against short-term trends. *E.g.* a contrarian may decide on a buying policy in a bear market. *See* **market, bear**.

contribution Money paid as an addition to another sum.

con trick = **confidence trick**

convenor Person who calls (convenes) a meeting. Most often used for the person in a trade union who organizes union meetings, and is the senior elected union representative at a particular site.

conversion Term with two meanings.
First, it is the changing of one thing into another that is equivalent.
Second, in a legal context, it is interference with the property of someone else, so as to deprive them of the right of ownership.

convertible Something that is easily capable of **conversion**.
The term has the more specific meaning of loan stock, bonds and debentures that are easily converted into ordinary shares. These are known as convertibles, or, in the USA, converts. *See* **currency, convertible**.

cooling off period Period of ten days (in the UK) during which a person who has agreed to a certain form of contract (such as a credit sale or hire purchase agreement) may withdraw that agreement and have his or her money repaid. Such a period exists in order to minimize the effects of hard selling that some companies undertake.

co-operative Group of people who come together to produce goods or services and who share all profits.

co-operative society Society of consumers and producers (or retailers) who share the profits of their co-operation.

copy Term with two meanings.
First, it is to reproduce something.
Second, it is text, or some form of written material.

advertising copy Verbal part of an advertisement.

certified copy Copy of a document that is certified as being identical.

fair copy Document that is a copy of an earlier draft, but without the mistakes and revisions. Also known as final copy.

hard copy Copy (on paper) of a document that has been written or stored on a computer disk or on microfilm.

knocking copy Advertising copy that relies on pointing out the faults of a competing product to sell its own.

top copy First (and most legible) sheet of a document, of which several carbon copies have been made.

copyhold Alternative term for **freehold**.

copyright Legal term for the right of ownership of an author over his or her own work. Copyright extends for fifty years after the author's death.

copywriter Person who writes advertising **copy**.

corpocracy If a company is involved in several mergers, its management is at risk of becoming cumbersome and confused. The resulting corporation thus labours under a large and inefficient bureaucracy and is known informally as a corpocracy.

Corn Exchange London commodities exchange that deals in such commodities as cereals and animal foodstuffs.

corner the market To build up a virtual **monopoly** in particular goods or services, so that the monopolist is able to dictate **price**.

corp Abbreviation of **corporation**.

corporate To do with a **corporation**.

corporate culture Culture that grows up within a company, among its employees. Corporate culture embodies such factors as dress, its employee's attitudes towards working and their expectations, and the style of working relationships.

corporate hospitality (CH) Hospitality extended to a company's most favoured clients (or potential clients) in the form of entertainment, *e.g.* tickets to the theatre or to prestigious sporting events.

corporate identity Identity of a company as displayed in the visual images it uses, *e.g.* logos and colours.

corporate image Image that a company presents to the general public. Some large companies are now spending large sums on improving their corporate image. *See also* **corporate identity**.

corporate licensing US Alternative term for **merchandising**.

corporate planning Activity undertaken to plan the future aims of a company, covering such subject areas as new products, sales targets and production targets.

corporate veil US Protection against liability that is afforded to multiple shareholders in a company as opposed to one single owner. *See also* **liability, limited**.

corporate venturing Practice of a company providing venture capital for another. Corporate venturing is usually undertaken to give the investing company a potential foothold in a new (or related) market or field, or to lay the foundations for a possible **takeover** at some future date. *See* **capital, venture**.

corporation Large **company**, usually with several **subsidiary** companies. In the USA, it is a company that has been incorporated under US law. Therefore, the term is a virtual synonym for company. Often abbreviated to corp. *See also* **corporate; tax, corporation**.

correspondent bank = **bank, correspondent**

cost Amount of money that has to be expended to acquire something.

accounting cost Total expenditure required to undertake an activity. *See also* **cost, economic**.

cost and freight (C&F) When exporting goods, a contract in which it is agreed that the exporter pays all costs up to the delivery point except for insurance.

See also **cost, insurance and freight; cost, insurance, freight and interest**.

cost centre For **accounting** purposes, location (*e.g.* a geographical area or department) or piece of equipment that can be isolated, with a view to ascribing specific costs to it. *See also* **cost unit; overheads**.

cost-effective Something that gives value for money. Often used as a relative term.
"Having discussed each of the alternatives, John decided that this would be the most cost-effective way of producing the goods."

cost, insurance and freight (CIF) Foreign trade contract stipulating that the exporter pays all costs up to the point of delivery, including insurance of goods in transit. *See also* **cost and freight; cost, insurance, freight and interest**.

cost, insurance, freight and interest (CIFI) Export contract, by which the exporter is bound to pay all costs to delivery, along with insurance on goods in transit and interest on the value of the goods. *See also* **cost and freight; cost, insurance and freight**.

cost minimization Practice of seeking the minimum cost at which a company is able to produce the output it requires.

cost of living In national terms, the amount of money each person has to spend in order buy food and accommodation. *See also* **index, retail price**.

cost-plus System of charges whereby the buyer pays the cost of the item plus a commission to the seller.
"Peter decided to charge for the goods on a cost-plus basis."

cost unit One article, to which a cost may be ascribed for **accounting** purposes. Cost units may include simple articles such as raw materials (*e.g.* a plank of wood), or articles in production (although these are more complicated in that they require the accounting to take into account direct and indirect costs). *See also* **cost centre**.

economic cost Total expense involved in undertaking a certain activity. Economic cost includes accounting cost and opportunity cost. *See* **cost, accounting; cost, opportunity**.

historical cost Cost of an asset at the time it was acquired, rather than the cost of its replacement. *See also* **accounting, historical cost**.

incremental cost Extra cost incurred when a company agrees to take on a new project.

marginal cost Cost incurred in raising the level of output beyond the original target. Marginal cost calculations are used to justify going beyond that target (or, indeed, not doing so).

opportunity cost Cost involved in using an asset (*e.g.* machinery) for one purpose rather than another. *E.g.* a company owns a building, which it uses as storage space. The company could rent it to someone else for, say, £500 per week. That sum is the opportunity cost of the building.

selling cost Extra expenditure required to increase **sales**.

unabsorbed cost In accounting, the cost of production may be allocated to each unit over a specified level of output and represented as a percentage of that unit's overall cost to the producer. If the specified level of output is not reached, then some of this cost is not paid for, and is known as unabsorbed cost.

unit cost Cost of producing one item. Unit cost is calculated by taking the total cost of production and dividing it into the number of units produced. Unit cost helps a company to determine **price**.
See also **accountant, cost; accounting, cost; inflation, cost-push**.

costing Practice of working out how much a product will cost to produce, taking into account costs such as raw materials, labour, overheads, etc. A frequent alternative is costing-out.

costs Term with two meanings.
First, it refers to expenses incurred during a court case.
"Roger was fined £200 and ordered to pay costs."
    Second, it is the sum of the cost of each item used during production of goods or services.

direct costs Costs of materials, items or activities that are directly involved in the production of goods, and without which those goods could not be produced in the short run.

fixed costs Costs that do not vary with short-term changes in the level of output (such as heating costs or rates).

indirect costs Costs of items or activities, such as maintenance of buildings and machinery, which are not used in the production of goods, nor immediately necessary for their production.

labour costs Expenses incurred in providing labour in the production process. Labour costs can include not only wages and salaries, but also National Insurance contributions and contributions to pension schemes.

manufacturing costs All expenses incurred by the manufacturer in the production of goods and services. Also known as production costs.

operating costs Expenses incurred in the day-by-day running of a company.

production costs Alternative term for manufacturing costs. *See* **costs, manufacturing**.

running costs Alternative term for operating costs. *See* **costs, operating**.

semi-variable costs Costs that include both fixed and variable costs in the reckoning. Also known as stepped costs.

skunk costs US Costs already ascribed to a project, that will not be clawed back if the company decides to abort the project.

stepped costs Alternative term for semi-variable costs.

supplementary costs Alternative term for **overheads**.

variable costs Expenses incurred in production, that vary depending on output.

Council for Mutual Economic Assistance (COMECON or CMEA) Group of Communist bloc countries that combined in 1949, with the aim of producing a self-sufficient economic bloc that could be co-ordinated from a central point (and to consolidate Soviet influence in the area). COMECON has now begun to trade more actively with non-COMECON neighbours in an effort to stimulate their own economies and the supply of foreign **currency**. COMECON members are:

Bulgaria, Cuba, Czechoslovakia, East Germany, Hungary, Mongolia, Poland, Rumania, USSR, and Vietnam. Associated countries are Afghanistan, Angola, Ethiopia, Laos, Mozambique, Yemen and Yugoslavia.

counter Term with two meanings.
First, it is a (figurative) table across which goods are bought and sold. Second, it is a prefix meaning against.

counterbid Bid that is made (*e.g.* during a takeover battle or an auction) against a previous bid, going one better.

counterclaim Claim for damages made by a defendant against a plaintiff, in the hopes that the counterclaim will offset any **damages** payable to the plaintiff in the first action. *See also* **set-off**.

countermarketing Willful destruction of the reputation or credibility of a product, either by a competing firm or by a consumer action group. "Anti-smoking groups have recently launched a biting countermarketing strategy against tobacco products."

countermove Tactical action taken in response to moves made by an opponent, *e.g.* during a **takeover** battle.

counter-offer Offer (*e.g.* of a price on a property) made in response to a previous offer.
"Both companies wanted the premises so badly that offer after counter-offer was made, until the final price was astronomical."

countersign To sign a document that has been signed by someone else. "Please would you ask Bill to countersign this contract before I return it."

over the counter Something that is legal, above board. *See also* **market, over the counter**.

under the counter Something that is illegal.
"During the war, the grocer used to sell my mother eggs under the counter."

counterfeit Banknotes that have been forged.

countervailing credit Alternative term for **back-to-back credit**.

coupon Term with two meanings.

First, it is a document attached to a bond, that must be detached and sent to the paying party in order for the bond holder to receive **interest** payments. Each payment is detailed on the coupon for each payment period.

Second, it is an alternative term for interest that is payable on a fixed-interest security. *See* **security, fixed-interest**.

See also **cum coupon; ex coupon**.

covenant Term with two meanings.

First, it is broadly any form of **agreement**.

Second, and more specifically, it is an agreement taken out between two parties, stating that one party agrees to pay the other a series of fixed sums over a certain period of time. If the covenant covers a period longer than six years, then the payer is entitled to **tax relief** on the payments.

restrictive covenant Agreement between two parties that restricts the activities of one. *E.g.* a restrictive covenant may take the form of a **clause** in a **contract** to supply goods, that stops the supplier selling goods to a competitor of the second party. A restrictive covenant may not be upheld legally if it is seen to be against the general good (*e.g.* against the interests of free competition).

cover Term with several meanings.

First, it is any form of **security** (*i.e.* collateral).

Second, it is used in financial futures markets to refer to the buying of contracts to offset a short position. *See* **short selling**.

Third, it is the number of times a company could pay its dividends to shareholders from its earnings.

"This year's annual report shows that C & F White plc are three times covered."

Fourth, it is to make enough money in selling products or services to pay for their production.

"I am pleased to say that last year, we more than covered our costs."

Fifth, it is the amount of money that an insured person stands to receive from an insurer should he or she make a claim.

"Tim has $600,000 insurance cover for his small art collection."

Sixth, it is the constituent amount put up as **margin** per unit of quotation on a futures contract, which combined will dictate the margin.

CPP Abbreviation of current purchasing power (accounting). *See* **accounting, current purchasing power**.

crash Term with two meanings.

First, it is an informal term for a very severe drop in prices on securities, financial and commodities markets. The most famous was the Wall Street Crash of 1929, which led to the 1930s depression; the largest in recent years was the worldwide drop in share prices on 15 October 1987.

Second, it is an informal term for a computer failure. In the USA, this is also known as brownout.

crawling peg Form of fixed **exchange rate**, in which the rate is allowed to fluctuate according to supply and demand, but within certain specified minimum and maximum limits. Also known as a sliding peg.

credit Term with several meanings.

First it is a loan of money.

"Andrew found it difficult to obtain credit from any bank."

Second, it is to add a sum to an **account**.

"My building society credits my account with interest automatically."

Third, in book-keeping, it is a **balance** that shows a profit.

"When he had rationalized his extremely complicated personal finances, he found that he was in credit after all."

Fourth, it is the financial standing of a person or company.

"Their credit is very good, so you may feel confident about lending them money."

blank credit Credit facilities with no upper limit.

credit bureau Alternative term for credit agency. *See* **agency, credit**.

credit crunch US Situation in which short credit becomes scarce and thus more expensive than long credit. *See* **credit, long; credit, short**.

credit freeze Action by banks to restrict the extension of credit to customers. Also known as credit squeeze.

credit limit The maximum sum that a person is prepared to lend to another.

"At Christmas, I spent right up to my credit limit."

credit squeeze Alternative term for **credit freeze**.

extended credit Credit that is to be repaid over a very long period of time. *See also* **credit, long; credit, short**.

irrevocable and confirmed credit Credit facilities that are confirmed by a bank in London on an account held by a non-UK resident. *See also* **irrevocable documentary acceptance credit**.

irrevocable documentary acceptance credit Credit facilities arranged by an overseas customer with a bank in London, who is then presented with a letter of credit to facilitate foreign trade.

long credit Loan that may be repaid over a long period of time. *See also* **credit, extended; credit, short**.

open credit Credit that is extended to the customers of a bank who are deemed to be extremely creditworthy, and thus requiring no **security**.

revocable credit Credit facility extended by a banker who is willing to take **bills of exchange**, but revocable (*i.e.* repayable) at any time.

revolving credit Lending made by a bank that is automatically renewed at the start of each period (or as soon as the sum is repaid). *E.g.* a bank may arrange to lend a customer a certain amount each month. It will stop borrowing above that limit once it is reached, but allow borrowing to go on at the start of the next month. The US alternative is revolver.

short credit Loan that must be repaid over a short timescale. *See also* **credit, extended; credit, long**.

tax credit That part of a **dividend** payment on which a company has already paid **tax**, thus relieving the **shareholder** of the necessity of doing so.

See also **account, credit; agency, credit; balance, credit; card, credit; debit; note, credit; rating, credit; transfer, credit**.

creditor Person or company to whom money is owed.

preferential creditor Creditor entitled to repayment before the debts of other creditors are met. Secured creditors have preference over unsecured creditors, and in the case of the liquidation of a company, payment of outstanding tax and salaries have preference over the settlement of debts.

trade creditor Person or company to whom money is owed as a result of normal trading.

unsecured creditor Person who has made a loan but demanded no **security**.

creditworthy Person who, from his or her record, is deemed willing and able to pay back credit. Thus, a creditworthy person finds it easier to borrow (and to borrow larger sums) than someone who is deemed to be a credit risk.

CRT Abbreviation of composite rate tax.

cross Term with two meanings.
First, it is to mark a **cheque** with two parallel lines to indicate that it is not negotiable and so must be paid into the bank account of the named payee.
Second, it is the practice of buying and selling the same block of **shares** or **futures** contracts simultaneously by the same broker.
See also **rate, cross**.

cross-border accord *US* Agreement made between two countries that are neighbours, often with regard to trading.

crowd The people who wish to trade in a particular option or future, so named because to do so, they must gather around the relevant **pitch**.

crown jewel tactic Strategy undertaken by a company that is threatened by **takeover**, in which it sells, or offers to sell, the best part of its business to someone other than the **raider** (*e.g.* a **white knight**), in order to make the target seem less desirable.

CT Abbreviation of corporation tax. *See* **tax, corporation**.

CTT Abbreviation of capital transfer tax. *See* **tax, capital transfer**.

CUG Abbreviation of closed user group.

cum coupon **Security** that is passed from one holder to another with **coupon** (enabling the holder to claim **interest** payments) attached. *See also* **ex coupon**.

cum dividend Shares that are sold with the right of the new holder to claim the next **dividend** payment. Sometimes abbreviated to cum div. *See also* **ex dividend**.

cum new Shares that are sold with the right to claim participation in a **scrip** or rights issue. *See also* **ex new; issue, scrip**.

currency Coins and banknotes that are used as legal **tender**.

blocked currency Currency that may not be removed from a country, sometimes for political reasons.

convertible currency Currency that is easily exchangeable for another.

hard currency Currency, used in international trade, from a country with a stable and prosperous economy. Thus demand for it is high compared with the demand for the currencies of weak, unstable or legally restricted economies.

reserve currency Foreign currency held by a central bank in order to fund foreign trade. *See* **reserves**.

scarce currency Alternative term for hard currency. *See* **currency, hard**.

soft currency Currency of which there is a surplus on the market and thus, relatively cheap.

See also **devaluation, currency; exposure, currency**.

current Continuing state of affairs that is occurring or relevant at the present time, and is expected to remain so in the near future. *See also* **accounting, current cost; assets, current; ratio, current assets**.

curriculum vitae Latin for the course of life. Document that relates (most usually in tabular form) the education, qualifications, and career of a person. Known in the USA as a resumé.

customs and excise Body that exists to control imports and to assess and collect customs and **excise** duties. The full name is Her Majesty's Customs and Excise. *See also* **barrier, customs; duty, customs**.

cut a deal To agree on the basic principles of an agreement. Negotiation or finalization of details usually follows.

cyclicals *US* Shares in companies that are involved in basic industries, such as the provision of raw materials, metals etc. So-called because their prices on the stock market tend to rise and fall with the business cycle.

D

damages Civil court award of monetary compensation for loss or injury.

contemptuous damages Damages awarded if the court agrees that the defendant was at fault, but believes that the loss or injury caused was so minor that the case should not have been brought.

exemplary damages Punitive damages awarded in an attempt to compensate for damage to an intangible thing (such as feelings or reputation) or to deter others from repeating the action which resulted in the award.

liquidated damages Damages of an amount already specified in a **contract**. The terms of the contract provides for liquidated damages to be paid in the event of certain specified breaches of that contract. *See also* **damages, unliquidated**.

nominal damages Damages awarded by a court which is satisfied that the plaintiff is in the right, but has suffered no actual loss.

substantial damages Damages designed by the court to place the plaintiff in the financial position that he or she would have enjoyed had the loss or injury not occurred. If the monetary value of the loss or injury can be precisely calculated, the substantial damages awarded are said to be specific; if precise calculation is impossible, approximate (general) damages are awarded.

unliquidated damages Amount of damages determined by a court, rather than specified by a contract.

See also **damages, liquidated**.

data Items of **information**.

data acquisition Purchase of data, computing software, etc.

database Data organized to allow easy access to the most up-to-date information and its collation with older data. The term is generally applied to electronic storage devices (i.e. computers), which can store, organize and search for data much more rapidly than was hitherto possible.

dataprocessing Sorting and organization of data in order to produce the desired information, generally according to standard procedures.

data security Protection of data from electronic criminals. Data security generally entails the production of programmes intended to deny unauthorized persons access to a database by means of passwords and other identification procedures. *See* **electronic crime**.

datel service British Telecom service that enables the transmission of computer data via telephone lines.

date The day, month and year. In the UK these are recorded numerically in that order (*i.e.* 1:2:89 February 1st 1989). However, in Europe and in the USA, they are recorded in the order month, day, year (*i.e.* 1:2:89 January 2nd 1989).

average due date If the due date falls within a range of days, the average due date is the mid-point of that range. *See* **date, due**.

back date To date a document with a date previous to that on which it was actually signed. Back dating indicates that the provisions of the document became effective on the back date rather than the date on which the document was signed.

base date Alternative term for base year. *See* **year, base**.

due date Date on which a **bill of exchange** is due to be paid. Instruments not payable on demand, on sight or on presentation are allowed three days of grace.

effective date Date on which a **contract** is concluded and becomes effective.

expiry date Date on which an agreement lapses.

indebtedness date Alternative term for indebtedness day. *See* **day, indebtedness**.

maturity date Date, specified in advance, on which a financial instrument may be exchanged for its cash value.

redemption date Date on which a **loan** or **debenture** is to be repaid. Redemption dates (plural) are those on which a **stock** is redeemable at par. In the case of Treasury stocks, the precise date of repayment is decided by the government. *See* **parity**.

settlement date The account day; the date on which stock exchange dealings must be settled. It falls ten days or six business days after the end of an **account**. *See* **account day**.

day Period of 24 hours

day book Ledger in which transactions are listed on a daily basis prior to transfer to ledgers which deal with transactions on a subject basis. It is usual to keep separate purchase and sales day books.

days of grace The period of three days still permitted in the UK for the payment of any **bill of exchange** except **bills of sight**. Days of grace have been abolished in most other countries.

day order Order given by an investor to a **stockbroker** which is valid only on the day it was given. A day order also specifies a price limit on the transaction envisaged. If not completed on the day in question, the transaction is automatically cancelled.

day to day loan US Alternative term for overnight loans, particularly to financial institutions which are temporarily illiquid. The money is leant by companies wishing to be paid **interest** on money earned in the previous day's trading. **Interest rates** on day to day loans are high and variable.

impact day Day on which a company is scheduled to publish details of a new issue. *See* **issue, new**.

indebtedness day When a company issues a prospectus, it must make known the day on which its statement of debt (the extent of its indebtedness) was made. It is assumed that the indebtedness figure was correct at that time.

last trading day In trading in financial futures, the last day on which trading may take place before delivery. See **futures, financial**.

lay day Day on which a vessel may unload cargo without incurring port charges.

name day On the Stock Exchange, the day before **account day**, on which sellers of **securities** are supplied with the names of those who have bought from them during the last **account**.

running days A number of consecutive lay days including weekends and public holidays. *See* **day, lay; day, weather working**.

settlement day Alternative term for **account day**.

trading day Day on which trading takes place on a stock exchange. On the UK stock exchange, every day is a trading day with the exception of weekends and public holidays.

weather working day Day on which work is able to go ahead because the weather conditions are favourable, *e.g.* in construction work or in loading or unloading a ship in port.

See also **account day**.

DCE Abbreviation of **domestic credit expansion**.

DCF Abbreviation of **discounted cash flow**.

dead cat bounce *US* Brief rise in the stock **index** of a falling market. The term refers to the supposed ability of a cat always to land on its feet. If a falling cat bounces, it must be dead. *See also* **bottoming out**.

deadheading *US* Term with two meanings.
First, it is the promotion of a junior member of staff over the heads of more senior members.
Second, it is the movement of a company vehicle from one location where it is not needed to a location where it is, and transporting employees at the same time.

dead in the water *US* A project that has failed completely, often before it is properly underway.

deadweight Debt not covered by or incurred in exchange for real assets. *E.g.* that portion of the National Debt taken on to pay for war is a deadweight debt.

deal Agreement or transaction; in particular, any bargain made on a stock market.

bought deal Practice common in the USA, and now becoming more common in to the UK, of a major financial institution purchasing a large **portfolio** of **securities** which it then passes on to its clients piecemeal.

cash deal Agreement or transaction concluded with a cash payment; on the stock exchange, a deal to be completed on the next trading day.

package deal Deal that is all-inclusive, *i.e.* one that makes provision for the settlement of most or all the outstanding issues between the parties concerned.

upstairs deal Deal arranged upstairs and behind closed doors — usually in the boardroom. Many takeovers are settled by upstairs deals.

dealer Anyone who is engaged in trading on a financial market.

primary dealer US Regulated dealer in government securities. *See* **securities, government**.

dealing Activity of dealers.

after hours dealing Alternative term for early bargain. *See* **bargain, early**.

dealing for the account Speculative stock market trading in which shares are bought and sold in the very short term. Because accounts do not have to be settled until **account day**, it is possible for a dealer to buy thousands of pounds worth of stock without having to pay for them. If the stock is then sold before account day, the dealer can keep any **profit** resulting from price fluctuations while the stock was held. Conversely, **bears** may sell stock which they do not actually possess in the belief that they will be able to buy back the stock at a lower price as the market falls. This practice is known as selling short.

forward dealing Accepting or awarding a contract (most usually on a **commodities** market) for settlement or delivery by a pre-arranged future date. *See also* **futures**.

margin dealing Term with three meanings.
   First, it is the method of dealing commodities or financial futures, in which only a proportion of the value of the contract is put up. *See* **cover**; **margin**.
   Second, it refers to high-gear dealing on the edge of a security's price; *i.e.* betting for low stakes on a high-risk change of price.
   Third, it describes transactions conducted on the margin of a loan from a broker to a speculator. The speculator deposits stock as collateral, but may still trade with any surplus accumulated as the result of a rise in market price.

option dealing Buying and selling in **options** to buy or sell goods or shares at some future date and at a pre-arranged price.

See also **insider dealing**.

death valley curve Period of time during which a start-up company uses venture capital at an extremely fast rate, to the point where it is using equity capital to fund overheads, an unhealthy state of affairs.

death valley days Nickname for 'dry' periods on the financial markets; days on which little trading takes place. *See also* **valium picnic**.

debentures Long term loans to companies made at a fixed rate of interest and usually with a specified **maturity**, generally between 10 and 40 years. Debenture holders are numbered with the company's creditors, and in the event of **liquidation** have preferential claims on the firm. Debentures may be treated as tradeable **securities**.

mortgage debenture Debenture secured by the mortgage of a property or other asset owned by the institution concerned.

naked debenture Alternative term for unsecured debenture. *See* **debenture, unsecured**.

perpetual debenture Debenture that may not be repaid on **demand**.

simple debenture Alternative term for unsecured debenture. *See* **debenture, unsecured**.

unsecured debenture Debenture that gives the holder no legal redress if full repayment has not been received by the specified repayment date. In such a case, the holder of an unsecured debenture must wait until the company has been wound up before claiming payment. For this reason, most debentures are secured against company property or financial assets. Also known as a simple or naked debenture.

See also **capital, debenture; issue, debenture; register of debentures**.

debit A sum owed or a charge made against a person.

debit card Plastic card issued by a bank to its customers which may be used in place of a **cheque** book. By accessing the bank's electronic records, the debit card makes direct debit of an account possible. *See* **debit, direct**.

direct debit Practice of debiting a bank account with the sum owed on the authorization of the account holder, but without his or her direct involvement (e.g. in issuing a **cheque**) at the time.

debit side In **accounting**, the side of a **ledger** on which debits are listed. Hence, in informal use the negative points in an argument.
See also **balance, debit; note, debit**.

debt Sum of money, or value of goods and services, owed by one person, group or company to another. Debt arises because the seller allows a purchaser **credit**. Assignable debts may be transferred in whole from one person to another; such debts therefore become negotiable instruments. In commerce, the term is also used to describe the whole of a company's borrowings. *See* **instrument, negotiable**.

bad debt Debt which has not been, and is not expected to be, paid. Such losses are practically unavoidable, (and allowances are almost always made for such instances) although some may be sold to a **factoring** company which attempts to recover the debt on its own account.

book debt Debt recorded in an account book.

debt-for-equity The proportion of a company's debt that is covered by its share capital. *See* **capital, share**.

debt servicing Payment of **interest** on a debt.

floating debt Short-term government borrowing *e.g.* Treasury bills. *See* **bill, treasury**.

funded debt Broadly, any short-term debt that has been converted into a long-term debt.

judgement debt Debt that has come before the courts and which has been ordered to be repaid.

National Debt Debts owed by the government, *i.e.* the sum of government borrowing, covering such things as National Savings, Treasury bills, and government bonds. The US equivalent is called the Federal Debt.

secured debt Debt that is advanced against some asset (the security) of the debtor. In the event that the debt is not paid, the creditor has rights to the security.

senior debt Oldest existing debt owed by a person or firm; hence, the one which will be repaid first, **ceteris paribus**.

statute-barred debt Debt that may no longer be called in because it has been outstanding too long.

trade debt Debt incurred by a company during the normal course of business as the result of the non-payment of bills.

unfunded debt That portion of the National Debt that is in the form of fixed-term securities. It consists of the floating debt, listed securities and small-scale savings. *See* **debt, floating; Debt, National**.

unsecured debt Debt that is not secured in any way. Thus, the creditor has no protection should the debt go unpaid.

debtnocrat Bank official who specializes in high-level lending, often to Third World nations.

debtor A person or company who owes money, goods or services to another.

debut Arrival on the stock markets of the shares of a new company and the first day's trading in that company's stock.

decentralization The distribution of the constituent parts of a company or government to a variety of geographical locations. The advantages include the availability of cheaper labour (this is likely to be initially offset by the cost of relocating key personnel), increased efficiency and, in the case of government, the provision of incentives to industry to consider non-metropolitan locations.

decertification *US* Removal of a trade union as the official negotiator on behalf of the workforce.

decontrol Alternative term for **deregulation**.

de-diversification Shedding of interests and companies acquired by a corporation in the process of **diversification**, so as to reduce the variety of business in which the company engages.

deduction Money deducted from wages and salaries at source and allotted to pay taxes and (in the UK) National Insurance contributions.

deductions at source Income tax deducted by the employer from the employee's pay before he or she receives it. The sum deducted is then paid by the company to the Inland Revenue. Deduction at source helps to prevent **tax evasion**. *See* **Revenue, Inland; tax, income.**

deed Document recording a transaction and bearing the seals of the parties concerned to testify to its validity ('signed, sealed and delivered').

title deed Document giving the holder **title** to a land or (more loosely) to property. Title deeds are often accepted as **collateral** for a **loan**. Also known as deed of title.

deep-pocket view Theory that some **subsidiaries** may have access to more funds than an independent firm of similar size. The deep-pocket view argues that the subsidiary may call upon the greater resources of its parent company to engage in competition with independents in its sector.

de facto By virtue of existence, rather than by any legal right. *E.g.* the de facto owner of a property may be the person in occupation, whether or not he or she has legal title to the land.

default Failure to comply with the terms set out in a **contract**. Legal proceedings generally follow if the matter cannot be settled amicably.

defensive tactics The strategy used when a 'player' feels threatened by aggression. Thus the subject of a hostile **takeover** bid sometimes arranges defensive tactics with the aim of making the takeover more difficult, *e.g.* by pushing up its own share price. Examples of defensive tactics are the **Lady Macbeth strategy** and the **poison pill**.

deferment Postponement, *e.g.* of a payment. *See also* **annuity, deferred; liability, deferred; pension, deferred; taxation, deferred**.

deficit Excess of **expenditure** over **income**, or **liabilities** over **assets**.

budget deficit Budgetary imbalance, caused by excess of **expenditure** over **income**. In the case of British government budgets, the deficit is generally funded by the authorization of an increase in the National Debt. *See* **Debt, National**.

trade deficit Excess of **imports** over **exports**, resulting in a negative **balance of payments**.

deflation Persistent decrease in prices, generally caused by a fall in the level of economic activity within a country. Deflation should not be confused with **disinflation**.

deflationary gap The difference between the actual level of **investment** and the level necessary to restore full employment.

See also **inflation**.

defray To settle an **account** or to lay out money in payment for goods or services.

defunct Company or organization that no longer functions as such.

degearing Reduction of **risk** or **leverage**. Examples include cutting **borrowing** and reducing **exposure** to forces which the company or **dealer** cannot control. *See* **hedging**.

de-industrialization Decline in the relative importance of manufacturing. *See also* **industry, sunrise; industry, sunset.**

del credere (agent) Person who accepts goods on consignment from exporters, agreeing (in return for an additional **commission**) to pay for them in the event that the original purchaser defaults.

delegation Term with two meanings.
First, it is a body of accredited representatives to a gathering (*e.g.* a conference).
Second, it is to cede responsibility to other, usually junior members of staff.

trade delegation Group of delegates sent to promote trade and negotiate agreements with a foreign trading partner.

delegatus non potest delegare Latin for a delegate cannot delegate, principle guarding against subcontracting if the client feels it vital to deal directly and exclusively with the principal agent.

delivery Handing over of **property** or monetary **assets**. In the City the term has two more specific meanings: it describes a transfer of

securities, and the receipt of the financial instrument or cash payment specified in a financial futures contract. *See* **futures**.
See also **cash on delivery; note, delivery**.

delta Stock exchange classification of shares that are traded on the USM and third market. They are generally relatively inactive and stable shares in small companies. *See also* **alpha; beta; gamma**.

demand Term with two meanings.
First, it is the desire for possession of a particular good or service at a specific price expressed by those able and willing to purchase it.
Second, it is a request, such as a request for repayment of a **debt**.

effective demand The quantity of an article or service actually purchased at a particular price. *See also* **demand, pure**.

pure demand Demand that may not be expressed by purchase for a variety of reasons. *See also* **demand, effective**.

See also **deposit, demand; inflation, demand-pull; supply and demand**.

demonetization Term with two meanings.
First, it is the process of removing a particular note or coin from circulation and declaring it to be illegal tender. In the UK, the farthing, half-penny, three-penny and six-penny bits, and the pound note, have all been demonetized.
Second, it is the abandonment of the use of a precious metal (gold, silver) as a monetary standard. *See* **gold standard**.

denationalization The **privatization** of a previously nationalized industry by floating the company involved on the stock exchange and selling shares to members of the public or institutions. In the UK, recently denationalized industries include British Telecom, British Gas and British Airways. A change in government may subsequently lead to the renationalization of the industries.

denomination The face value of something, *e.g.* the unitary classification of coinage, or the nominal value of **bills** and **bonds**. "The US government issues Treasury bonds in denominations of $10,000."

depauperization New term meaning the relief of poverty (generally through economic growth.

deposit Goods or money placed with a bank or other financial institution; an initial payment made on an item to reserve it.

certificate of deposit Record of a deposit that establishes its ownership.

demand deposit US Deposit of a sum of money with a bank, that may be withdrawn at only a moment's notice. *See also* **deposit, fixed**.

deposit slip Document that records the time and place of a deposit and its value.

fixed deposit Money placed in a deposit account, *i.e.* in an account from which it cannot be withdrawn without suitable notice being given. The US equivalent is time deposit. *See* **account, deposit**.

lessee deposit Deposit that is paid to the lessee on rented property, intended to cover the lessee against damage and returnable on termination of the **lease**.

safe deposit Well-protected **depository**; one that is guarded and/or armoured to prevent theft, *e.g.* a safe deposit box.

time deposit US Alternative term for fixed deposit. *See* **deposit, fixed**.

See also **account, deposit; hire purchase; society, deposit**.

depository Secure place where money or goods are stored (deposited), *e.g.* Fort Knox. Depositories may be distinguished from banks in that they do not transact other financial business and do not necessarily offer ready access to the assets stored. *See also* **deposit**.

depreciation Progressive decline in real value of an **asset** because of use or **obsolescence**. The concept of depreciation is widely used in **accounting** for the process of writing off the cost of an asset against profit over an extended period, irrespective of the real value of the asset. *See also* **accounting, historical cost**.

accelerated depreciation In accounting, practice of depreciating an **asset** at a rate greater than the actual decline in its value in order to gain **tax concessions**. Accelerated depreciation need not occur throughout the life of the asset; a substantial proportion of its total value is often written off in the first year, and reduced allowances for depreciation are made thereafter.

accumulated depreciation In accounting, the total value of an asset that has been written off so far. *See* **write off**.

depreciation rate Rate at which depreciation occurs. *See* **depreciation, straight-line**.

free depreciation In accounting, depreciation of an **asset** over any time period the company thinks fit.

reducing balance depreciation Method of accounting for depreciation by calculating it in a period as a fixed proportion of the residual book value of an **asset** at the start of the period.

straight-line depreciation Method of calculating the **depreciation rate**. A fixed proportion of the total original value of the **asset** is written off in each accounting period, making allowance for its current resale value, either as a useful asset or as scrap. *See* **write off**.

depression Major and persistent downswing of a trade cycle, characterized by high **unemployment** and the under-utilization of other factors of production. A less severe downswing is known as a slump or recession.

deregulation Removal of controls and abandonment of state supervision of private enterprise. The most notable recent instance of deregulation is that of the London Stock Exchange, (commonly termed the **Big Bang**).

detinue Legal term meaning action to recover something that has been detained.

devaluation Reduction in the relative value of a **currency**. The devaluation may be relative to an absolute value (e.g. the **gold standard**) or to other relative values (e.g. other currencies). The pound sterling was devalued against the US dollar in 1949 and again in 1967. *See also* **revaluation**.

develop To begin to realize the potential of, *e.g.*, a product or company.

developing country Country that is beginning to industrialize, but which is still too poor to do so without **foreign aid**. Developing countries are characterized by improving standards of health, wealth (standard of living), education, capital investment and productivity, and by a broadening of the economic base.

development aid Financial and material aid to a **developing country**.

development area Economically depressed area suitable for reindustrialization. Development areas are designated by the state and incentives are provided to help develop businesses in the area, to encourage the relocation of existing businesses, and to enhance the prospects for employment.

development expenditure Corporate **expenditure** on the research and development of new products. Development expenditure may be tax deductible.

See also **research and development**.

dies non Day that is not counted for some purpose. *E.g.* Saturday and Sunday are not counted as days of the working week.

differential The difference between two values, *e.g.* prices or salaries. *See* **wage differential**.

dilution Term with two meanings.
First, it is the reduction in the skill of a workforce overall, as comparatively unskilled workers are recruited in response to a rise in **demand**.
Second, it is a deliberate increase in the number of shares on the market that has the effect of reducing the price of each individual share.

dilution of equity Reduction of individual stakes in a company by the issue of further shares. *See* **dilution of shareholding**.

dilution of shareholding Reduction in the relative value of a share in the event of a new issue. For example, if a company has a capital of £1,000 in £10 shares, each share represents 1% of the total capital. If a new issue of 5,000 £10 shares is made, a shareholding of £10 represents only 0.16% of the firm's capital. Thus the relative power of each existing shareholder to influence corporate affairs is reduced.

See also **issue, rights**.

dime Popular term for a US coin worth 10 cents (1/10 of a dollar).

diminishing Something that is declining or falling.

diminishing balance (method) Method of calculating **depreciation** by writing off a fixed proportion of the total residual value of an asset each year.

diminishing marginal product Alternative term for **diminishing returns**.

diminishing returns Concept that suggests that as additional units of one factor of production are added, the relative increase in output will eventually begin to decline. *E.g.* a factory can increase its output by employing more labour, but unless the other factors of production (*e.g.* machinery) are also increased each additional employee will be working with a smaller proportion of the other, fixed, resources available.

direct Immediate or unobstructed.

direct action Attempt to take control of a company by purchasing a controlling interest of shares, rather than by negotiation with the company itself. *See* **raid, dawn**.

direct mail Form of advertising. Individual potential customers receive promotional material and information through the post.

See also **debit, direct; expenses, direct; labour, direct; production, direct; taxation, direct**.

director One of the principals of a company, (in a public limited company) appointed by its shareholders. Most companies have a group of directors who act collectively as the senior management of the company, being responsible to the shareholders for its efficient running and future development. The duties and responsibilities of a director are defined in the Companies Acts. They include the compilation of an annual report and the recommendation of an annual **dividend** on shares. *See* **report, annual**.

alternate director Person who shares a directorship with another. Each member of a pair of alternate directors has a vote on the board.

associate director Director who is a member of the **board** but lacks full voting powers. The position is normally held by able but comparatively junior managers; it rewards their enthusiasm and reinforces their commitment without giving them real power.

board of directors Decision-making group comprising all the directors of a company. The board of directors is specifically charged with the management of the company and in the case of a public limited company is elected by the shareholders at the company's annual general meeting (**AGM**). *See* **company, public limited**.

directorate Alternative term for board of directors. *See* **directors, board of**.

directors' valuation In **accounting**, the right of a board of directors to estimate the value of the firm's shareholding in an unquoted company. The directors' valuation is called for only if the value of the shares concerned has changed since they were purchased. *See* **company, unquoted**.

managing director Senior executive director of a company, junior only to the **chairman**, and charged with implementing the decisions made by the **board**.

non-executive director Member of the **board** of directors who plays no active part in the day-to-day running of the company. He or she may attend board meetings and offer advice. Non-executive (or outside) directors are often well-known public figures whose appointment lends -cachet to a company, or whose presence on the board is valued for their expertise, impartiality or wide-ranging contacts.

outside director Alternative term for non-executive director. *See* **director, non-executive**.

working director Director who takes an active part in the management of a firm.

See also **director, non-executive**.

discharge Term with two meanings.
First, it is to dismiss a member of staff from one's employment.
Second, it is to pay a debt such as a **bill of exchange**.

disclaimer Clause in a **contract** that states that one of the parties does not take responsibility for some occurrence. *E.g.* the owners of many car parks advise drivers that they disclaim any responsibility for loss or damage to their cars.

disclosure Revealing of relevant information. The term has two major uses.

First, it is the requirement that a limited company must disclose its financial dealings and position by the publication of accounts, and deposit at Companies House lists of directors and shareholders in the company.

Second, it is the requirement that parties to any contract should disclose relevant information. *E.g.* a person holding a life assurance policy must notify the assurers of his or her medical history.

discount In commerce, term with five specialized meanings.

First, it refers to the amount by which a new share issue stands below its par value. *See* **parity**.

Second, it refers to the price of a share whose price/earnings ratio is below the market average. *See* **ratio, price/earnings**.

Third, it refers to the amount by which a currency is below par on the foreign exchanges.

Four, to discount is to make a reduction in the face value of some article, generally in order to make purchase more attractive to the customer.

Five, on financial markets it is the charge made for cashing an immature **bill of exchange**, the discount being proportional to the unexpired portion of the bill.

cash discount Reduction in the price of goods in return for payment in cash.

discounted cash flow (DCF) Method of assessing a company's investments according to when they are due to yield their expected returns, in order to indicate the present worth of the future sum. In this way it is possible to determine preference for one of a number of alternative investments.

quantity discount Discount offered to the purchaser of bulk goods.

settlement discount Discount offered for the early settlement of an account.

trade discount Discount offered to trade customers, *i.e.* to customers likely to place large and regular orders. A trade discount therefore recognizes the importance of the customer concerned.

See also **house, discount; market, discount; rate, discount**.

discounting Act of making a **discount**. More specifically, it is the practice of selling a debt at a discount to an institution.

invoice discounting **Discount** offered on unpaid **invoices** sold to a **factoring** company, which will then try to claim the money owed on its own account. The discount will reflect the likely difficulty of securing payment.

See also **bank, discounting; factoring**.

discretionary Something that is not compulsory, but is left to the discretion of the person or authority involved. *See also* **account, discretionary; grant, discretionary**.

disenfranchise To deprive of the right to vote.

dishonour To refuse to accept or discharge a **bill of exchange** when it falls due for payment. Cheques are sometimes dishonoured ('bounced') by a bank if there are insufficient funds in the drawer's account to make the payment. *See also* **acceptance for honour supra protest**.

disinflation The curbing of **inflation** by the adoption of mild economic measures such as the restriction of **expenditure**. Other measures include increasing **interest rates** and the deliberate creation of a budget surplus. Disinflation is a mild form of **deflation**, which by contrast indicates an uncontrolled fall in prices.

disintermediation Withdrawal of a financial intermediary from a negotiation. The term may also be applied to the flow of funds from lenders to borrowers without the intervention of an intermediary (*e.g.* a mortgage broker).

disinvestment Withdrawal or sale of an investment. Governments and companies sometimes decide to disinvest from nations whose economic or political complexion offends them. *E.g.* there has been widespread disinvestment from the Republic of South Africa.

dismissal Notice of redundancy served on an employee.

constructive dismissal Redundancies that are made for the purpose of improving the efficiency of a business. They may be agreed between the parties concerned or may be unilateral. Constructive dismissals include those achieved by the implementation of early retirement schemes.

unfair dismissal Redundancy that is made on insufficient or unfair grounds. A company found to have dismissed an employee unfairly is normally expected to re-employ the person concerned.

wrongful dismissal Redundancy that a court of law decides was illegal. A company responsible for wrongfully dismissing an employee is normally expected to re-employ the person concerned, and may also be liable to pay some form of **compensation**.

disposables Non-durable goods; those that are consumed during their use. Food, drink, and petrol are all disposables.

dissident shareholder = shareholder, dissident

dissolution **Winding up** of a company, usually by the legal process of **liquidation**. In the case of a **partnership**, dissolution may be occasioned by the death or retirement of one or more partners, by **bankruptcy** or by the expiry of a specified time period, without recourse to law.

distraint The legally-authorized seizure of **assets** to compel a debtor to pay a **debt**. If the debt remains outstanding, goods obtained by distraint may be sold in order that the **creditor** may obtain satisfaction.

distress merchandise Goods and assets made available for sale by a company facing or already consigned to **bankruptcy**. Most distress merchandise is placed on the market on the orders of an official **receiver** in order to provide liquid sums for the payment of creditors. *See* **receivership**.

distribution Term with three meanings.
     First, it is the transportation, apportioning and placement of raw materials or goods to and from the factory to warehouses and shops.
     Second, it refers to payments made by a company from its profits (*e.g.* **dividends**).
     Third, it is the apportioning of a **scrip** or rights issue of shares. *See* **issue, rights**.

distribution slip Document that describes the goods that have been distributed, their location and eventual destination.

primary distribution Distribution of raw materials to manufacturers.

distributor Wholesaler; person or company that acts as an agent in the distribution of goods to **retail** outlets.

diversification Extension of the range of goods or services offered into new areas, either material or geographical. By extension the term may also be applied to attempts by local authorities or central government to attract a variety of industries to an area heavily dependent upon a single industry, particularly one in decline.

geographical diversification Diversification into new geographical areas. *E.g.* a company that owns a chain of stores in Scotland may diversify by acquiring similar shops in Wales and England.

horizontal diversification Diversification into industries or businesses at the same stage of production as the diversifying company. *E.g.* a suit manufacturer might diversify into leisurewear, and a yacht builder into the construction of motor boats. *See also* **diversification, vertical; integration, horizontal**.

product diversification Decision to begin the manufacture of new products, usually by horizontal or vertical diversification. The main purpose is to lessen the risk of commercial failure caused by a sudden fall in demand for a particular product. Diversification is also attractive to firms dependent upon seasonal or cyclical business.

vertical diversification Diversification into industries or businesses at different stages of production to the diversifying company. *See also* **diversification, horizontal; integration, vertical**.

divestment Sale or **liquidation** of parts of a company, generally in an attempt to improve efficiency by cutting loss-making businesses and/or concentrating on one product or industry. Divestment is therefore the opposite process to **merger**. *See also* **de-diversification**.

divestiture Act of **divestment**.
"RCF plc today announced the divestiture of its unprofitable subsidiary, MG Ltd."

dividend A share in the profits of a limited company, usually paid annually. Dividends are generally expressed as a percentage of the nominal value of a single ordinary share. Thus a payment of 10p on each £1 share would be termed a dividend of 10%. Dividends are determined by the **directors** of a company and are announced at the annual general meeting (**AGM**) of the firm. *See* **share, ordinary; value, nominal**.

accrued dividend Dividend payment due to shareholders but not paid, the capital being retained by the company to fund expansion.

cum dividend Latin for including dividend, denoting the right of the purchaser of a share to receive the next dividend payment. Shares cum dividend are, of course, more valuable than equivalent shares carrying no such right.

dividend per share (in pence) Expression of a dividend in pence per share rather than as a percentage of the total value of a share. Thus a 10% dividend on a share worth £1 would be termed a '10p per share dividend'.

dividend cover Degree to which a dividend payment on ordinary shares is covered by profits earned. Thus a company that declares after-tax profits of £10m and makes a total dividend payment of £2m on ordinary shares is said to be 'covered five times'. An uncovered dividend, on the other hand, is a payment made at least partly from reserves rather than current profits. *See* **profit, after-tax**.

dividend equalization reserve Also known as the dividend equalization account, a **reserve** from which a company may make a dividend payment during periods of low profits or trading loss. The firm pays profits into the reserve during years of significant **profit**. The purpose is to maintain shareholders' confidence in the company.

dividend limitation Government instruction to companies to limit increases in their dividend payments as part of a prices and incomes policy. Dividend limitation curbs the **income** of shareholders and the management in the same way that wage restraints limit increases in the salaries paid to workers.

dividend mandate Mandate signed by a shareholder and delivered to a company, instructing it to pay dividends directly to a third party (generally into a bank account).

dividend restraint Policy of minimizing increases in dividend payments, generally implemented by a company wishing to build its reserves for investment and corporate growth.

dividend stripping Technique of **tax avoidance** that makes it unnecessary for a company to make dividend payments and enables it to avoid tax on undistributed profits. *See* **profit, undistributed**.

ex dividend Latin for without dividend, denoting that the purchaser of a share does not have the right to receive the next dividend payment due on that security. However, he or she has the right to receive subsequent dividends.

interim dividend Any dividend other than the final dividend declared at the conclusion of each trading year. Interim dividends may be made as a reward for a particularly good economic performance or simply as an effective advance on the final dividend, which will be correspondingly reduced in value. Most British companies quoted on the stock market make one interim dividend payment per annum; it is unusual for a firm to exceed this number of interim payments.

See also **policy, dividend; tax, dividend; yield, dividend**.

DM Abbreviation of Deutschmark, the West German unit of currency.

dogsbody Person who performs a number of mundane tasks on behalf of others. In the USA a dogsbody is known as a gofer.

dollar US unit of currency, divided into 100 cents. The economic predominance of post-war USA has made the dollar the most important medium of international trade. It is also the name of the unit of currency used in Australia, New Zealand, Canada, Bermuda, the Bahamas, the West Indies, Malaysia, and Hong Kong. *See also* **eurodollar**.

dollar gap Shortage of dollars caused by the flow of US funds and aid to Europe in the immediate post-war period.

hard dollars Dollars traded on the foreign exchange markets, for which demand is persistently high because of a US trade surplus. The value of hard dollars tends to rise. *See* **surplus, trade**. *See also* **dollar gap**.

soft dollars Dollars traded on the foreign exchange markets for which demand is persistently low because of a US trade deficit. The value of soft dollars tends to fall. *See* **deficit, trade**.

dole Informal term for any variety of social security payments, but particularly unemployment benefit. *See* **benefit, unemployment**.

dolphin *US* Informal term for a person who buy shares in new issues and proceeds to sell for high profit immediately trading opens. *See also* **flip**.

domestic Concerning the internal economy of a nation.

domestic credit expansion (DCE) Measurement of the growth of a nation's **money supply** which allows for changes in the **balance of payments** by deducting net foreign currency reserves from the figure for money supply itself. It is thus a measure of domestic **liquidity**.

domestic production Total production of a good or goods within a nation.

See also **economy, domestic; market; domestic; sales, domestic**.

domicile A person's place of residence for legal and tax purposes. A person domiciled in the UK is liable to pay British taxes and is subject to British law.

donee Person in receipt of a donation.

donor Person who gives a donation.

double Something multiplied by two.

double bottom In the analysis of share market trends, a term that describes a price that hits a low point equal to the last low point. The prediction is that once two similar low points have been reached, the price will tend to rise. *See also* **double top**.

double or quits Terms offered in a wager or **speculation**; the losing speculator offers another wager on the same terms as before, but for twice the money. As a result, the winning speculator either doubles the sum earned or is left in the same position as before. Offering and acceptance of such terms implies that each of two possibilities have an equal chance of occurring.

double top In the analysis of share market trends, a price that rises twice to similar high points. The prediction is that after the double top, the price will tend to fall. *See also* **double bottom**.

See also **book-keeping, double-entry; inflation, double-figure; insurance, double; option, double; pricing, double; time, double**.

down and dirty *US* When a company is in financial difficulties, the practice of arranging a refinancing package that would severely dilute the holdings of minor shareholders were they not to participate. *See* **dilution**.

downgrade To reduce the status of someone or something. *E.g.* a person downgrades his or her shareholding by selling part of it.

downside The amount a person stands to lose when taking a **risk**. *E.g.* the amount by which a share price may fall, or the amount a person is likely to lose by making a speculative investment.

downsize *US* To reduce the size of a company's workforce in the interests of economy.

downstream (activity) Economic activity in or close to the **retail** sector, *i.e.* that involving the distribution and selling of goods and services. The term is, *e.g.* frequently applied to the oil industry, in which context the petrol station is downstream and the oil rig is **upstream**.

downtick Transaction concluded at a lower price than a similar previous transaction. It is also a small and temporary fall in the price of a share. *See also* **uptick**.

downturn Point at which something begins to fall. *E.g.* a share price that has been rising and begins to fall, or productivity that is beginning to decline.

DPS Abbreviation of **dividend per share** (in pence).

draft Written **order** from a customer to a financial institution, requesting that money is paid from the customer's account to a third party. To draft is to draw up any document, especially a **contract**.

bank draft **Cheque** drawn on a bank by a person whose creditors are unwilling to accept a personal cheque. A bank draft must be honoured, because it is drawn on the bank itself rather than on the debtor's account. The debtor must pay the bank the sum drawn in advance.

banker's draft Draft instructing a **bank** to pay a specified sum to the person or organization named.

dollar draft Cheque or banker's draft denominated in **dollars.**

sight draft **Bill of exchange** payable upon presentation (*i.e.* on sight).

drawback Repayment of customs and excise **duty** on certain goods to an exporter who has already paid duty on imported raw materials. *E.g.* drawback may be claimed on tobacco imported to make cigarettes when the cigarettes are exported. *See* **re-export**.

drawdown *US* The sum of money borrowed.
"The drawdown on that project was $100,000."

drawee Person or company to whom a **bill of exchange** is adressed. *E.g.* the bank **account** on which a **cheque** is drawn, or the **acceptor** of a bill of exchange.

drawer Person who draws a **bill of exchange**, *i.e.* presents it for payment. *E.g.* the person to whom a **cheque** is made out.

drip-feed Steady payment of money at regular intervals. Pejorative term that implies that the recipient is dependent upon the payment of funds. Often applied to **foreign aid** to the Third World. Also used by venture capitalists for venture capital payments made to a start-up company in stages. *See* **capital, venture**.

drive Concerted effort.

economy drive Effort to improve the efficiency of a company by cutting unnecessary **expenditure** and costs and making better use of resources.

sales drive Effort to improve **sales** and create **demand**. Techniques include reducing prices, increasing the sales force, providing free samples and distributing point-of-sale advertising material.

drop dead date *US* Date on which it is expected that a company will run out of funds.

drop dead fee Payment offered to a bidder by the **target** of a (usually **takeover**) bid in an effort to induce the bidder to withdraw the bid.

drop dead rate Amount demanded by a would-be corporate **raider** to withdraw the bid.

drop lock Loan stock issued when a specific **interest rate** is reached. The purpose is to convert short-term borrowing into long-term loans. *See* **stock, loan**.

dual capacity Stock exchange system that makes no distinction between the functions of **stockbrokers** and **jobbers**. One person may therefore both buy and sell stocks and shares on the **exchange**. The London Stock Exchange was converted to dual capacity in October 1986. *See* **Big Bang; single capacity**.

dud Informal term for something that is worthless or forged.
"She was very angry to find that she had been given a dud cheque."

due Something that is owed to someone, or something that belongs to someone by right.
"Last Friday, my rent for next month became due."
"Each year she paid her dues to the union."

See **date, due**.

dummy Something that is false and has no substance.
"I discovered that it was a dummy company."

dumping Sale of surplus goods overseas at extremely low prices.
"Several countries in the Pacific basin have been dumping electronic components onto Western markets."

duopoly Market in which there are only two competing companies. Because competition between duopolists is particularly fierce and destructive, there tends to be some form of implicit or explicit agreement to share the market, *e.g.* on a regional basis. *See also* **monopoly**.

duopsony Market in which there are only two purchasers of a type of goods or services, but a number of competing suppliers. *See also* **duopoly; monopsony**.

durable Goods that are not consumed by their use, but which endure for a reasonable period of time. Manufacturers of durables tend to build in some form of **obsolescence** to ensure a continuity of demand. *See also* **disposable**.

consumer durable Consumer goods of some technological sophistication that yield utility over a period of time. *E.g.* clothing, cars, washing machines, etc.

duty Broadly any **tax** levied by a public authority, particularly that imposed on imports, exports and manufactured goods.

ad valorem duty Duty charged as a percentage of the total value of goods or services being taxed. Value-added tax is a form of ad valorem duty. *See* **tax, value-added**.

back duty Also known as back tax. Retrospective tax levied on profits or goods on which no duty was paid at the time.

customs duty Duty levied on imports by the Customs and Excise, either as a protectionist measure, or simply to raise **revenue**.

duty-free Goods on which no duty is charged. In the UK, the term is most usually applied to goods which, although sold elsewhere in the UK, are available to those about to leave the country (from duty-free shops at ports). It is assumed that these goods are for consumption overseas or for personal consumption.

duty-paid Authenticated statement attached to goods on which duty has been paid, to facilitate their passage through customs.

excise duty Duty levied on home-produced goods, either to control consumption and thus influence spending, or to raise revenue. Goods that currently attract excise duty are tobacco and alcohol.

stamp duty Duty levied on the completion of certain transfer documents. *E.g.* stamp duty is paid when a person signs property transfer documents.

transfer stamp duty Duty levied on the transfer of securities on the stock exchange. It is therefore a form of capital transfer tax. Transfer stamp duty is not imposed upon government stocks, nor on securities bought and sold within one **account**.

See also **tax**.

dynamics Analysis of the behaviour of variable elements.
"There have been changes in the dynamics of stock exchange trading since Big Bang."

dynamization Giving new dynamism to a company, generally by importing a new management team.

E

E & OE Abbreviation of **errors and omissions excepted**.

earning Act of generating **income**.

earning capacity Value of an employee's services to a company. *E.g.* the earning capacity of an advertising sales executive is equivalent to the **revenue** he or she brings in. The term is also applied more colloquially to describe the maximum wage that could be earned in a specific job.

earning potential **Net** present **value** of an person's expected future earnings. Earnings potential is as a key determinant of **creditworthiness**.

earning power Value of an person's services at a specified time and in a free market. Earning power is indicated by the salary which could be commanded if that individual was to change jobs.

earnings Return, monetary or otherwise, for human effort. Broadly, however, earnings may be defined as wages plus bonuses for overtime worked. The term is also used to describe the **income of a company.**

average available earnings **Profit** available for distribution to shareholders.
See also **earnings per share**.

earnings per share (in pence) (EPS) Method of expressing the **income** of a company, arrived at by dividing the annual net income attributable to the shareholders by the number of shares. Earnings per share can then be used to calculate the price/earnings ratio of a company. *See* **ratio, price/earnings**.

gross earnings Earnings before **tax** has been deducted.

invisible earnings **Income** earned from payment for services rather than goods, on a national scale. Invisible earnings include profits from shipping, the provision of **insurance**, and other financial services.

retained earnings That part of a company's post-tax earnings not distributed to shareholders, and thus retained by the firm to finance the day-to-day running of the company and any future expansion. Retained earnings are added to reserves and hence appear on the firm's **balance sheet**.

See also **pension, earnings-related; yield, earnings**.

earn-out Employee incentive scheme whereby the employee is offered **share** options that give him or her an **interest** in the company for which he or she works.

EAS Abbreviation of **Enterprise Allowance Scheme**.

easement Legal term that refers to the right of a landowner to take or use something from a neighbouring piece of land. Right of way is an example of easement.

negative easement Right of a landowner to prevent a neighbour from exploiting or affecting his or her land.

echelon Level in the hierarchy of a company.
"He rose very quickly to the higher echelons".

ECI Abbreviation of **equity capital for industry**.

econometrics Branch of statistics that uses mathematical models to test economic hypotheses, describe economic relationships, and forecast economic trends. Econometrics is used to produce correlated quantitative data rather than to prove economic causation.

economic Term with two meanings.
First, it is something that concerns the study of economics.
Second, it is something that is cost-effective.

economic development Per capita increase in national income. Broadly, the rate of economic development is a way of expressing the growth of an economy and can be used to determine the relative growth of a number of competing or allied economies. The rate of economic development is often used as a simple guide to the health of an economy.

economic refugee Person who leaves his or her country for economic (rather than political) reasons. The term embraces both tax exiles and those who leave a country in which employment prospects are bleak. Irish emigrants to the United States and (in the post-war period) British emigrants to Australia were economic refugees. *See* **tax exile**.

See also **cost, economic; indicator, economic; profit, economic**.

economy Term with two meanings.
First, it is the financial and productive apparatus of a nation.
Second, it is frugality.

black economy Illegal economic activity conducted largely for cash by companies and individuals who pay no taxes on the proceeds. *See also* **moonlighting; tax evasion**.

capitalist economy Economy in which business is conducted for the profit of the companies and persons engaged in it.

closed economy Economy that is self-sufficient in that it makes neither imports nor exports.

controlled economy Economy in which the government tries to control elements of economic activity by legislating for key areas rather than taking direct charge of the factors of production. *See also* **economy, planned**.

domestic economy Internal economy of a nation.

economies of scale Reductions in the average cost of production made possible by the large size of a firm or industry. Internal economies of scale are defined as those enjoyed by a single large company or organization and are, broadly, made possible by the distribution of indirect costs and improvements in technology which increase the optimum level of output.

External economies of scale are those associated with an industry or location. For example, a concentration of shipbuilding companies on a river leads to the creation of a large pool of skilled labour which can be drawn on if one company is in the process of expansion.

free market economy Economy in which the allocation of resources is determined by the level of **demand** and **supply** without intervention by the state. No pure free-market economies exist.

mixed economy Economy in which elements of free-market and planned economies co-exist.

natural economy Economy in which barter is the most common form of **exchange**.

planned economy Economy in which some or all economic activity is planned and undertaken by the state, directly or indirectly, irrespective of the market forces of **demand** and **supply**, and without the intervention of private **enterprise**. *See also* **economy, controlled**.

service economy The total output of the service, or tertiary, sector of an economy. It is also an economy that is based on service rather than manufacturing industries.

share economy Aggregate value of companies quoted on the stock exchange. Also known as 'Quoted UK plc'. It is also an economy in which many people are shareholders.

sleeping economy Informal term for an economy that contains substantial resources that are not fully exploited and having substantial unrealised trade potential. The People's Republic of China is a good example of a sleeping economy.

socialist commodity economy Technologically advanced socialist economy in which all factors of production are controlled by the state.

underground economy US That part of an economy controlled by organized crime. The underground economy is better-controlled and more concentrated than the black economy. *See* **economy, black**.

wage economy Informal term for the total earned income in an economy. It is also an economy in which the majority of people's income is from wages. *See* **income, earned**.

econospeak Economic jargon.

ECU Abbreviation of **European Currency Unit**.

EDP Abbreviation of electronic data processing.

EEC Abbreviation of **European Economic Community**.

effective Actual, real or capable of producing a desired outcome. *See* **cost-effective; date, effective; demand, effective; yield, effective**.

efficiency Use of resources so as to get the most output from the least input.

absolute efficiency Efficiency that depends on discovering and putting into effect the most effective possible combination, distribution, allocation or utilization of limited resources.

relative efficiency A company is relatively efficient if it combines, distributes, allocates or uses limited resources more effectively than a rival. Thus if two firms have the same input but different outputs, the firm producing the larger output is said to be the more efficient of the two.

EFT Abbreviation of **electronic funds transfer**.

EFTPOS Acronym for **electronic funds transfer at point of sale**.

EGM Abbreviation of extraordinary general meeting, any meeting of company shareholders except the annual general meeting (**AGM**).

electronic Something that works by electronics, *e.g.* calculators or computers.

electronic cottage US Popular term for the home of someone who makes use of computer communications to enable him or her to dispense with travelling to an office.

electronic crime Criminal activities conducted with the help of computers. It generally involves breaking into other computer systems via a modem, often by using special programs to run combinations of letters and numbers until a password is discovered. Expert users can then manipulate records and data to their own advantage.

electronic data processing Collection, interpretation and transmission of data by electronic means. Most electronic data processing is performed by computers, which receive information inputs from their own keyboards or from other computers, interpret it using computer programs and transmit it electronically via cables or telephone lines.

electronic funds transfer (EFT) Transfer of funds by computer. *See also* **chequeless society**.

electronic funds transfer at point of sale (EFTPOS) Automatic, computerized transfer of funds from a retail customer to the retailer through credit and debit cards.

electronic mail Service provided by a number of organizations (notably Prestel in the UK), which allows two computer users linked by modem to deposit messages on each other's machines. Sometimes abbreviated to Email.

electronic point of sale (EPS) **Retail** computer system that debits a customer's credit card at the till, and simultaneously updates stock records.

elephant Informal term for a large corporate entity that is slow but dominant and displays a tendency towards the creation of monopolies. *See* **monopoly**.

Elves of Wall Street *US* The US banking and stockbroking community centred on **Wall Street**. The term is an Americanization of Harold Wilson's description of the Swiss banking community as the **gnomes** of Zurich.

email Abbreviation of **electronic mail**.

embargo Prohibition of the import or export of specified goods from or to a particular country or bloc, generally for political reasons.

embezzlement Theft by an employee of money belonging to his or her employer.

emolument **Salary**, particularly that paid to the holder of high office.

employer Person or company that employs a workforce in exchange for **wages and salaries**. Employers are charged by law with certain responsibilities, such as that for industrial safety, and are responsible for the deduction of certain taxes from the wages paid. *See* **Insurance, National; pay-as-you-earn**.

employment The act of employing somebody, the provision of work, or the state of having a job.

employment bureau Organization that acts as an intermediary between employers and employees, supplying labour in exchange for a commission payment.

full employment Term with two possible meanings. The precise definition is, however, in dispute.

First, it may be a situation in which the entire labour force, excluding those who are in the process of moving from one job to another (frictional unemployment), is in full-time employment. *See* **unemployment, frictional**.

Second, it may be a situation in which the number of full-time vacancies paying the standard wage for the job concerned exceeds the number of people unemployed.

full-time employment Long-term employment that entails an employee putting in a full working week.

part-time employment Long-term employment that entails an employee putting in less than a full working week.

self-employment Being in business on one's own account. The self-employed include those who run their own companies, either alone or in partnership, and professional people such as doctors. The self-employed must pay higher National Insurance contributions than other employees. *See* **Insurance, National**.

temporary employment Full- or part-time employment in the short term, sometimes with a specified time-limit, and often without formal contract.

emptor The purchaser.

EMS Abbreviation of European Monetary System.

endorse To sign one's name on a **bill of exchange** (*e.g.* a **cheque**) to certify its validity.

endorsee Person who signs an **endorsement**.

endorsement Term with two meanings.
First, it is a signature or explanatory statement on a document. Cheques cashed at a bank or transferred by the payee to a third party must bear the payee's endorsement on the reverse.

Second, it is a confirmatory statement.

blank endorsement Term with two meanings.
First, it is a blank cheque endorsed on the reverse. *See* **cheque, blank**.
Second, it is a reference that may be freely used by the endorsed person, *e.g.* a statement given by a referee for distribution with a **curriculum vitae**.

facultative endorsement Special endorsement to a **bill of exchange** that waives a duty toward the endorser. *See* **waiver**.

restrictive endorsement Endorsement that restricts the negotiability of a document.

endowment Term with two meanings.
First, it is payment of a fixed sum to an insured person, *e.g.* an endowment mortgage. *See* **mortgage, endowment**.
Second, it is an alternative term for an **inheritance**.

education endowment Endowment assurance in which the capital sum is paid in instalments, providing the funds to pay school or university fees. *See* **assurance, endowment**.

See also **assurance, endowment; mortgage, endowment**.

engineer Person who designs, constructs or maintains mechanical objects.

civil engineer Person who designs or constructs works of public utility such as roads, bridges and hospitals.

knowledge engineer Person who collects and files information on a sophisticated computer system, in order to produce knowledge rather than data.

enterprise Any undertaking, but particularly a bold or remarkable one, or the quality of boldness and imagination in an undertaking.
"He showed great enterprise in developing an entirely new market."

Enterprise Allowance Scheme (EAS) UK government scheme set up to encourage the establishment of new businesses by the unemployed, by, among other incentives, offering grants and tax concessions.

enterprise zone Geographical area in which economic activity is promoted by the government. Small businesses are encouraged, and the relocation of firms and industries to enterprise zones is helped by the provision of incentives. *See also* **Enterprise Allowance Scheme**.

free enterprise Economic system under which individuals or groups may own the factors of production and exploit them for their own benefit within the limits of the law.

private enterprise Undertaking by an individual or a private group working without significant support from the state.

state enterprise Undertaking initiated and controlled by the government, generally for the benefit − direct or indirect − of all its citizens. *E.g.* nationalized industry. *See* **industry, nationalized**.

entrepreneur Person who controls a commercial enterprise − the risk-taker and profit-maker − the person who assembles the factors of production and supervises their combination. The term also has the connotation of someone who has a brilliant idea and then finds the money to back it.

entrepreneurial veteran Entrepreneur with extensive experience of business. Often, someone who has taken many risks, and been **bankrupt** at least once.

entrepreneurial virgin Entrepreneur with little experience.

entry Term with two meanings.
First, it is the appearance of a company on a certain market.
Second, it is an item of information entered onto a record, *e.g.* in double-entry **book-keeping**.

contra entry In double-entry **book-keeping** an item that is entered to balance out another. Its purpose is to negate the original item, often because that entry was made in error.

credit entry Item of **credit** recorded in a **ledger** for accounting purposes.

debit entry Item of **debit** recorded in a ledger for accounting purposes.

entry and exit Refers to the appearance of companies in an industry and the disappearance of other companies, as new companies are established and others diversify or go into **liquidation**. *See* **barrier to entry**.

entry charge Cost of entry into a building, market, etc. Stock exchanges levy entry charges on firms applying for a listing.

EPOS Acronym for **electronic point of sale**.

EPP Abbreviation of executive pension plan. *See* **pension**.

EPS Abbreviation of **earnings per share** (in pence).

equalization Return on **capital** invested in a **unit trust**. All investors in a trust receive an equal sum per unit held, although some may only have invested in the period since the last **distribution**. The distribution paid on the latter's stock therefore comprises the **dividend** and an equalization that brings the return up to par. *See* **parity**.

equalization of estates Equal distribution of an **estate** among two or more parties. Equalization of estates normally results from a court case in which a beneficiary applies unsuccessfully for a greater share of the estate, the court ruling that all beneficiaries have equal rights.

equities Alternative term for ordinary shares. Equities entitle their holder to share in the issuing company's profits. Ordinary shareholders bear the ultimate risk, in that they have no entitlements in the event of **liquidation**. *See also* **share, ordinary**.

equity Term with four meanings.
First, it refers to the ordinary share capital (risk capital) of a company. *See* **equities**.
Second, it is the residual value of the variation and initial margins of a liquidated **future**. *See* **margin, initial; margin, variation**.
Third, it is the residual value of common **stock** over the debit balance of a margin account. *See* **account, margin**.
Fourth, it is used to describe the concept of fairness, of central importance to a branch of law distinct from common law, and as such it has significant effect on all kinds of contracts, dealings and trusts.

equity dilution Reduction in the unit value of ordinary shares effected by a bonus issue. *See* **issue, bonus**.

equity-linked policy Pension or savings plan whose payments are linked to fluctuations in the stock market.

equity play Any investment strategy operated on the stock market.

quasi-equity Loan stock or debt **instrument** that offers its holder rights and benefits similar to those offered to the holders of shares. *See* **stock, loan**.

shareholder's equity Equity held by shareholders rather than by the company itself.

sweat equity US Practice of providing labour in exchange for shares when personal **capital** is unavailable.

See also **capital, equity; switchings, equity**.

ergonomics Study of workers and the choices that confront them in ordinary working situations. Ergonomics has as its goal an increase in the efficiency of the workforce and therefore in productivity. *See also* **time and motion**.

ERM Abbreviation of **exchange rate mechanism**.

errors and omissions excepted (E&OE) Denial of responsibility for clerical errors and omissions, often included in invoices as a safeguard.

escheat Confiscation of a property. Escheat is a legal doctrine that states that property or titles revert to the crown in the event that the owner or holder dies intestate and without heirs. *See also* **intestacy**.

escrow Document held in **trust** by a third party. *E.g.* deeds and titles may be held in escrow until a person reaches the age of majority, or until some specified condition has been met.

establishment charges Overheads of a department store or shopping centre which are divided up and paid by the individual departments or shops. Establishment charges include rent, rates, taxes, light, and heating.

estate Term with two meanings.
First, it is the residual possessions of someone who has died.
Second, it is land, most especially a large area of land owned by one person.

industrial estate Area of land set aside for (usually light) industry.

real estate Any immovable property, particularly land with permanent buildings on it.

estimate Approximate valuation of an uncertain quantity.

It may be an approximate price quoted by a company before it undertakes work. In making such an estimate, the firm binds itself to complete the work at that price unless there is a change in the price of some key variable. An estimate therefore differs from a contractually-binding **quotation**. *E.g.* a printer's estimate could be revised if an increase occurred in the cost of paper.

The term also refers to UK government documents that set out proposed **expenditure** that accompany requests to Parliament for funds. *E.g.* naval estimates.

estoppel Legal restriction on a person's actions. The law insists that a person must bear liability for previous actions. Estoppel is generally used to prevent a denial of responsibility. *E.g.* the parties to a **contract** cannot subsequently claim that they were unaware of its conditions.

ethical Action that conforms to the moral constraints of an industry or society. 'Professional ethics' restrict a number of undesirable practices that are not strictly illegal. *E.g.* it is unethical but not illegal for a **stockbroker** to advise his or her clients to buy a **share** when he or she fully intends to sell his or her own holding.

euroaussie Popular term for an Australian government bond traded **offshore**, but not necessarily in Europe.

eurobond Medium- or long-term bearer bond denominated in a **eurocurrency**. Eurobonds are issued by governments or multinational companies. The eurobond market developed in the 1960s and is independent of the stock market. *See* **bond, bearer**.

eurocheque Cheque issued by an administrative consortium of European Community banks that may be cashed (without additional charge) at EEC banks outside the country of origin.

eurocurrency Currency of any nation held **offshore**. The eurocurrency markets deal in very large scale loans and deposits rather than the purchase or sale of foreign exchange. *See* **exchange, foreign**.

eurodollars US dollars held outside the USA. The term is particularly applied to dollars circulating in Europe. The post-war economic ascendancy of the USA has made the eurodollar an international currency medium. *See also* **eurocurrency**.

euromarket Market in which **eurocurrency** is traded.

European Currency Unit (ECU) Unit of account used by the **European Economic Community** since 1979. The value of the ECU is calculated by taking a weighted average of the current value of EEC member-states' own currencies. It exists only on paper, but it is used to settle intra-Community debts and in the calculation of Community budgets. Because it is an inherently stable currency, the ECU is increasingly favoured in the international money markets and as a medium for international trade.

European Economic Community (EEC) An association of some twelve European nations joined by a customs union and committed to the promotion of free trade within the boundaries of the community. It is intended that in the long run all the factors of production may be moved within the community at will, and remaining customs barriers are expected to be removed by some time in the 1990s. The EEC operates a protectionist policy by maintaining common tariffs on imports, and generates a substantial portion of its income from import duties and value added tax. Often abbreviated to European Community (EC), and also known as the Common Market.

euroyen Japanese currency held **offshore**. *See also* **eurocurrency**.

eurosclerosis Popular term for a 'seizure' (breakdown) in the **euromarkets** caused by **illiquidity** or some other financial panic.

ex ante Latin for from before. What is expected to be the position after some future event. *See also* **ex post**.

exceptional items Below-the-line **costs** and **revenues** that arise outside the normal business activities of a quoted company. The sale or purchase of new buildings or plant are examples of exceptional items.

exchange Term with two broad meanings.
First, it is to give one thing and take an equivalent in return.
Second, it is any place where goods or stocks are traded.

commodity exchange Exchange where the titles to commodities are traded. (It is now uncommon for the goods themselves to be exchanged.) Commodities exchanges may deal in either the **spot** or **future** markets.

exchange control Control of foreign exchange dealings by the government, either by means of restrictions on trade or by direct intervention in the market. Exchange controls help a government to exert some influence over the international value of its own currency.

exchange dealings Trading of stocks shares, and other financial instruments on an exchange.

exchanger Person who exchanges one currency for another.

exchange restrictions Exchange control that enables a state to limit the sale or purchase of foreign or domestic currency, usually in order to maintain the exchange rate for its own currency at an artificial level.

foreign exchange (FOREX) Buying and selling of currencies.

produce exchange Alternative term for a commodity exchange. *See* **exchange, commodity**.

share exchange Alternative term for stock exchange.

stock exchange Essentially, a place where **securities**, **stocks** and **shares** are bought and sold.

See also **bill of exchange**.

exchange rate The price at which one currency may be exchanged for another. Such transactions may be carried out on either the spot or forward markets, and are usually conducted either to permit investment abroad or to pay for imports. There is, in addition, considerable speculation on the exchange rates. *See* **market, forward; market spot**.

fixed exchange rate Exchange rate that the government attempts to control and fix in the short term by instructing the Bank of England to buy or sell foreign exchange reserves, or by introducing **tariffs.**

floating exchange rate Also known as a free exchange rate, an exchange rate that is not in any way manipulated by a central bank, but which moves according to **supply and demand**.

A clean floating rate is determined entirely by market forces, without any government intervention.

A dirty or managed float results from the imposition of some exchange controls, the value of a currency being allowed to fluctuate between set limits. *See* **exchange rate, pegged**.

pegged exchange rate Form of floating exchange rate in which the value of the currency is pegged between a pre-determined maximum and minimum value.

Exchequer Broadly, the central depository of government funds. As the department charged with the supervision of the nation's economic affairs, the Treasury is responsible for ensuring that all monies due to the government are paid into the Exchequer, and all spending approved by Parliament is paid for from Exchequer funds.

excise Duty charged on goods produced for home consumption before their sale and in the UK administered by the Customs and Excise department. British cars, beer, cigarettes, electrical goods, etc, are all liable to excise duty. *See* **duty, excise**.

Customs and Excise UK Government department charged with levying indirect taxes, including value added tax and **duty** on goods imported into the UK or produced in the UK for home consumption (**excise**). *See* **tax, value-added**.

ex coupon Stock that does not give the purchaser the right to the next interest payment due to be paid on it.

ex dividend Stock that does not give the purchaser the right to the next **dividend** payment, or to any dividend payment due within a specified period, generally the next calendar month.

executive Person charged with decision-making, specifically a member of the management of a company.

account executive In the UK, most commonly used for a person in advertising responsible for service to one client. In the USA, it is an alternative term for **stockbroker**.

executor Person appointed to see that the terms of a will or bequest are carried out.

exercise To make use of a right or option.

exercise notice Formal notification that a call option is to be taken up. The price paid is known as the exercise price. *See* **option, call**.

See also **price, exercise**.

ex factory A near-synonym for **ex warehouse**, indicating that the goods concerned are collected from the manufacturer's factory rather than his warehouse. The manufacturer therefore pays no storage costs.

ex-gratia Latin for from gratitude. Payment made in thanks, for example a tip, or **golden handshake** payment to a retiring worker.

ex-growth Euphemism for decline.

exhaustive events Set of possible events which collectively cover every possible occurence in a given context. A useful concept in corporate planning.

exit To leave a **market** by selling all relevant stocks and shares, or to cease production.

ex new Alternative term for **ex rights**.

ex officio Latin for by virtue of office. The concept is used to justify actions, or to appoint people to certain posts or groups.

expansion Development or growth of a business, either by **takeover** or **merger**, or by an increase in sales, production or investment by a firm.

expectations Prospects; that which is anticipated. Expectations of future business activity are one of the most significant influences on **investment** and thus have a significant effect on the level of **employment**.

expenditure Money spent on attaining some object.

above-the-line expenditure Alternative term for current expenditure, so called because these items are recorded before the total in a statement of account. *See* **expenditure, current**.

below-the-line expenditure Alternative term for capital expenditure, because such expenditure is listed below the line recording the total in a statement of account and is regarded as an additional cost. *See* **expenditure, capital**.

capital expenditure Expenditure on capital goods *e.g.* fixed assets such as plant or on trade investments and current assets. Capital expenditure is classed as below-the-line for accounting purposes. *See* **investment, trade; asset, current; asset, fixed**.

current expenditure Expenditure on assets for resale, such as raw materials rather than on fixed assets. Also known as above-the-line expenditure. *See* **asset, fixed**.

expenses Costs incurred by a business in the course of its normal activities.

administration expenses One of the general expenses. In company accounting, this is a blanket term covering expenses incurred in the overall management of a company, but not positively attributable to any particular department or operating arm.

allowable expenses Expenses that are tax-deductible.

direct expenses Expenses that may be attributed to one or another factor of production. *See also* **expenses, indirect**.

entertainment expenses The expense of entertaining business associates and potential clients, *e.g.* the cost of meals in restaurants.

fixed expenses Expenses that are incurred regardless of the level of other activities. *See* **overheads**.

general and administrative expenses (G&A) Administrative expenses plus operating costs. *See* **cost, operating**.

general expenses Non-specific expenses incurred in the day-to-day running of a firm.

incidental expenses Minor expenses not directly relevant to the running of a business.

indirect expenses Expenses incurred in production, but not directly attributable to any one factor of production.

overhead expenses Sometimes used for **indirect expenses**, sometimes for **fixed costs**, and sometime for both. Its precise meaning varies from company to company.

preliminary expenses Costs incurred during the formation of a company, including registration and promotion.

running expenses Also known as direct expenses or variable costs. Expenses incurred in the running of a business and which vary with output. Running expenses and costs include those incurred in purchasing the factors of production and in the marketing, advertising and distribution of goods.

See also **account, expense**.

export To take goods and services for sale outside the country of origin.

export declaration Statement provided to the Customs and Excise detailing the cost, price, destination and nature of goods leaving the country. *See* **excise**.

export duty Tax levied on exports. Because they tend to discourage export and adversely affect the **balance of payments**, export duties are seldom raised.

export house Company that assists other companies involved in the export trade, either by providing short- or medium-term credit (*e.g.* an export finance house) or by acting as an overseas agent for companies that do not maintain their own representatives in the countries to which they export.

export incentive Government incentives to promote exports. Export incentives include direct-tax incentives, subsidies, favourable terms for insurance and the provision of cheap credit.

export leasing Practice of selling goods for export to a leasing company in the country of origin. The leasing company ships them overseas and leases them to a foreign buyer.

See also **import**.

exports Goods or services manufactured or produced in one country and sold to another.

invisible exports Services (rather than goods) provided to foreign people, organizations and countries. Invisible exports include banking, shipping and insurance services.

temporary exports Short-term 'export' of cash or goods to an **offshore** location, often for the purpose of **tax avoidance**.

visible exports Also known as visibles, goods sold to foreign buyers and shipped abroad. The difference between the value of visible exports and visible imports is the **balance of trade**.

See also **import**.

ex post The position that arises after a certain event has taken place. *See also* **ex ante**.

exposure Extent of **risk**.

currency exposure Risk of holding assets in a foreign currency. The risk is incurred because their value, relative to that of the host nation's currency, is unstable. It is possible to hedge against currency exposure by selling foreign currency on the **forward** markets. *See* **hedging**.

overexposure Overabundance of risk. *E.g.* if a **stockbroker** is paid a salary largely dependent on the performance of the company, and if he or she also maintains a substantial shareholding in the firm, he or she is over-exposed to the possibility of a downturn in the broking business.

expropriation Dispossession; the confiscation of, *e.g., an* **estate** or **property**.

ex quay Goods that are sold for collection after they have been unloaded from a ship. The seller therefore pays freightage and the charge of unloading.

ex rights Also known as ex new, a stock exchange term for shares that are sold minus the right to take up bonus issues. *See* **issue, bonus**.

ex ship Goods sold to a purchaser who must pay the cost of unloading. The seller therefore pays only the cost of freightage.

extended Prolonged or offered. *See* **credit, extended**.

external Something that is outside. *See* **account, external; trade, external**.

extraordinary Additional items, expenditure, etc., acquired or incurred in addition to normal business.

extraordinary items Non-recurrent material items listed below the line on an **balance sheet**. *E.g.* the sale or purchase of an office building would be listed as an extraordinary item. *See also* **exceptional items**.

See also **EGM**.

ex warehouse Price exclusive of all delivery costs. The purchaser must arrange and pay for the collection, loading and distribution of the goods concerned from the seller's warehouse.

ex works Price exclusive of all delivery costs except those of loading. The purchaser must arrange for the collection and distribution of the goods concerned.

F

face value Alternative term for nominal value. *See* **value, nominal**

factor Company that undertakes **factoring** or, in Scotland, the manager of an estate of land.

factoring Activity of managing the trade debts of another firm. Commonly, a company sells due debts to a factor at a discount. The factor then makes a profit by recovering the debts at a price nearer the face value. Factoring relieves companies of the burden of administering debts and gives them access to ready cash before payment is due. *See* **debt, trade; value, nominal**.

failure investment *US* Practice of buying shares in companies that are doing badly, in the hope that their performance will improve.

fair price provisions (fair-price amendments *US*) Clause in a corporate charter whereby a buyer of the company's shares must pay the same amount or make the same consideration for all shares purchased. Used as a defensive tactic against **bootstrapping**.

fallen angel *US* Company, or shares in a company, whose **rating** has recently fallen significantly.

FAS Abbreviation of **free alongside ship**.

FASB *US* Abbreviation of Financial Accounting Standards Board.

FCA Abbreviation of Fellow of the Institute of Chartered Accountants. *See* **accountant, chartered**.

Fed Abbreviation of **federal reserve system**.

federal fund *US* Deposits held by federal reserve banks that bear no interest. *See* **bank, central**.

federal funding rate *US* **Interest** rate at which one federal reserve bank borrows funds from another. It is regulated by the federal reserve board to control the growth of bank reserves and the **money supply**. *See* **bank, federal reserve; money supply; rate, interest**.

Federal Reserve Board = **federal reserve system**

federal reserve system US central bank system, under which 12 regional federal reserve banks are governed by the Federal Reserve Board in Washington, appointed by the President. Like the Bank of England in the UK, it sets banking policy and controls the **money supply**. *See* **bank, federal reserve**.

fee Amount charged in return for a service performed. A stockbroker charges a fee for buying and selling shares for clients, and accountants charge fees for company audits.

fee simple Property held in fee simple may be bequeathed and inherited without limitation. Effectively the highest form of land ownership for any citizen, ending only if the owner dies **intestate**, without heirs, in which case the property passes to the crown.

redemption fee **Premium** paid to shareholders who surrender redeemable shares when asked to do so by a company.

feemail *US* Popular term describing the exorbitant fees charged by lawyers who handle **greenmail** cases.

fiduciary Person or body acting in trust. Anyone holding, say, cash in trust for another is said to be acting in a fiduciary capacity.

fiduciary issue Money issued by the Bank of England backed by securities, mainly in the form of the government's debt to the Bank. It is called fiduciary because of the public's trust that the government will repay the debts backing the issue.

FIFO Abbreviation of **first in first out**.

fight the tape *US* Practice of selling when prices are rising and buying when prices are falling. The tape is the ticker tape that once relayed prices to brokers.

fill or kill On a **futures** market, an order to trade that must be either fulfilled immediately or cancelled.

FIMBRA Acronym for Financial Intermediaries and Brokers Regulatory Authority, a recognized **SRO**.

finance Term with two meanings.
First, as a noun, it means resources of money and their management. "He is trying to raise the finance to float another company."
Second, as a verb, it means to supply money for a certain purpose. "He finally found a backer who would finance the whole operation."

Finance Act Annual legislation enforcing the measures set out in the UK government's spring **budget**.

mezzanine finance Money leant to a small and growing, but financially viable, company. So-called because the risk of making the loan falls between that of advancing venture capital and the safer course of putting the finance into established debt markets. *See* **capital, venture**.

See also **house, finance**.

financial Of or to do with **finance**.

Financial Accounting Standards Board US (FASB) Private regulatory body that sets the accounting standards for US public companies. *See also* **SEC**.

financial advisor Person (or institution) who gives advice on raising, lending or managing money, or on particular transactions, usually for a **fee**.

Financial Services Act (FSA) Came into force on April 29 1988 in the UK, to prevent abuse of the de-regulated stock exchange system, principally by placing all people or institutions involved in financial services under the authority of an **SRO**.

financial supermarket Financial institution that provides more than one type of financial service. A significant number sprang up after **deregulation**. A financial supermarket may also be known as a **boutique**. *See also* **Big Bang; Chinese wall**.

See also **accountant, financial; year, financial**.

financial institution = house, finance

fine Money paid as a penalty, usually for an illegal act.

fine bill = bill of exchange, fine

firm Commonly used to refer to any company or business. Strictly, a firm is a partnership of professionally qualified people, such as lawyers, accountants, surveyors or civil engineers. In this case, firms are legally distinct from companies and do not, for instance, issue shares. Also, the **liability** of individual partners is not (and legally cannot be) limited. *See also* **incorporation**.

first class paper **Bills** issued by financial institutions of high standing, *e.g.* the **Treasury**.

first in first out (FIFO) Accountancy principle whereby **stock-in-trade** is assumed to be issued to customers in the order that it is received. Thus, stock currently held may be valued at current prices. *See also* **last in, first out**.

fixed Unchanging, not subject to movement. The term is commonly found in phrases such as fixed **assets**, fixed **capital**, fixed **charge**, fixed **costs**, fixed **deposit**, fixed exchange **rate, fixed interest securities,** fixed **trust**.

fixture Any **chattel** attached or annexed to land. In this case it becomes part of the property.

landlord's fixture Object, *e.g.* a fence, provided by the landlord of a property. Otherwise, a fixture provided by a tenant that may not be removed, either because an agreement has been made between landlord and tenant or because the tenant has not removed it on vacating the property.

tenant's fixture Fixture provided by a tenant. A tenant's fixture may be removed before his or her tenancy ends.

flip *US* Practice of buying and then selling shares (usually in the manner of a **stag**) at high speed in order to make a fast profit. *See also* **dolphin**.

float Term with two broad meanings.

First, it is cash or funds used either to give change to customers or to pay for expenses.

Second, to float is to sell shares in order to raise share **capital** and obtain listing on the stock exchange. Also now more frequently used to mean to start a new company.

clean float Floating exchange rate that is completely uncontrolled by the central bank. *See also* **float, dirty.**

dirty float Partly-managed floating exchange rate. The central bank continues to intervene in the market for its own currency. In practice all floats tend to be dirty. *See also* **float, clean.**

See also **exchange rate, floating.**

floor Usually refers to the trading area of an exchange. *See also* **trader, floor.**

flotation Act of selling shares in a company to raise capital and be listed on the stock exchange. *See* **float.**

fluctuation Movement of prices up or down on a market. Downward fluctuation is also known as slippage.

maximum fluctuation Upper limit to which a price may change on any exchange in one day's trading. It is fixed in advance as a percentage of the current price, and trading in a contract is halted for the rest of the day if the maximum fluctuation price is reached.

minimum fluctuation Also known as the basis point, lower limit to which a price may fall in one day's trading on an exchange. As with the maximum fluctuation, it is fixed in advance and trading is halted for the day if the minimum fluctuation is reached.

FOB Abbreviation of **free on board**.

foreign aid Aid, most often in the form of loans or investment, to developing and Third World countries.

FOREX Acronym for foreign exchange. *See* **exchange, foreign.**

foreclose If a property has been mortgaged, *i.e.* stands as security against a loan, the lender may take possession of the property if the borrower fails to pay off the loan. Such an act of possession is known as foreclosure.

forward Verb meaning to send something on to someone (*e.g.* to a new address) or something (*e.g.* a **futures** contract) to be completed some time in the future, or an adjective describing something (such as a transaction) in the future.

forward dating Practice of dating documents in advance. *E.g.* an invoice or a cheque may be dated sometime in the future. Also known as postdating.

See also **buy forward; market, forward; price, forward; purchase, forward**.

franchise Licence bought by a retailer or supplier of services that entitles him or her to sell the goods of a particular manufacturer under a particular trading name. This system enables the manufacturer to have direct control over who sells the goods, and often gives the seller exclusive rights to sell those goods in his or her area.

franco Alternative term for **rendu**.

fraud Illegal practice of obtaining money from people under false pretences. *E.g.* fraud is committed if the facts pertaining to a contract are purposefully misrepresented. Fraudulently diverting ones company's or employer's money for one's own use is **embezzlement**.

free contract Alternative term for **rendu**.

free alongside ship (FAS) An exporter who sells goods FAS pays for their carriage up to the point when they are standing on the dockside waiting to be loaded. *See also* **free on board**.

free on board (FOB) An exporter who sells goods FOB pays for their carriage up to the point where they are loaded aboard ship. *See also* **free alongside ship**.

freehold Land or buildings that are owned freehold are owned absolutely by the freeholder. *See also* **leasehold**.

freeze Broadly, act of stopping something (*e.g.* wages or prices) from moving.

"The Government has decided to freeze wage levels of certain public-sector employees for the next twelve months."

freeze-out Situation in which a company successfully out-competes its competitors, causing a new ice-age for them and thus freezing them out of the market.

friendly Used more and more frequently to mean something that is sympathetic to the needs of a particular person or group.

user-friendly Originally, computer software that is easily used, even by a novice. Now often used for anything that is easy to use.

See also **society, friendly; takeover, friendly**.

fringes *US* Popular abbreviation for fringe benefits. *See* **benefit, fringe**.

front company Company established to conceal its true ownership or the true activities of its owners.

front door Popular term for the Bank of England's practice of lending money to discount houses in order to inject cash into the money market. *See also* **back door**.

front-end *US* The marketing (rather than the manufacturing) side of a company.

front end load In a transaction covering a period of time, to distribute the benefits towards the early part of the period. **Bootstrapping** is a form of front-end loading.

front money Alternative term for seed money. *See* **money, seed**

FSA Abbreviation of **Financial Services Act**.

fund As a verb, to make finance available.

"He was unable to raise sufficient capital to fund the project."

As a noun, money set aside for a specific purpose (*e.g.* from which to pay pensions or insurance claims), or lent to an institution or government.

More specifically, it is the money that the UK government borrows from institutions and the public by issuing various forms of government bonds. *See* **bond, government**.

captive fund Fund for venture capital held by a large financial services group. *See* **capital, venture**.

closed-end fund Alternative term for investment trust. *See* **trust, investment**.

consolidated fund Essentially the bank account of the UK Exchequer. Taxes are paid into the consolidated fund and money for government expenditure is withdrawn from it.

discretionary fund Sum of money left with a stockbroker, to be invested at his or her discretion. *See also* **fund, managed; trust, unit**.

fund of funds Unit trust, organized and managed by an institution to invest in other of its own unit trusts. *See* **trust, unit**.

index fund Investment fund that is linked directly to a share **index**, in that it has investments in shares on that index.

International Monetary Fund (IMF) International organization set up in 1944 after the Bretton Woods conference, to organize and administer the international monetary system. It was designed to help countries in financial difficulties, especially with their **balance of payments**. It makes loans and provides financial advisors.

low-load fund Mutual fund that charges a low initial fee.

managed fund Fund that is set up by an intermediary, and invested (using a **stockbroker**) on behalf of an investor.

money market fund Unit trust, the income from which is invested in high-yield, short term instruments of credit. Money market funds are particularly popular when interest rates are high. *See* **trust, unit**.

mutual fund US Alternative term for unit trust. *See* **trust, unit**.

no-loan fund US Form of unit trust that employs no salesmen and therefore incurs no commission or distribution costs. An investor thus avoids paying a commission on shares purchased, the only expense remaining being a relatively modest management fee. *See* **fund, mutual**.

open-end fund US Alternative term for unit trust. *See* **trust, unit**.

pension fund Pool of money from which pensions are paid.

sinking fund Sum of money set aside for a specific purpose and invested so that it produces the required amount at the right time. *See also* **debt, funded**.

funding Practice of providing money for a specific purpose. *See* **fund; tranche funding**.

fundamentalist *US* Stock market analyst who predicts stock exchange price movements after making an analysis of the performance of the company involved, rather than of market trends.

fungible Stock market term for **securities** that are in hand, *i.e.* that have not yet been settled.

futures Contracts that are made for delivery of *e.g.* currencies or **commodities** on a future date. Futures markets provide an opportunity for **speculation**, in that contracts may be bought and sold (with no intention on the part of the traders to take delivery of the goods) before the delivery date arrives and their prices may rise and fall in that time.
  "Following reports that bad weather in Brazil had seriously damaged the coffee crop, coffee futures rose sharply today."

deferred futures Futures contracts that are furthest away from **maturity**. *See also* **futures, nearby**.

financial futures Contracts for the delivery of financial instruments (*i.e.* a currency) on a future date. Financial futures are used to **hedge** against the rise and fall of interest and exchange rates.

index futures Futures contracts that are based on the figures provided by indices.

interest rate futures Financial futures purchased as a hedge against an adverse change in **interest rates**. If interest rate changes on the hedger's financial instruments produce a loss, the futures contract offsets it. *See also* **hedging**.

nearby futures Futures contracts that are closest to maturity. *See also* **futures, deferred**.

See also **market, forward**.

FX Abbreviation of foreign exchange. *See* **exchange, foreign.**

FY Abbreviation of fiscal year. *See* **year, fiscal**.

G

G5 countries Group of Five leading industrial nations (France, Japan, West Germany, the UK and the USA), which meet from time to time to discuss common economic problems.

G7 countries Group of Seven leading non-communist industrial nations consisting of the **G5 countries**, Canada and Italy.
"The G-7 countries managed to keep exchange rates close to the targets set out in the Louvre Accord."

GAAP *US* Abbreviation of generally accepted accounting principles, a code of practice set out by the Financial Accounting Standards Board. *See* **FASB**.

gadfly *US* Shareholder who appears at shareholders' meetings and asks awkward questions.

gain Alternative term for **profit**.

capital gain Gain made from a capital transaction, *e.g.* the buying and selling of **assets**.

gainsharing Alternative term for **profit sharing**.

galloping inflation = **hyperinflation**

gambling Applied figuratively to the commitment of money on any highly **risky** venture. Gambling on a stock market is similar to **speculation** in that it is shorter term, riskier and less serious-minded than **investment**. *See also* **bet the ranch**.

gamma shares Shares that are traded infrequently and in small quantities. *See* **share**.

G & A Abbreviation of general and administrative expenses. *See* **expenses**, **general** and **administrative**.

GATT Abbreviation of General Agreement on Tariffs and Trade, an international organization with more than eighty member countries, whose object is to negotiate on matters of trade policy, notably the reduction of **tariffs** and other barriers to free trade. *See also* **clause, most-favoured nation; barrier, trade**.

gazetted Refers to the London Gazette (in Scotland, the Edinburgh Gazette), a weekly publication that includes details of appointments, bankruptcy orders, notices of winding up, changes in company constitutions, etc. If information is gazetted, it is assumed that everybody in the nation has been notified, even if they have never even seen or heard of the publication.

gazump To raise the asking price of a property after an offer has been agreed verbally or in writing and before exchange of contracts, in order to take advantage of rising prices.

GDP Abbreviation of gross domestic product, a measure of the value of goods and services produced within a country, normally in one year. *See also* **GNP**.

gearing The proportion of long-term debt to equity finance on the balance sheet of a company. More specifically, it is the ratio of borrowed capital against total capital employed, expressed as a percentage. Sometimes also known as leverage.

general Not specific, covering all eventualities. *See also* **AGM; clearing, general; EGM; offer, general; partner, general; reserves, general**.

ghost worker Person who appears on the payroll of a company but does not work.

GIGO *US* Acronym for garbage in, garbage out, a precept in the world of computing, meaning that the data delivered by a computer is only as good as the data supplied to it.

gilt Common term for a **gilt-edged security**.

gilt-edged Security that carries little or no **risk**, in particular, government-issued stocks. Known as a gilt for short. In the United States, however, gilt-edged refers to bonds issued by companies with a good reputation for **dividend** payment and with a good profit record. *See also* **Consol**.

gilt switches Process of selling one gilt and investing the entire proceeds in another. One reason for gilt switching may be to take advantage of changes in **interest rates**, when a long-dated gilt may be switched for a short-dated gilt, or vice versa.

long-dated gilt Gilt with a redemption term of more than fifteen years.

medium-dated gilt Gilt with a redemption term of between five and fifteen years.

short-dated gilt Gilt with a redemption term of less than five years.

giro Banking system whereby money may be transfered from one bank account to another without a cheque being written; also known as bank giro.
   Giro also refers in the UK to the Post Office banking service, and is slang for a cheque received as a social security payment.
" Please transfer this money to his account by giro."
" He has just gone to cash his giro."

Glass-Steagall Act *US* 1933 Act of Congress which separated the activities of commercial and investment bankers.

global Worldwide.

global equities market Worldwide market in equities, still in its infancy, involving principally the exchanges in London, New York and Tokyo. "Global equities have been hailed for two years now as the new era in securities markets."

globalization Increasing internationalization of all markets, industries and commerce.

global village Term coined by Marshall McLuhan to describe a world closely interconnected by modern telecommunications, especially television, which greatly reduce the intellectual, cultural and trading isolation formerly caused by geographical separation.

GM Abbrevation of gross margin.

GmbH *GER* Abbreviation of *Gesellschaft mit beschrankter Haftung*, the West German eqivalent of a UK private (limited) company. *See also* **AG**.

GMP Abbreviation of guaranteed minimum pension. *See* **pension, guaranteed minimum**.

gnome Rhetorical term for a remote and detached financial operator, as in the 'Gnomes of Zurich' blamed by UK Prime Minister Harold Wilson for the fall in the international value of the pound sterling during the Labour Government of 1966 to 1971.

GNP Abbreviation of gross national product, a measure of the value of all goods and services produced by a country, including those produced overseas, usually in one year. *See also* **GDP**.

godown Far East term for a **warehouse**.

gogo (fund) *US* Investment fund that is being actively traded, producing high capital gains and high market prices.

gold Precious metal, widely and historically used as a primary medium of exchange independent of the value of national currencies.

gold and dollar reserves Stock of **gold** and US national currency held by the US government or central bank.

gold and foreign exchange reserves As above, with national currencies other than the US dollar included in the stock.

gold bug US Investor who uses gold **reserves** as a cushion against **inflation**.

gold standard Historical arrangement whereby the comparative value of national currencies such as the pound sterling or US dollar, was determined by a fixed price for gold.

golden handcuffs Contractual arrangement between a company and its employee whereby the employee has a very strong financial incentive (other than loss of normal salary) to remain with the company, such as a low-interest mortgage or share options which expire if the employee resigns.

golden handshake Gratuitous payment made by a company to an employee who is leaving, or has recently left. Such a payment may be made out of goodwill, or to maintain good relations with the employee, or to induce the employee to resign where there are no grounds or dubious grounds for statutory dismissal or redundancy.

golden hello Payment other than normal salary made to an employee on joining a company in order to induce him or her to do so.

golden parachute Term in a contract of employment whereby the employer is bound to pay the employee a substantial sum of money in the event of dismissal or redundancy.

gold fixing Activity that occurs twice a day when the five dealers of gold bullion on the London exchange meet to determine the price of gold.

See also **share, gold**.

good faith = bona fide

goods Physical items manufactured, sold or exchanged; contrasted with **services** where no physical items are transferred.

capital goods Goods (such as machines) that are used for the production of other goods. Ships are also sometimes regarded as capital goods.

consumer goods Goods that are consumed in use, either over a short period (*e.g.* foodstuffs), or over a longer period, such as motor vehicle tyres (or even the motor vehicles themselves). *See also* **durable, consumer**.

Giffen good Good that violates the laws of demand. When the price of a Giffen good increases (such as a cosmetic), demand increases, instead of falling off as would normally expected.

goods on approval Goods delivered to a customer for which payment is not required unless the customer is satisfied. If the customer is not satisfied in a stated period of time the goods are returned to the vendor. A retailer may also hold goods on approval, and return them if they are not sold.

goods on consignment Method of trading in goods whereby they are sent to an agent on consignment. Although the agent has no title to the goods he may sell them on to a buyer. If the goods are not sold, they are returned to the owner.

hard goods US Consumer durables, *e.g.* furniture and household appliances.

perishable goods Goods that are liable to deterioration over a relatively short period of time. The term is most frequently applied to foodstuffs.

red goods US Goods, such as food, that are produced and consumed quickly.

spot goods As opposed to **futures**, spot goods are commodities available for immediate delivery, rather than forward delivery.

good-till-cancelled (GTC) **Order** that remains in force unless it is expressly cancelled. Cancellation is usually dependent upon a satisfactory profit level being reached. Also known as a resting order or an open order.

goodwill Value of a business over and above the book value of its identifiable or physical assets. Or the amount paid on acquisition of a business over its current stock market valuation. Can refer *e.g.* to the literal good will of the established customers of a retail business (shop or restaurant) whose benevolent habit (or custom) of using it cannot be shown in the accounts.

go-slow Form of industrial action whereby workers decrease their rate of production as a protest.
"A prolonged go-slow by car workers has reduced the company's output by 20%."

graft *US* Informal term for money made in illegal dealings undertaken while in public office.

Graham-Rudman Amendment *US* Legislation, currently being introduced in stages in the USA, aimed at amending the Constitution to make it unconstitutional to run a budget deficit.

grant Funds provided by a government, government body or other institution (*e.g.* the Leverhulme Trust or the Nuffield Foundation). "The theatre company received a smaller grant from the Arts Council this year than last."

discretionary grant Grant that is not automatically paid, but is made at the discretion of the authority concerned. *See also* **grant, mandatory**.

grant price US In instances where employees have a preferential option on their company's stock, the grant price is the price at which they may exercise that option.

investment grant Grant of money made available by the government to companies for certain purposes.

mandatory grant Grant that must be paid to all people or organizations that fall into the qualifying categories. Most maintenance grants to first degree students are currently mandatory. *See also* **grant, discretionary**.

gratuity Payment made voluntarily in excess of statutory or contractual obligation, *e.g.* a tip in a restaurant or a bonus payment on retirement.

gray *US* spelling of **grey**.

Great Yellow Father *US* Popular name for the Kodak Corporation.

greenback Informal name for the US dollar.
"The central bank has no plans to cut its support of falling currency despite a stronger greenback."

green baize door Alternative term for **Chinese Wall**.

green book Informal name for the *Unlisted Securities Market*, published by the London Stock Exchange, setting out requirements for entry into the **USM** and regulations.

green grass project Project for the construction of a new factory or processing plant where none has existed before (by contrast with the extension or replacement of an existing facility). Also known as a green field project.

greenmail Procedure whereby a person with a sufficient shareholding in a company seeks a sum of money, or the repurchase by the company of his shares at an unreasonably high price, in order to induce him or her to refrain from making a **takeover bid**.

green pound Notional unit of currency used in the administration of the Common Agricultural Policy of the European Economic Community to determine the relative prices (and hence subsidies) of farm produce from different countries in the EEC.

green shoe *US* When a company goes public it may grant its underwriting firm an option on extra quantities of shares. This prevents the underwriter making a loss should the issue be oversubscribed and the underwriter have to buy shares on the open market to cover a short position.

grey (gray *US*) Normally describes something that is ambiguous, shady or too far off to identify properly.

grey knight In a **takeover** situation, a third party acting as a counterbidder, whose intentions towards the target company are not at all clear. Grey knights are normally unwelcome to both the **target** and the original **raider**. *See also* **white knight**.

grey market Trading in shares before they are officially issued. Trading on the grey market acts as a pre-issue indicator of the likely performance of shares after they are issued.

grey wave Normally used in venture capital circles to decribe a company or new industry that shows potential but whose realization is, however, a long way in the future. *See also* **capital, venture**.

gross Term with two meanings.
First, a gross is twelve dozen (144) units.
Second, it is an amount calculated before the deduction of certain items, the items being conventionally specified according to context. *E.g.* a salary or interest paid 'gross of tax' is paid before deduction of tax, in contrast to 'net of tax' where the amount is deducted before payment.

grossing up Calculation of a gross amount from the net amount by adding back the item deducted.

gross mark-up Amount by which a **trader** increases the purchase price of an item in order to sell it at a **profit**, usually expressed as a percentage of his purchase price.

gross margin (GM) Similar to **gross mark-up**, but expressed as a percentage of the trader's selling price. Also sometimes used instead of **gross profit**.

gross profit **Profit** on a transaction or series of transactions before deduction of **indirect expenses**, interest or taxation. *I.e.* the sales revenue or fees minus only those costs directly incurred in the purchase, manufacture and delivery of the goods concerned.

See also **value, gross annual**

gross domestic product = GDP

gross national product = GNP

group Another name for a **conglomerate**.
  "The A & G Group plc now has 10 subsidiary companies."

Group of Ten Also known as the Paris Club, the Group of Ten is
  Belgium, Canada, France, Italy, Japan, the Netherlands, Sweden, the
  UK, the USA and West Germany. These countries signed an agreement
  in 1962 to increase the funds available to the IMF and to aid those
  member countries with **balance of payments** difficulties.

growth Process of increase in any entity, activity or quantity.
  "Strong demand from our customers has led to growth in sales."
  Growth may also be the speed or rate of increase in any entity, activity
  or quantity.
  "The growth in GDP forecast for the current year is 2%."

  growth stocks **Stocks** or **shares** that are expected to provide the investor
    with a larger proportion of capital growth (*i.e.* growth in the value of
    the stock or share) to income (in the form of dividends) than other
    shares.

  growth recession US Situation in which the **GNP** and **unemployment**
    are both increasing slowly.

  higgledy-piggledy growth Term coined in the 1960s for the theory that
    share prices, dividends and stock market earnings are relatively
    unpredictable.

See also **EMH; random walk theory**.

  natural rate of growth Used in theoretical economics to describe a rate of
    growth in an economy that is in equilibrium, *i.e.* an economy with no
    inflation and with **unemployment** at its natural level.

GTC Abbreviation of **good-till-cancelled**

guarantee Term with two meanings.
  First, it is a document stating that goods or services are of good
  (merchandizable) quality.

"The washing machine came with a five-year guarantee."
Second, it is a promise to pay the debts of someone else in the event that the debtor defaults. A guarantee is not to be confused with an **indemnity**.

fidelity guarantee Guarantee of the trustworthiness of a person for employment purposes.

See also **pension, guaranteed minimum**.

guarantor Person who guarantees, if necessary, to pay someone else's debt.
"Her father agreed to act as guarantor for her loan."

guinea Former unit of British currency valued at 1 pound and 1 shilling (£1.05 sterling), occasionally still referred to in transactions with a marked ceremonial or traditional aspect.

gyration Fluctuation on the financial markets.
"The deregulation of the London Stock Exchange has helped to cushion the London market against recent wildly gyrating trading."
See also **whipsaw**.

H

hack Writer-to-order or journalist. The term has recently gained a new meaning in the field of computing. To hack is to enter a computer database illegally by breaking the security codes, *e.g.* in order either to steal computer time, steal data or 'amend' files.

hacker Someone who is enthusiastically knowledgeable in the field of computers or one who spends his or her time breaking into other people's computer systems.

haggle To discuss a price or the terms of an agreement in an attempt to reduce or improve them.

haircut *US* Normally, a **discount** on the market **value** of a **bond**. It may also be any discount or deduction from the normal value, or the cutting of a budget for a particular project or operation without harming the project itself.

half-commission man Person whose business is to introduce new clients to a **stockbroking** firm, receiving in return a share of the **commission** received from those clients.

hallmark Mark imprinted onto precious metals and their alloys (*e.g.* platinum, gold or silver) to show that the metal is of a certain quality. The term has also come to mean any sign of high quality. *See also* **assay**.

hammering Stock Exchange term that refers to the announcement of the inability of a member to pay his debts.

hammer out To enter into extended negotiations and to discuss the details of an agreement at length.
"We managed to hammer out an agreement, but it took us several months of negotiations."

hancock = annuity, hancock

hard Reliable or tangible.

hard numbers US Financial projections that can be relied upon.

See also **currency, hard; dollars, hard; goods, hard**.

haulage Charge made for transporting goods by road. It does not normally include a charge for loading and unloading.

headage Per capita payment for livestock.

headhunter Person or agency that finds suitable (usually high-grade) staff for posts that companies have vacant, taking a commission from the company involved in relation to the 'head's' salary.

hedging Method of protecting oneself from price fluctuations. Hedging happens commonly on the commodities **futures** market.

hereditament Piece of land, originally just large enough to support one family, but now used to mean any plot of land.

hidden Adjective which refers to something that is not obvious. *See* **price increase, hidden; reserve, hidden; tax, hidden; unemployment, hidden**.

high-end Adjective, normally used of **goods** produced for the top of the market and consequently very expensive.

high seas Waters that are not part of the territorial waters of any particular country.

High Street bank = big four

hightech Any business that makes extensive use of modern technology, particularly electronic systems.

hike *US* Increase.
"He took a large pay hike when he changed jobs."

hire To pay a sum of money (usually expressed as so much per hour, day, week, etc) for the use of goods (*e.g.* equipment or transport).

hire purchase (HP) Form of **credit**, normally extended on consumer **goods**, whereby the customer takes and uses the goods and pays for them in instalments (with interest) over an agreed period of time.

plant hire Hire of extra machinery, often in order to cope with a sudden surge in demand.

hit bid Bargain in which a dealer sells immediately at a price a buyer is willing to pay, instead of waiting for a possibly better price.

hive off Splitting off of an operating arm of a company to make it into a **subsidiary** company, it is said to hive off that part of its operation.

holder Someone who owns something or owns rights in something, such as shares, bills, bonds, credit cards or insurance policies.

holder for value Person who holds a **bill of exchange** for which a value has at one time been given.

holder in due course Person who has taken up bill for value before payment is due, and who has no good reason to suspect the title of the previous holder.

See also **bearer**.

holding Investment in a company or in any **security**.

holding company = company, holding

hold over To defer settlement of a deal on the Stock Exchange until the next settlement day.

hollowization What happens when a country suffers a relatively sudden loss of skilled workers, **capital** and technology; similar to a **brain-drain**.

honorarium Money paid to a professional such as an **accountant** or a **solicitor**, when the professional does not request a **fee**.

honorary Term referring to a person who is not paid for his or her services. *E.g.* honorary secretary, honorary president. *See* **secretary, honorary**.

house A business or **company**. The term is usually preceded by a verb denoting the activity of the company. The house is also a popular nickname for the London Stock Exchange.

clearing house Institution that specializes in clearing debts between its members. The best known type of clearing house is a banker's clearing house, which clears cheques between the major banks.

discount house Company whose main activity is the discounting of bills of exchange. *See* **bill of exchange; discounting**.

finance house Also known as a finance company or an industrial bank, a company that provides finance (credit), *e.g.* to operate **hire purchase** transactions on behalf of retailers.

issuing house Connecting link between those who need **capital** and those who are willing to lend. Often, an issuing house also operates as a share issue **underwriter** or merchant bank. *See* **bank, merchant**.

wire house US Informal term for a large stockbroking firm.

HP Abbreviation of **hire purchase**.

hustle *US* To work hard to make sales and profits. The term has connotations of forwardness or aggression.

hyperinflation Inflation that is running extremely high; also known as galloping inflation.
"After the First World War, Germany suffered a crippling period of hyperinflation."

hypothecation A firm of shippers may borrow money from a **bank** using cargo they are currently shipping as **security**. In this case, the bank takes out a **lien** on the cargo and this is conveyed in a letter of hypothecation.
   In the United States, hypothecation is putting up securities as collateral on a **margin** account.

I

IAS Abbreviation of internal audit system. *See* **audit, internal**.

ICC Abbreviation of International **Chamber of Commerce**.

ignorantia juris neminem excusat Latin for ignorance of the law is no defence. Doctrine which warns that people who break the law will be punished, regardless of whether or not they are aware that they are committing a crime.

illiquidity Situation in which an **asset** is not easily converted into cash, or in which a person is unable to raise cash quickly and/or easily. *See also* **liquidity**.

illegal Something that is against the law. *See also* **unlawful**.

imperfect Broadly, actual rather than purely theoretical economic structures and transactions; more precisely, any economic state that is not perfectly efficient. 'Imperfect competition', for example, is defined as any environment between pure **monopoly** and a state of perfect **competition**. *See also* **competition, imperfect; oligopoly, imperfect.**

IMF Abbreviation of **International Monetary Fund**.

implied terms Terms of a **contract** that are not expressly stated, but that the law considers necessary to the sense of the contract and therefore implicit.

import Goods and services brought into a country for sale, from abroad.

import ban Ban of specified imports, often for political rather than economic reasons.

import specie point Point in the variation of exchange rates at which it becomes cheaper for a nation on the **gold standard** to import gold than buy foreign **currency**.

invisible imports Imports of intangible products, such as services, rather than of goods. *See also* **imports, visible**.

visible imports Tangible products; imports of goods rather than services. *See also* **imports, invisible**.

See also **quota, import**.

importation The act of importing.

importers' entry of goods The customs regulations in force in the country to which exports are being despatched, and which the exporter must note and observe.

imputation system UK **taxation** system, established in 1973, which partly governs the payment of corporation tax. By which the shareholder's **dividends** are taxed at source, and he or she is issued with a **credit** for the tax imputed. *See also* **tax, corporation**.

IMRO Acronym for Investment Managers' Regulatory Organization, a recognised UK **SRO**.

inactive Something that is not moving or working.
See also **active; market, inactive**.

Inc Abbreviation of incorporated. *See* **incorporation**.

incentive Positive motive (sometimes artificially generated) for performing some task. *See also* **bonus, incentive**.

incestuous share dealing Dealing in the shares of associated firms in order to win tax concessions. Incestuous share dealing is often illegal, but need not necessarily be so.

incidentals Non-material items, particularly those referred to in a company's **accounts**. Incidentals normally amount to no more than 5% of total **costs**.

income Money, goods or services received from any activity. Income may be either a return on one of the factors of production - a **salary**, **rent**, **interest** or **profit** - or a transfer payment made for some other reason, such as unemployment benefit. The definition includes non-monetary income such as the benefit derived from the possession of **assets**. *See* **benefit, unemployment**.

disposable income That part of a person's income that he or she may dispose of in any way, *i.e.* what is left after such things as accommodation and food have been paid for.

earned income Income received in exchange for labour, rather than derived from investments (the definition does, however, include some **pension** and social security payments.)

income statement Alternative term for profit and loss account. *See* **account, profit and loss**.

non-taxable income Income which for one reason or another is not subject to normal income tax. Non-taxable income includes **dividends**, money received by charities, and interest on bank deposit accounts.

notional income Non-financial benefit that an owner receives from an **asset**. Most usually applied to the benefit received by the owner-occupier of a property. In such a case, the notional income is equal to the amount which would otherwise have had to be spent on **rent**.

taxable income Income on which taxes are levied. Taxable income is calculated by deducting personal allowances from **gross** income. *See* **allowance, personal**.

unearned income Income received from investments (and not from the provision of goods or services), including **dividends** and **interest** payments.

See also **bond, income; tax, income**.

inconvertible Money that cannot be exchanged for gold of equal value. UK currency has been incovertible since the country came off the **gold standard**, in 1931.

incorporation The process of setting up a business as a legal entity.

increment Amount of increase.

annual increment Amount by which money (often a salary) or goods increase in the course of one year.

incremental increase Increase that occurs in stages or steps, or successive increases by one unit.

See also **cost, incremental**.

indebtedness State of owing money or services to someone else, or the amount of money owed. *See also* **day, indebtedness**.

indemnity Undertaking that gives protection against **loss** or damage. Indemnity may be in the form of replacement or repair of property lost or damaged, or provision of cash to the value of the property. With the exception of personal insurance, **insurance** contracts are based on an offer of indemnity made in return for the regular payment of **premiums** by the person insured.

letter of indemnity Letter sent with a shipment for **export**, that states that the manufacturer is prepared to rectify any damage that occurs during transit, due to inadequate packing, handling, etc.

professional indemnity Form of **insurance** cover that is desgined to protect the insured from the legal consequences which his or her actions (in a professional capacity) may have for some third party. *E.g.* a doctor would use a professional indemnity insurance as a protection against legal action brought as a result of incorrect diagnosis or a mistake made in the operating theatre.

indent Order for goods from abroad, often placed with an **agent**.

closed indent Order for goods placed with an agent abroad that specifies the supplier from whom goods are to be obtained.

open indent Order for goods which does not specify a particular supplier. The agent receiving the indent may purchase suitable goods from any manufacturer at his or her own discretion.

indenture **Deed** or **instrument** to which there is more than one party. So called because such deeds were formerly cut or torn (indented) into portions, one for each party, to prevent forgery and provide proof of each person's involvement in the transaction. Indentures were formerly widely used to bind an apprentice to his master.

independent Someone who is free to act unilaterally and who does not depend on any other person or organization. *See also* **company, independent**.

index Form of measurement or comparison; listing giving an indication of change.

index-linking System of linking costs, prices, or wages to the price fluctuations of an economy in order to allow for **inflation** and maintain value in real terms. Index-linking is most often used to relate **income** to the retail price index. In a year of 4% inflation, therefore, it would be usual for an indexed salary to rise by the same amount. *See* **index, retail price**.

index number Weighted average that permits the comparison of prices or production over a number of years. The components selected for comparison are weighted according to their importance and then averaged. Figures are compared to those for a base year, selected for its typicality and given the index number 100. *See* **year, base**.

retail price index Analysis of trends in retail prices, expressed as an index number and used to evaluate changes in retail prices with reference to **inflation**. *See* **price, retail**.

misery index Index that estimates the relative ill-health of the economy by incorporating variables such as the level of **inflation**, **unemployment** and economic growth.

share index Index that shows the average change in value of a number of individual shares. Share indexes therefore give an overall guide to movements in the financial markets. Examples include the Financial Times 100-share index, the Nikkei-Dow average and the Dow Jones industrial average.

tax and price index (TPI) Index launched in 1979 to compare levels of **taxation** with **retail prices** and relate them to average wage levels. The TPI is used to calculate the real spending power of the nation.

See also **fund, index; futures, index**.

indexation Form of **index-linking** that ties **income** to the retail price index and therefore prevents a fall in real wages during a period of **inflation**. *See* **index, retail price**.

indicator Measurable variable used to suggest overall change among a group of linked variables too complex to yield to simple analysis. Thus a variety of economic indicators — such as **price**, **income**, **imports**, **exports**, **money supply** and so on — are studied in an attempt to estimate the state of a national economy.

economic indicator One of several measurable variables used to study change in an economy. In addition to the variables mentioned above, economists study production indexes, unemployment trends, the amount of overtime worked and levels of **taxation**.

leading indicator Measurable variable (such as factory construction) that moves in advance of the indicated item (such as the level of employment).

indirect Associated with, but not immediately connected to; at one remove. *E.g.* indirect **taxation** consists of taxes levied on **expenditure** rather than **income**. *See also* **costs, indirect; expenses, indirect; taxation, indirect**.

industrial Concerning **industry**.

industrial espionage Attempt by one company or group to gain access to confidential information about another, generally in order to acquire commercial advantage and improve efficiency by imitation.

industrial sabotage Unfair competition between competitors. The term applies to any dubious tactics, not just physical sabotage.

industry Agglomeration of companies involved in the production of goods. Usually applied as a generic term for a group of companies manufacturing very similar products, *e.g.* "the car industry".

constructive industry Companies and people involved in secondary production, *e.g.* manufacturing. *See* **production, secondary**.

extractive industry Companies and people involved in primary production, *e.g.* fishing, farming and mining. *See* **production, primary**.

infant industry Newly-established national industry in the early stages of growth.

manufacturing industry The aggregate of companies that produce goods rather than providing services.

nationalized industry Industry that is owned by the state and controlled by the government, which was previously in private ownership. *See also* **nationalization; privatization**.

173

service industry Businesses engaged in the service, or tertiary sector, such as a shop or hairdressing business.

smoke-stack industry One of the 'traditional' manufacturing industries, such as an ironworks, mill, or engineering works. So-called because the smoke-stack was a typical feature of the early industrial skyline.

sunrise industry Industry, such as those surrounding computer technology and biotechnology, that is rapidly becoming more important. *See also* **industry, sunset.**

sunset industry US Industry that, because of the march of technological progress, is becoming less important. *E.g.* the iron and steel industries. *See also* **industry, sunrise.**

inertia State of inactivity, or resistance to movement. *See* **selling, inertia**.

inflation Persistent general increase in the level of prices. Strictly defined, inflation includes neither one-off increases in price (occasioned by *e.g.* a sudden scarcity of some product) nor any other increases caused by real factors. Its causes include an excess of demand over supply and increases in the money supply, perhaps brought about by increased government expenditure, which cause a decline in the real value of money.

cost-push inflation Theory that inflation is caused by increases in the cost of the manufacturing process, thus pushing overall prices to the consumer up.

demand-pull inflation Theory that inflation is caused by excess of demand over supply, thus pulling prices up.

double-figure inflation Inflation that has reached the rate of over 10 per cent.

inflation accounting Alternative term for current cost or current purchasing power accounting. *See* **accounting, current cost**.

inflation-adjusted Wages modified to maintain real income by increasing pay in line with inflation. The term may also be applied to the economist's technique of discounting price changes to obtain a truer picture of quantitative changes in output.

monetary inflation Inflation that is caused by an increase in the **money supply**.

repressed inflation Alternative term for suppressed inflation. *See* **inflation, suppressed**.

suppressed inflation Inflationary trend that has been slowed down or completely halted, usually by extensive government intervention in the economy. Also known as repressed inflation.

See also **tax, inflation**.

infopreneur Person who makes a living by collecting, assessing and selling information to interested parties.

information Items of knowledge or news.

information float US The time it takes to relay information from one person or organization to another. *E.g.* the information float using the postal service is at least one day, whereas the float using computer link-up could be a matter of seconds.

information services Economic sector in which information is traded and sold. *E.g.* most financial services are information services, as are the City pages of newspapers.

information technology (IT) Area of micro-electronics that combines computing and telecommunications technologies in the organization, storing, retrieval and transfer of information.

infrastructure Public utilities of a nation. Also known as social overhead capital, the infrastructure includes roads, railways, airports, communications systems (*e.g.* telephones), housing, water and sewage systems and other public amenities. The existence of an infrastructure is a necessary precondition of most economic development, and provision of an adequate infrastructure is vital if new industry is to be attracted to an area.

inheritance Possessions or titles passed to one or more persons on the death of another. *See also* **tax, inheritance**.

initial First, or something that ocurrs at the beginning of something.

initial public offering (IPO) First share offer made by a firm going public.

initial public offering window (IPO window) Period of time between the announcement of an IPO and the start of dealing in the shares offered on a stock market. Grey market trading takes place in the IPO window. *See* **market, grey**.

See also **allowance, initial; units, initial**.

injunction Restraining order issued by a court. An injunction instructs a named person to perform a certain duty or forbids him or her to commit a specific act. Failure to comply with an injunction is considered contempt of court.

Mareva injunction Injunction that prevents the transfer of funds overseas until a case concerning them has been heard in the UK courts.

innoventure Venture capital scheme based on an innovative product or service. Such schemes are particularly risky. *See* **capital, venture**.

in play Quoted company for which a **takeover** bid is expected to be launched in the very near future. *See* **company, quoted**.

insider Person with special knowledge derived from holding a privileged position within a group or company. *See also* **SUPSI**.

insider dealing Also known as insider trading, illegal transactions made on the basis of privileged information. Most insider dealing concerns trading in stocks and shares whose value is likely to be affected by the release of news of which only a few people are aware.

insider trading Alternative term for **insider dealing**.

insolvency State in which total liabilities, excluding equity capital exceed total **asset**s; therefore, the inability to pay **debt**s when called upon to do so. If insolvency is chronic, **bankruptcy** or **liquidation** generally follow. *See* **capital, equity**.

instalment Part payment of a **debt**. Instalment payments fall due at fixed and specified intervals and when totalled equal the original debt, usually with the addition of **interest** payments. *See also* **hire purchase**.

instant Often abbreviated to inst., little-used term meaning 'of this month'. E.g. a letter written in October mentioning the '13th inst.' refers to October 13. *See also* **ultimo**.

institution Organization, particularly one concerned with the promotion of a specific subject or some public object (*e.g.* the Royal United Services Institution). The term 'The Institution' is used to denote the collective of institutional investors.

institutional investor Corporate rather than individual investor; a company which invests funds on behalf of clients, generally intending to reap profit only in the long run. Institutional investors include **insurance** companies, **pension** funds, unit trusts and **banks**. At present institutional investors hold from 50%-70% of all negotiable securities. *See* **trust, unit; security, negotiable**.

instrument Broadly, any legally binding document.

investment instrument Any medium of investment, including **stocks**, **shares** and **securities** of all kinds, unit trusts and funds, grouped investment media and so on. *See* **trust, unit**.

negotiable instrument Document that may be freely exchanged, usually by **endorsement**, and which entitles the **bearer** to a sum of money. Negotiable instruments include, **cheques**, **bills of exchange**, certificates of deposit and promissory notes. *See* **deposit, certificate of; note, promissory**.

insurance Contract under which the insurer agrees to provide **compensation** to the insured in the event of a specified occurrence, *e.g.* loss of or damage to property. In return, the insured pays the insurer a much smaller sum – known as a **premium** – at fixed intervals. The premium varies according to the insurer's estimate of the probability that the event insured against will actually take place; thus it costs much more to insure an astronaut against injury than it does an astronomer. *See also* **assurance**.

accident insurance Broad category of insurance against all manner of mishaps, accidents, and liabilities, including public and professional **liability** and some deliberate acts such as burglary or theft by employees.

comprehensive insurance Form of motor insurance that provides more comprehensive cover than third party insurance. Comprehensive insurance normally includes protection for the driver, the vehicle and its contents, and third parties.

double insurance Insurance cover against the same risk, with two different insurers. In practice, however, it is impossible to receive more than the value of the cover, and in many cases one insurer would claim a contribution to the claim from the other.

endowment insurance Form of insurance in which payment is made either on death or after a set number of years. Pure endowment insurance policies pay benefits only if the insured survives the specified period.

fire insurance Insurance against losses due to fire. In general, fire insurance covers only cases in which actual ignition took place, and in which the insured was not culpable. Most policies also provide limited cover in the event of damage caused by lightning or explosion.

fraternal insurance US Insurance cover provided by mutual assistance or Friendly Societies. Fraternal insurance is a very old-established form of pension or unemployment insurance, and was initially developed in the seventeeth century. *See* **society, friendly**.

hull insurance Insurance of a vessel and its machinery. A policy is generally taken out during construction which covers the ship for the whole of its useful life. Most hull insurance provides cover against accidents caused by the negligence of crew or stevedores.

insurance claim Claim made by a person who is insured, upon an insurance company for payment under the conditions of a policy.

insurance cover Sum of money guaranteed to the insured in the event of the circumstances insured against actually occurring.

key man insurance Insurance to cover the health of an essential employee (the key man) in a company. This form of insurance covers the cost of replacing such personnel at short notice with equally qualified temporary staff.

loss of profit insurance Insurance policy that covers the insured against loss of trade and profits resulting from some disaster such as fire. In the latter instance the policy would typically pay a business the equivalent of the expected net profits lost while repair work and restocking were carried out, plus salaries, rates and rent due in that period.

marine insurance Insurance of ships and their cargoes against partial or total loss. *See* **loss, partial; loss total**.

medical insurance In the UK, insurance that covers the cost of medical treatment in private rather than NHS hospitals and clinics. Medical insurance policies normally offer to pay the cost of specialist treatment and home nursing, but no cover is provided for emergency treatment, which is still provided by public hospitals.

motor insurance Specialized form of accident insurance. Insurance of motor vehicles has been compulsory in Britain since 1930. Owners must be covered against any death, injury or damage to property they may cause to their passengers, other drivers, passers-by and so on. *See* **insurance, accident; insurance, comprehensive; insurance, third party**.

National Insurance (Fund) UK Government fund into which employees and their companies pay contributions. The fund is administered by the Department of Health and Social Security and covers the National Health Service and payments of state **pension**s and social security payments etc.

permanent health insurance (PHI) Insurance against the possibility of long-term illness or disability.

pluvial insurance Alternative term for weather insurance. *See* **insurance, weather**.

term insurance Life assurance provided for a fixed term only. Term assurance is one of the oldest forms of insurance and the cheapest form of life assurance. Term insurance policies are valid only if the assured dies within a set period; it is therefore commonly used to insure against death on a particular voyage. *See* **assurance, life**.

third party insurance Insurance policy that covers injury or damage suffered by a third party (one other than the insurer and the insured). In the UK all motor vehicle owners must be protected by third party insurance; this provides injured third parties with a means of redress in the event that the driver at fault is too poorly off to pay compensation himself.

weather insurance Also known as pluvial insurance, insurance against losses caused by inclement weather, usually rain, available to farmers and the organizers of outdoor events.

whole-life insurance Life assurance policy which pays out only upon the death of the insured. He or she pays **premium**s until death or (sometimes) retirement. *See* **assurance, life**.

See also **broker, insurance**.

integration Amalgamation of two or more companies to improve efficiency. Also, an industry is said to be integrated if products from different companies are compatible.

backward integration Amalgamation of a company that operates at one stage of production with another that is located farther back in the chain. *E.g.* a manufacturing company amalgamates with a company that provides raw materials.

forward integration Taking on by a company of activities at a subsequent stage of production or distribution (which are carried out by another company). *E.g.* many oil production companies undertook forward integration when they invested in refineries, tankers and petrol stations.

horizontal integration Amalgamation of companies in same stage of production, and which are therefore likely to possess similar skills.

vertical integration Amalgamation of companies involved in different stages of production in the same industry, for example to produce one company capable of extracting raw materials, using them to produce goods and then distributing and selling the manufactured product.

intellectual property Expression of the theory that ideas as well as tangible inventions and innovations are unique to one person or group and should be patentable. Intellectual property currently has no clear standing in UK law, other than in copyright.

intensive Most commonly used to indicate something that is extremely important to something else.

capital-intensive Industry in which **capital** is the most important and costly factor of production. Thus, an industry in which the major cost is the purchase and maintenance of machinery is capital-intensive.

labour-intensive Industry in which labour is the most important and costly factor of production. Thus an industry in which the major cost is the payment of salaries, incentives and bonuses is labour-intensive.

intent Planned action or intention.

letter of intent Letter outlining some intended action sent to establish intent in the eyes of the law.

interbank Term with two possible meanings.

First, it is an association of some 3,000 US banks collectively responsible for the issuing and administration of the Mastercharge credit card.

Second, it is also used to describe a **market** in which financial institutions lend each other (frequently large) sums of money for short periods. The **interest** rate offered is known as the London inter-bank offered rate (LIBOR). Interbank loans developed as a way of averting short-term liquidity crises.

interest Term with three possible meanings.

First, it is a charge made by a lender to a borrower in exchange for the service of lending funds.

"The bank made me a loan on 10% interest."

Second, it is a payment made by a bank or building society to customers on some forms of savings account.

"My building society pays 7% interest."

Third, it is money that is invested in a company, usually in return for **equity** or **shares**, thus making the investor 'interested' in the performance of the company. In this sense, an interest may be in anything that yields a return.

"He has an interest in several small companies."

accrued interest Interest payment that is due, but that has not yet been received.

back interest Alternative term for accrued interest. *See* **interest, accrued**.

beneficial interest Possession or involvement that gives a person the right to take some form of **benefit** (*e.g.* profit or use) from a property.

compound interest Rate of interest calculated by adding interest previously paid to the capital sum. Interest is subsequently paid on the capital sum plus previous interest payment. *See also* **interest, simple**.

insurable interest Some possession or involvement ('interest') whose loss or damage would cause measurable financial disadvantage to the owner equal to the insurance cover provided.

interest cover Ratio of earnings to the fixed-interest payments necessary to service loan **capital**.

interest rate Expression of the amount of interest charged on a loan in a specified time period. Interest rates are usually expressed as a percentage per annum.

majority interest Shareholding that gives the holder control of a company, *i.e.* one of over 50%. *See also* **interest, minority**.

minority interest Shareholding that does not give the holder control of a company, *i.e.* a holding of less than 50%. *See also* **interest, majority**.

natural rate of interest Rate of interest at which the demand for and supply of loans is equal.

short interest Interest rate charged on loans over a period of three months or less.

simple interest Rate of interest calculated by keeping interest that has already been paid separate from the capital sum. Thus, when calculating the next interest payment, the capital sum, but not the interest already paid, enters the calculation. *See also* **interest, compound**.

vested interest Reason (*e.g.* an investment or possible benefit) that a person may have for maintaining a certain state of affairs.

See also **futures, interest rate**.

interim In the meantime. Usually refers to the halfway point in a financial year. *See also* **dividend, interim; receiver, interim; report, interim**.

intermediary Person who acts between and deals with two parties who themselves make no direct contact with each other.

internal Something that is inside something else.

internal check System of **accounting** that ensures that each person's work and financial dealings are checked by an independent third party within the firm. Together with the internal audit, internal checks act to promote efficiency and prevent fraud. *See* **audit, internal**.

internal control Combination of self-regulatory measures by which a company ensures that each employee is accountable, safeguards its **assets** and institutes an accurate system of **accounting**, therefore enhancing its own efficiency.

internal rate of return Term with two meanings.

First, it is a hypothetical **interest rate**, equivalent to the marginal efficiency of **capital**, which is used to assess the investor's **yield** and therefore determine the viability of an investment. If the internal rate of interest is higher than the current rate of interest at which the investor could borrow, the investment would be worthwhile.

Second, it is the discount rate which, applied to the expected pattern of cash expenditure and income of a capital project, would give a net present value of zero. It may be compared with the return on alternative investments, or on some target rate of return.

See also **audit, internal**.

intestacy Situation in which a person dies without making a will, leaving the estate without a designated heir. If a person dies intestate, the Crown divides the estate between surviving relatives, making provision first for the spouse, and then for any children. If neither spouse nor children are living, other relatives are entitled to share in the estate. If no relatives can be traced, the estate goes to the crown.

in the window Anything obviously for sale. For example, a company may put an unquoted subsidiary in the window by discreetly inviting potential purchasers to make themselves known. The term is also a virtual synonym for in play.

intracapital *US* **Capital** placed at the disposal of an **intrapreneur**.

intrapreneur *US* Member of the staff of a company who is given relative autonomy in order that he or she may make use of entrepreneurial skills to the advantage of the company. *See also* **entrepreneur**.

introduction Means of offering a new share issue to the public, through the medium of a stock exchange but without the publication of a **prospectus** and the provision of an application form. Introductions are possible only if there is a large number of potential shareholders and no large **bargains** have been struck to market the **stock**.

inventory Term with two meanings.

First, it is a list of the stocks of raw materials, goods in production or finished goods owned and stored by a company, giving details of their **cost**, **value** and **price**.

Second, it is an itemized account of the contents of a rented property, against which the contents are checked when the tenant leaves.

inventory control Stock control. Most efficient businesses are managed, using inventories, in such a way that minimum levels of **stock-in-trade** sufficient to meet any likely demand are always maintained.

perpetual inventory Running record of all materials, parts or items of stock. Most frequently used in retailing, where stock turnover is relatively fast.

investment Term defined in two different ways by two schools of thought.

First, it is expenditure on real or financial assets rather than the funding of consumption. In this sense, expenditure consists of the purchase of any asset which is expected to increase in value.
"We have invested our money in short-term treasury bonds."

Second, to an economist, it covers spending that results in economic growth. *E.g.* money ploughed into the production of machinery or the building of plant which will produce goods and services for sale. Investment extends to funds applied to the improvement of the **infrastructure**, and the term may also be applied to expenditure on human resources.
"In an effort to improve the nation's economy, the government is investing in a huge road-building programme as well as making an enormous investment in the re-education of its workforce.

blue-chip investment Investment in the **stock** of one of the blue-chip companies. Hence, a safe but conservative investment. *See* **blue-chip**.

foreign investment Acquisition of another country's **assets** through any form of investment. It serves to stimulate economic growth in the investing nation and helps to maintain a favourable **balance of payments**.

investment adviser Person who advises individuals or institutions on financial matters related to investment in its widest sense. The function is performed by everyone from turf accountants to chartered accountants.

inward investment Alternative term for foreign investment. *See* **investment, foreign**.

long-term investment Investment for lengthy periods (strictly, 15 years or more). Such investment is risky, because it is impossible to predict interim fluctuations in the economy which may make other ways of generating capital more attractive.

safe investment Investment certain to yield the expected **return**.

short-term investment Investment for short periods. In the City, it refers to investment for a period of days; elsewhere, the period may be up to three months. Short-term investments are usually made in return for interest rates slightly lower than those available on long-term investments. *See* **investment, long-term**.

trade investment Investment in capital goods related to existing business, or in a new business in an established sector.

unquoted investments Alternative term for unquoted securities. *See* **securities, unquoted**.

See also **allowance, investment; banking, investment; grant, investment; trust, investment**.

invisible Something that is non-physical. *See* **asset, invisible; invisibles; trade, invisible; visibles**.

invisibles Income received by a nation from trading in services rather than goods. Invisibles include earnings from tourism, shipping and banking, together with profits on UK investments overseas. *See also* **visibles**.

invitation to treat Suggestion, made by one person to another, that he or she enter into negotiations which may result in a formal offer to trade. The difference between an invitation to treat and an **offer** proper is that an invitation does not bind the parties concerned to the conditions of the invitation, whereas the terms of an offer are legally binding.

invoice Document that summarizes a business transaction and often doubles as a demand for payment. An invoice lists and describes the goods (or services) ordered, details their price and records the dates and times of dispatch and delivery.

pro forma invoice Form of invoice submitted before goods are despatched and used to confirm an order and to advise of despatch.

See also **discounting, invoice**.

IOU Abbreviation of I owe you, a non-negotiable written note recording a **debt**.

IPO Abbreviation of **initial public offering**.

IRR Abbreviation of internal rate return.

irrevocable Something (*e.g.* an order) that is unalterable and cannot be revoked.

IRS Abbreviation of inland revenue service. *See* **revenue service, inland**.

issuance Procedure of issuing **securities**, carried out by a **company** or issuing house. *See* **house, issuing**.

issue Term with two meanings.
First, it is the quantity of a particular **stock** or **share** offered to the public.
Second, it is the total number of banknotes in print at a given time.

bonus issue Issue of **shares** made by a company wishing to reduce the average price of its shares. Shareholders receive a number of extra shares in proportion to the number already held. Also known as a capitalization issue.
"A & T Publications have announced a three-for-one bonus issue."

capitalization issue Alternative term for bonus issue. *See* **issue, bonus**.

debenture issue Issue of **debentures**, whether secured or unsecured, by a company wishing to raise loan capital. The debenture-holders become the company's principal **creditor**s and have the right to preferential repayment of their loans in the event that the firm encounters financial difficulties. *See* **capital, loan**.

hot issue Issue of shares expected to sell extremely rapidly.

issued price The published price of a stock or share.

new issue Stocks and shares that are about to be, or have recently been placed on the open market. New issues may consist of stock in a recently-established limited company or supplementary issues made by established companies. *See* **company, limited; market, open**.

rights issue Practice of offering existing shareholders the opportunity to buy more shares (*i.e.* subscribe more **capital**), in order to raise additional capital. Rights issues act as a protection for the shareholder, in that the total number of shares issued increases without decreasing the percentage holding of each shareholder.

scrip issue Alternative term for bonus issue. See **issue, bonus**.

share issue A limited company wishing to raise **capital** may issue a number of shares, each worth a fraction of the company's total value. The shares are placed on the market by **stockbroker**s acting on behalf of the firm in question and may, in most cases, be purchased by financial institutions, other companies and private individuals.

See also **bank, issuing; capital, issued; house, issuing**.

IT Abbreviation of **information technology**.

J

Jajo *US* Acronym for January, April, July, October, the months in which some stock options expire. *See* **option**.

jerry building Speculative construction of buildings (normally residential property at times of housing shortage) that leads to bad workmanship and use of poor quality materials.

job Regular work for which a person is paid either a salary or wages, or a particular project or piece of work.
"After two years unemployed he eventually found a job."
"The price for the job was £500."

job description Document setting out the duties and responsibilities entailed in a particular job. Sometimes, the job description forms part of a contract of employment.

job enrichment Making a job seem as attractive as possible.

job evaluation Evaluation of the skills and qualities necessary for a person to be able to perform a particular job, or of the ability of a person to do a job.

job-share Also known as a time-share, employment that is held by two people, each working part-time.

job specification Often shortened to job spec, a description of what a particular position or job entails.

See also **lot, job**.

jobber Also known as a stockjobber, a member of the London Stock Exchange who deals in securities with stockbrokers and other jobbers, but not with the public. Before the **Big Bang**, the London Stock Exchange was the only exchange in the world on which the activities of stockbrokers and jobbers were kept separate. This practice has now been discontinued and jobbers have been replaced by **market makers**.
In the USA, a jobber is any middleman between a wholesaler and a retailer *or* a person on a stock exchange who deals in securities that are

worthless (*e.g.* junk bonds). The US synonym for jobber in the UK sense is **dealer**.

See also **book, jobber's; turn, jobber's**.

jobbing backwards Looking back at past decisions, often – with hindsight – regretting them.

joint Something that is a combination of two or more things, *e.g.* companies or people.

joint and several Concept by which joint debtors (*e.g.* two or more partners in a company) are responsible for the debt, both jointly and as individuals. Joint and several liability gives the lender recourse to each of the partners in the debt in the event of default.

See also **account, joint; bank, joint stock; company, joint stock; tenancy, joint**.

Jonestown defence *US* Any form of defensive tactics against a hostile takeover bid that is so extreme as to appear suicidal.
See also **poison pill**.

journal In accounting, a book in which daily transactions are recorded before being transferred to the books of account.

house journal Periodical magazine that carries company news, distributed by larger companies to their employees.

sales journal In book-keeping, an account book in which the record of a sale is first made.

judgement Ruling made by a court in a particular case (also spelled judgment). *See* **debt, judgement**.

jumpy Description of a market in which dealers are nervous and so likely to jump at the slightest movement.

K

K 1,000, often in finance expressed in units of currency.
"She was earning 50K as a consultant."

kaffir Stock exchange nickname for shares in South African mining companies.

kangaroo Stock exchange nickname for shares in Australian companies, especially those dealing in tobacco, property and mining.

Kaufmanized *US* Markets in securities are said to be Kaufmanized when they react to information from the mouth of the American economist Henry Kaufman.

kerb On the London Metal Exchange, a period of time during which all metals are traded simultaneously. *See also* **trading, ring**.

kerb market Trading in securities that takes place outside an official exchange.

kerb trading Closing a deal on a financial futures market after hours. Known as such because originally traders would emerge from the exchange after official trading closed for the day and remain there to close any unfinished business.

late-kerb Trading in metals that goes on after hours, usually over the telephone.

key money Premium paid by a new tenant of a property to the previous leaseholder in return for the granting of the lease or licence.

Keynesianism School of economic thought, named after John Maynard Keynes (1883-1946), an economist greatly influential in the late 1930s. Keynesians believe that the best way to bring about economic change is by government intervention in the form of market controls and public investment. *See also* **monetarism**.

kick-up Chance offered to holders of bonds to convert them into shares at a profit.

"By offering an equity kick-up, the company was able to offer lower coupons on the issue."

kick upstairs To promote a senior executive to a position in which he or she has relatively little influence and can therefore do no (more) harm.

kite Another name for an **accommodation bill**.

kite flying Raising money by way of an **accommodation bill**.

kiting *US* Fraudulent issuing of a cheque that is not backed by funds in the account.

knee-jerk Reflexive movement in a market that is sudden and largely artificial.

knight Third party who appears at the scene of a **takeover** battle. *See also* **white knight; grey knight**.

knock-on (effect) Series of effects caused by a single action.
"The failure of that one machine had a knock-on effect all the way down the production line."

know-how Saleable knowledge of techniques or processes.
"A & G are the only company with the know-how to produce such state-of-the-art equipment."

know-how licence *US* Licence to use knowledge about a particular process or technique for commercial purposes.

L

labour People used in the production of goods or services.

direct labour Members of a company's workforce who are directly
involved in the production of goods or services. *E.g.* a welder is part of
the direct labour force, whereas an estimator is not.

laches Legal term for negligence in performing a duty, asserting a right
or claiming a privilege.

lacklustre Term with two similar meanings.
First, it is uninspiring corporate performance, normally indicated by a
poor stock market rating. *See* **ratio, price/earnings**.
Second, it is a relatively inactive day on the stock exchange.

See also **valium picnic**.

Lady Macbeth strategy During a hostile **takeover**, a strategy
undertaken by a party who seems at first to be acting as a **white knight**,
but subsequently joins the aggressor.

laesio enormis Latin for extraordinary injury. Doctrine (derived from
Roman law) which states that a contract price must be fair and
reasonable. An unreasonable or unfair price is grounds for terminating
the contract.

lame duck Weak individual or firm; one ripe for **takeover** or unable to
provide effective competition.

landmail *US* Practice of buying the shareholding of an actual or
potential corporate **raider** in return for land as opposed to cash. *See
also* **greenmail**.

last in first out (LIFO) Term with two meanings.
First, it is an accounting term for a system of stock-keeping, whereby
the latest items manufactured or bought are used or sold before old stock
is cleared. In a period of deflation this has the effect of maximizing

profit, because new goods or materials have cost less to manufacture or buy. *See also* **base stock method; first in first out**.

Second, it is the process whereby some companies are said to make employees redundant, on the basis of length of service. Thus, the last people to be employed are the first to be laid off. *See also* **laying off**.

LAUTRO UK **SRO**, governing the trading and operation of **unit trusts**. *See also* **Financial Services Act**.

lawyer Somebody licensed to practise law. The term may be applied to a solicitor, but is most usually (and loosely) used as a synonym for 'attorney' or 'barrister'.

laying-off Making an employee redundant, either temporarily or permanently, usually because there are insufficient orders for the whole workforce to be employed.

laundering Method of disguising the origin of funds by moving them rapidly from one account or country to another. It thus becomes a complicated business to trace their origins, movements and eventual destination.

LBO Abbreviation of leveraged buyout. *See* **buyout, leveraged**.

LCE Abbreviation of London Commodities Exchange. Now also known as London FOX (Futures and Options Exchange).

lead manager In a **syndicate**, the company that does the administration. For this service, the lead manager usually receives a higher **commission** than the other members of the syndicate.

lease Contract giving temporary possession of a property, often in areas where prices are appreciating so rapidly that it is not in the owner's best interests to sell. Buildings are the most common subjects of a lease, although it is also possible to lease land and other possessions, such as vehicles and machinery. Long-term leases are often mortgaged, bought and sold.

lease-back Arrangement by which a property is sold on condition that it is immediately leased back to the original owner. **Capital** tied up in property is therefore freed for other uses.

lease financing Form of off-balance-sheet financing whereby goods (*e.g.* machinery) are leased rather than purchased outright. Lease financing is therefore generally thought of as a type of disguised **borrowing**. It is generally frowned upon by accounting authorities.

leasehold Property held by **lease**. On leasehold land, the lessee pays ground rent to the **freeholder**. *See* **rent, ground**.

ledger Book in which trade transactions, credits and debts are recorded. The term is most accurately applied to the principal volume in a series of account books, which collates the details made in the **books of original entry**.

leg One of the divisions of a corporation or company.

lender of the last resort Central bank that is prepared to lend to the banking system as a whole, including to commercial banks. In the UK the lender of the last resort is the **Bank of England**. It must be prepared to advance money to discount houses which have insufficient funds to balance their books, preventing their bankruptcy. It therefore gives confidence to the markets and helps to prevent a damaging run on the banks. By acting as lender of the last resort, the Bank of England is able to influence the **money supply** and **interest rates**. *See* **bank, central; house, discount**.

lending Temporary grant of money, goods, people and so on, made on the understanding that the thing lent, or its equivalent, will be returned, often with an additional (**interest**) payment.

letter Written document of agreement, often listing the terms and conditions of a business relationship.

letters patent Document issued by the Patent Office attesting the holder's right to possession of a **patent**.

See also **administration, letters of; allotment, letter of; indemnity, letter of**.

leverage *US* Alternative term for **gearing**; the ratio of a company's debt to total **capital** or shareholder's funds. In a buoyant market, a high proportion of debt has a beneficial effect on share earnings, because it is usually possible for the company to earn more on its loan capital than it is paying in **interest**. In such circumstances, high gearing is beneficial to shareholders; conversely, a fall in demand or a rise in interest rates affects a highly-geared company adversely. A company's leverage or gearing often has a significant effect on its share price in an open market. *See also* **buyout, leveraged**.

liability A company's debt. Long-term (or deferred) liabilities are usually distinguished from current liabilities, as are secured debts from unsecured debts. *See* **debt, unsecured**.

deferred liability Liability that does not fall due until after a period of a year.

limited liability Restriction of the owners' loss in a liquidated company to the amount of **capital** each has invested. The loss of the individual shareholder in such an eventuality is therefore limited to the value of his or her holding. In the event of **liquidation** the company itself remains liable for its outstanding debts; creditors are generally paid by selling off or dividing up the bankrupt company's **assets**. *See also* **company, limited**.

long-term liability Debt that need not be repaid in the next three years. In **accounting**, the term is sometimes applied to loans that are not due to be repaid in the current accounting period.

LIBOR Acronym for London inter-bank offered rate. *See* **rate, London inter-bank offered**.

lien The right to the possession of property until such time that an outstanding **liability** has been repaid. A lien gives a **creditor** the right to retain or sell the property of a **debtor** in lieu of payment.

equitable lien Lien that arises from a dispute over **equity**.

general lien The right to take possession of **assets** at will after default.

lien on shares The right to take possession of **shares** if a borrower defaults on repayment.

particular lien The right to take possession of specified **assets** in the event of default. A particular lien cannot be transferred to other goods or assets.

LIFFE Acronym for London International Financial Futures Exchange.

LIFO Acronym for **last in first out**.

limited In a business context, something of restricted **liability**. *See also* **company, limited; liability, limited; partnership, limited**.

limit (order) On a stock or commodity exchange, an instruction given by a client to his or her **stockbroker**, which specifies the maximum price the broker is authorized to pay to buy a shareholding, or the minimum he is to demand before selling.

limit (up/down) The maximum and minimum limits within which the price of a financial and some commodity futures are permitted to fluctuate in one day's trading. *See* **fluctuation; futures, financial**.

liquid Something that is readily accessible, such as **assets** that can be immediately realized in **cash** form. **Money** is by definition fully liquid, and cash kept in a bank is the most obvious liquid asset. Treasury bills, money at call and Post Office savings are similarly liquid. *See also* **assets, liquid; ratio, liquid assets; damages, liquidated**.

liquidation The **winding-up** of a company. So-called because the company's **assets** are liquidated – converted into cash money – in order that outstanding **creditors** may be paid (in whole or in part).

compulsory liquidation Liquidation of a company that has become insolvent. In this case, the Official Receiver is initially in charge of the disposal of the company's assets. *See* **insolvency; receivership**.

long liquidation Long-term **self-liquidating** company.

self-liquidating Something that has a pre-determined life and liquidates itself at the end of that period. In the investment trust sector, for example, a closed-end fund with a stock exchange listing is self-liquidating. *See* **fund, closed-end**.

voluntary liquidation Liquidation of a company that has decided to cease trading, rather than one which has gone **bankrupt**.

liquidity The ease with which an **asset** can be converted into money. Cash deposits in current bank accounts may be quickly withdrawn and are said to be highly liquid; money in most deposit accounts is slightly less so because notice must be given before withdrawal.

listed company = **company, listed**

listing Flotation of a company on the stock exchange; the sum of the actions that permits **securities** to be traded on a stock market. So-called because the issued shares are then listed in the exchange records and its price fluctuations recorded and published. *See also* **agreement, listing; Official List**.

Livingstonization Popular term, recently coined, for the control of local companies by Labour-controlled local authorities. So-called after the last leader of the Greater London Council (GLC), Ken Livingstone. *See also* **nationalization; privatization**.

Lloyds of London Incorporated association of insurers who specialize in marine insurance. Formally established by Act of Parliament in 1871, the corporation developed from a seventeeth century group of **underwriters** who met at Edward Lloyd's coffee house in London.
  Lloyds supervises about 22,000 individual insurers ('names') grouped into some 400 **syndicates**, each of whom has unlimited **liability** and accepts a fraction of the **risk** of business brought to them by one of more than 200 registered **brokers**. Lloyd's involvement in marine insurance currently comprises less than half of the total business transacted by Lloyd's underwriters. *See* **insurance, marine**.

LME Abbreviation of London Metals Exchange.

load The difference between the price of a unit trust or insurance **premium** and its actual value. Load on unit trusts is generally charged only on purchase. It is levied to meet expenses and the cost of administration. *See* **trust, unit**.

part load Portion of the part of the share capital of open-ended investment companies not covered by underlying **assets**. *See* **capital, share**.

loan Sum of money borrowed by one person or organization from another, generally for a specified time and often at an agreed rate of **interest**.

loan back Alternative term for **lease-back**.

loan guarantee scheme (LGS) UK government scheme introduced in 1981 to promote the establishment and development of small businesses. The government agrees to underwrite 70% of approved loans made to such firms in exchange for a 2.5% annual **premium** on this portion, and on condition that the lending institution underwrites the balance of 30%.

margin loan Loan commonly made on limited **security**. *E.g.* a group of several lenders may advance money secured on property to 75% of its value. A margin loan would then be secured on the remaining 25%. This would carry higher risk and therefore attract a slightly higher rate of interest. Also known as a top-up loan.

personal loan Loan made (usually by a bank, but now increasingly by registered brokers) to a private individual. This form of loan is generally fairly modest and intended for some specific purpose, such as the purchase of a car.

soft loan Loan that carries an unusually low rate of **interest**, often advanced as a form of **foreign aid**.

term loan Fixed loan made for a specified number of years.

tied loan Loan made by one country to another on condition that the money concerned is spent in the lending nation. Tied loans are a common form of **foreign aid**, because they create employment and have no effect on the lending nation's **balance of payments**.

See also **capital, loan; stock, loan**.

local *US* Basic unit of an American labour union, equivalent to a British branch or chapel.

lock box Security chest or safe for personal use. The term also covers safe-deposit boxes provided by some banks.

lock-out Industrial action taken by an employer, who prevents the workforce from entering their office or factory until they accept the terms set out by the management.

lock-up On financial markets, an investment expected to yield profit only in the long term, and in which capital will therefore be 'locked up' for some time.

locus poenitentiae Latin for opportunity to repent. It is an option open to the parties to an illegal **contract**, who may save it by deciding not to carry out that part which is against the law.

lollipop Corporate incentive or reward.

long Position taken by a **bull** speculator, who acquires quantities of a **stock** or **commodity** in excess of the amount contracted for, in expectation that the price will rise and permit the surplus to be sold at a **profit**.

US Usage refers to a **security** which a person has bought and actually owns.
See also **liquidation, long**.

longs Fixed-interest securities with redemption dates more than 15 years in the future. *See* **security, fixed-interest**.

long-term Period exceeding 15 years, but more loosely applied to **stocks** issued for an indefinite period of time or in perpetuity. In the City, the phrase 'long-term' is loosely applied to any period over one year. *See also* **liability, long-term**.

loop Circular chain of **shareholdings**. *E.g.*: A owns 20% of the stock of B; B owns 20% of the stock of C; C owns 20% of the stock of D; and D owns 20% of the stock of A.

loophole Any circumstance that permits the evasion of a custom or rule, but especially a legal inexactitude that offers an escape from a **contract**.

loss Disadvantage, forfeiture of money or goods, or negative profit.

constructive total loss Ship not actually lost at sea but which is damaged beyond economic repair, or a cargo so damaged that it is no longer of use for its intended purpose.

loss leader Product or service offered for sale at a substantial loss in order to attract customers. The hope is that shoppers who come to buy the loss leader will also purchase other goods in the same store.

partial loss In marine **insurance**, loss caused by damage to a ship or its cargo.

particular average loss In marine insurance, loss incurred by damage to a ship or its cargo, resulting in the payment of hull or cargo insurance. Average is a marine term for partial loss. *See* **loss, partial**.

stop-loss selling Sale of shares or futures contracts in a declining market, usually at a predetermined price, in order to prevent further loss.

tax loss Loss sustained by a person or business which may, once incurred, be offset against a demand for income tax, capital gains tax or corporation tax. Tax losses are frequently incurred deliberately in an attempt to reduce the real cost of tax-paying. *See* **tax, capital gains; tax, corporation; tax, income**.

total loss In marine **insurance**, the loss at sea or complete destruction of a ship and/or its cargo.

trading loss Loss incurred while taking a principal (trading) position in a **market**. The loss must be recorded on the profit and loss account of a company. A trading loss is thus often disguised, where possible, by such tactics as 'redefining' it as a fixed asset investment or including it as an extraordinary or **below-the-line** item in the accounts. *See* **accounts, profit and loss**.

See also **insurance, loss of profit**.

lot Method of deciding by chance which **stocks** will be redeemed in a given year.

job lot Collection of **stocks** or **goods** sold together, perhaps to somebody who wants only a portion of them.

odd lot Collection of **stocks** or **shares** so small or varied that they inconvenience the **broker** who agrees to deal them, and which he or she will therefore buy only at a low price.

round lot Large or heterogeneous collection of **stocks** or **shares** which a **broker** agrees to deal in the usual way. *See also* **lot, odd**.

Luddite Person belonging to a group of disaffected early nineteenth century workers who smashed industrial machinery in the belief that mechanization would lead to unemployment. Hence, a contemptuous term now applied to anyone who stubbornly opposes necessary change.

lump sum Sum of money paid to someone all at once, as opposed to being paid as a series of separate sums. *See also* **lump system**.

lump system System of payment under which workers receive a **lump**

sum for each day's work or for the fulfilment of a daily quota. The lump system is common in the building industry, but frowned upon because it can enable employees to avoid **taxation**.

Lutine bell Bell that hangs in the underwriting room at **Lloyds of London**, rung before the announcement of important news – for example that concerning the fate of a missing ship.

M

M0 = money supply

M1 = money supply

M2 = money supply

M3 = money supply

£M3 = money supply

macroeconomics Study of broad or **aggregate** economics. Macroeconomics concerns itself with the relationship between such major aggregates as prices, incomes, total consumption and total production, together with interest and exchange rates, savings and investment. *See also* **microeconomics**.

mail order System for buying and selling by post; the customer purchases goods direct from the manufacturer or distributor without the intervention of a **middleman** or retailer.

maintenance Broadly, the financial provision made by a husband for his ex-wife and any children after a divorce.
   In law, also used to describe a contribution towards the cost of a legal action made by a person who has no legal or moral interest in the case.

major *US* American equivalent of a **blue chip** company; a very large firm within its market sector.

making a price Action of a stockbroker or market-maker when he or she quotes a bid or offer price for a stock or share. *See* **price, bid; price, offer**.

making up day Alternative term for settlement day. *See* **day, settlement**.

mala fide Latin for in bad faith; fraudulent. *See also* **bona fide**.

management Control and supervision of a firm, asset or operation; the group of people who control and administer a firm, as distinct from the workforce. The effectiveness of a firm's management is often of vital importance to its **performance**, and management is therefore sometimes taken as a factor of production. *See* **production, factor of**.

asset management Broadly, the efficient control and exploitation of a firm's assets, most commonly used to describe the management of any **fund** by a fund manager.

line management Management system in which a chain of command is formed from top executives, down the line to junior staff. Line management is concerned only in the major activities of the company. *See also* **management, staff**.

passive management Form of mutual fund management, increasingly popular in the USA, in which a fund's investments are selected arithmetically to match the exact performance of a stock index. *See* **fund, managed**.

staff management Management of the support services that enable a company to fulfil its major function. Staff management is involved in the management of such activities as accounting, cleaning, maintenance, etc. *See also* **management, staff**.

total quality management (TQM) Management concept in which employees at every level are involved in quality and product control.

See also **accountant, management; buyout, management; company, management; director, managing**.

M & A Abbreviation of **mergers and acquisitions**.

mandate Written authority empowering one person to act on behalf of another. Mandates are issued when the mandator dies, is declared bankrupt, or certified insane. They are generally used to give access to the mandator's bank accounts.

MAP Abbreviation of **manufacturing automation protocol**.

margin Term with three meanings.

First, it is the proportion of the total cost of a product or service that represents the producer's profits.

Second, when trading financial or commodities futures, it is the proportion of the value of the contract that is put up.

Third, it is the proportion of the total price of a **share** paid by the purchaser to his **stockbroker** when the broker buys **securities** on **credit**. The practice is more common in the USA than in the UK, where most dealing is done on account.

gross margin Difference between the selling price of an article and the direct cost of the materials and components used in its manufacture.

initial margin **Deposit** that must be paid on selling or buying a **contract** on a **futures** market. *See also* **equity**.

net margin Difference between the selling price of an article and all the costs incurred in making and selling it.

operating margin Operating profit expressed as a proportion of price or operating costs.

profit margin Gross **profit**, usually expressed as a percentage of net **sales**, or as simple **net** profit. Company policy generally specifies some profit margin below which it is hardly worthwhile producing goods.

variation margin When dealing in contracts on a **futures** market, the gain or loss at the end of a trading day that is recorded on a person's account. If the variation margin falls below the initial margin required, the trader is required to deposit more funds. *See* **margin, initial**.

See also **call, margin; cover; dealing, margin; loan, margin**.

marginal In economics, the difference between two figures. *E.g.* a marginal unit is the last unit produced, or the first unit supplied, and is defined as the smallest additional amount that it is economically viable to produce or to buy.

marginal analysis Method used in **microeconomics** to study the effect of successive small changes in demand, output, prices and costs.

See also **cost, marginal; relief, marginal**.

market Term with three meanings.

First, it is a place where goods and services are bought and sold.

Second, it is the actual or potential demand for these goods and services.

Third, it is an abstract expression denoting any area or condition in which buyers and sellers are in contact and able to do business together.

bear market Condition in which share prices are falling. **Bear**s are speculators who sell shares in anticipation of falling prices.

black market Wholly illegal market; one that is illicit and uncontrolled. Black markets deal in scarce or stolen goods, and frequently come into existence in wartime, because the goods concerned are rationed, or because the market price is exceptionally high − in which case counterfeit or imitation goods often appear. Trading is often in kind, one valued commodity being exchanged for another.

bull market Condition in which share prices are rising. **Bull**s are speculators who buy shares in anticipation of rising prices.

capital market Market made up of the various sources of **capital** (long-term) for investment in new and already existing companies.

captive market Market in which there is a monopoly of production, allowing the consumer no option but to buy that company's product.

discount market That part of the London money markets that involves the buying and selling of short-term **debt** between the commercial banks, the discount houses and the Bank of England, which acts as the **lender of the last resort**. *See* **house, discount**.

domestic market Market for goods and services that exists within a company, as opposed to the international market that is reached by **export**.

down market Something that is poor-quality and often low-priced.

dull market Market on which little activity is taking place. *See also* **valium picnic**.

easy market Market in which there are few buyers. Therefore prices are low.

forward market Market in (contracts or options for) goods that are to be delivered at a future date. *See also* **buy forward; futures; market, spot.**

205

free market Term with two meanings.

First, it is a market that operates essentially by the laws of **supply and demand**.

Second, on the stock market, it is a situation in which a particular **security** is available freely and in reasonably large quantities.

grey market Any semi-legal market; one that keeps within the letter but not the spirit of the law. The term is most usually applied to the market dealing in any stock or share whose issue has been announced but which has not yet taken place. Traders therefore gamble on the eventual selling price of the issue when it comes onto the market.

imperfect market Any market that does not enjoy free competition, good communications, regular demand and uniform goods.

inactive market Alternative term for dull market. *See* **market, dull**.

market forces Forces of **supply** and **demand**, which together determine the prices of goods and services on the open market.

market if touched (MIT) Instruction to a broker to sell shares as soon as the price reaches a designated level.

market leader Company that has the largest share of a particular market. Individual products that have the largest share of a market are known as **brand leaders.**

market maker Market principal who encourages dealing by varying the prices of his stock to promote its sale or purchase. Used especially with reference to the stock market.

market order Order to buy or sell securities on the stock market or a financial futures exchange at the best obtainable market price.

market research Survey that is conducted to assess consumer demand. Companies carry out market research in order to maximize the efficiency of their output and also to determine potential markets which may be exploited in future. In addition, market research often suggests ways in which goods and services may be more attractively presented to the public.

market tending Control of a market's stock index, by intervention buying and selling.

market timer US Investment manager who operates by moving his or her investment from one instrument to another depending on market prices.

new issues market Alternative term for primary market. *See* **market, primary**.

non-contract market Alternative term for spot market. *See* **market, spot**.

open market Market in which goods are available to be bought and sold by anyone who cares to. Prices on an open market are determined by the laws of **supply** and **demand**.

outcry market On commodity markets, trading is recorded from the outcries of traders on the floor, although deals are sealed by private contract. Markets on which trading is carried on in this noisy manner are known as outcry markets and the style of trading is known as open outcry.

over-the-counter market (OTC) Market on which securities not listed on any registered stock exchange may be bought and sold. In practice, the OTC market is operated by a limited number of market-makers, often on the basis of matched bargains. *See also* **market, unlisted securities**.

primary market Market in new securities issues. Also known as the new-issues market. *See also* **market, secondary; market, tertiary**.

secondary market Market in securities that have been listed for some time, rather than new issues. Secondary market trading occurs on the stock exchange. *See also* **market, primary; market tertiary**.

seller's market Market that is more favourable to sellers than to buyers. Such a market often arises when demand is greater than supply.

spot market Market in which the goods sold are available for immediate delivery. Also known as the non-contract market. *See also* **futures**.

tertiary market Market in listed securities traded by non-exchange brokers on the over-the-counter market. *See also* **primary market**.

third market Stock Exchange market introduced in January 1987, with less stringent entry requirements than the USM. Also known as the third tier, and not to be confused with the OTC.

unlisted securities market (USM) Market for shares in companies that do not fulfil the entry requirements for a full quotation on the Stock

Exchange, or that do not wish to be quoted, but which do fulfil certain less stringent requirements.
See also **capitalization, market; risk, market; value, market**.

marketing Distribution, promotion and presentation of a product, or research carried out to determine the nature and extent of a market.

marketing research Alternative term for **market research**.

marking up Term with two meanings.
First, the adjustment of price (say, by a retailer) to allow for a profit **margin**. The retailer's mark up is equal to **gross profit**.
Second, the upward revision of prices of goods, including shares.

mark to market On a financial **futures** exchange, the adjustment of a customer's account to allow for profits or losses on his or her open contracts during the previous day's trading. *See* **contract, open**.

marzipan layer Broadly, middle management; that group of managers who are perceived, somewhat cynically, as unnecessary and indeed potentially harmful to a company's interests. The supposition is that the marzipan layer tends to develop into an overfed bureaucracy. Alternatively known as the marzipan men or marzipan set.

maturity Date on which the repayment of an instrument or security's **principal** is due.

maximum Greatest possible. *See also* **fluctuation, maximum; slippage, maximum**.

May Day 1 May 1975, the day on which the minimum commission system was abolished; the New York Stock Exchange's equivalent of the **Big Bang**.

meltdown Sizeable financial crisis; a severe crash. The term is taken from the nuclear power industry, where a 'meltdown' in a reactor would trigger a major disaster.

mergers and acquisitions (M&A) Field of arranging **merger**s between companies or **takeover**s of companies, or the department within a large company that is formed to carry out this function.

memorandum Broadly, a reminder, very often a document that records the terms of an agreement or sets out an argument. Often abbreviated to memo.

memorandum of association Public charter of a company, drawn up during its formation and listing its title, business, registered address, and authorized capital. The memorandum must also contain a statement of liability and details of proposed share issues. It must be signed by the founder members.

memorandum of satisfaction Document issued to certify that a **mortgage** has been repaid in full.

merchantable quality That quality possessed by goods deemed fit for sale; also termed merchandizable quality.

merger Fusion of two or more companies, as distinct from the **takeover** of one company by another. Mergers may be undertaken for various reasons, notably to improve the efficiency of two complementary firms by rationalizing output and taking advantage of economies of scale, and to fight off unwelcome takeover bids from other large companies. The firms involved form one new company and their respective shareholders exchange their holding for shares in the new concern at an agreed rate.

megamerger Merger of two major companies to form one gigantic corporation, *e.g.* the 1986 merger between British Petroleum and Standard Oil of Ohio.

mergermania Fever that is believed to grip sectors of the business world from time to time. Mergermania occurs after a well-publicized merger or series of mergers; other firms become concerned that they will be adversely affected by the creation of larger and more powerful rivals and seek to merge themselves with other concerns as a protective measure.

minimerger Merger between two small companies.

microeconomics Study of the individual components of an economy in isolation. Microeconomics examines the choices open to specific people, companies and industries and has been developed to enable the study of subjects such as utility, price mechanisms, **competition** and **margins**. *See also* **macroeconomics**.

middleman Intermediary, usually a wholesaler, retailer, or broker who acts as an agent between a buyer and a seller. Middlemen tend to push up prices by adding their own profit margin to the difference between buying and selling prices, and it may therefore be in the interests of the buyer and the seller to 'cut out the middleman' (as in **mail order).**

middle price Alternative term for middle market price. *See* **price, middle market**.

minimerger = merger

minimum Least possible. *See also* **fluctuation, minimum; lending rate, minimum; offer period, minimum**.

minor In British law, a person under the age of 18; one who cannot legally conduct certain transactions or purchase certain goods.

minority Term with two meanings.
 First, it is the period during which a person is a **minor**.
 Second, it is the smaller portion of something, *i.e.* less than half of the whole.
 See also **interest, minority; shareholder, minority**.

mint Institution licensed to make coins or tokens. In the UK, the Royal Mint at Llantrisant is charged with the manufacture of British legal tender, but there are several private mints that produce tokens, for example for gaming machines, coins aimed at collectors, and coinage for other countries.
 In the United States coins are manufactured by the Bureau of the Mint.

MIP Abbreviation of **maximum investment plan**.

MIRAS Acronym for **mortgage interest relief at source**.

misfeance summons Application requesting that a court investigate the actions and conduct of a director of a company in **liquidation**. The summons may be issued by any interested party, such as the official receiver, a creditor or a shareholder, and it requests the court to force the director concerned to compensate them for money misapplied or misappropriated.

misrepresentation Any false statement that encourages a person or company to enter into a **contract**. Misrepresentation may be either fraudulent, *i.e.* a deliberate intent to deceive, or innocent, *i.e.* the result of a genuine mistake. Under British law the injured party may have the contract dissolved and claim suitable damages. *See also* **mistake**.

mistake In legal parlance, any error, short of **misrepresentation**, that induces a person or company to enter into a **contract**. Mistakes may be mutual, *i.e.* common to both parties, or unilateral. Mutual mistakes include the innocent purchase or exchange of goods which are not in fact for sale; unilateral mistakes include more deliberate deceptions. Both mutual and unilateral mistakes may invalidate a contract, but they do not necessarily do so.

MIT Abbreviation of **market if touched**.

mitigation Reduction in the severity of something.

mitigation of damage Minimization of a **loss**. Mitigation of damage is the responsibility of the sufferer, and must be attempted if he or she is to win full **compensation** in court. Mitigation of damage, therefore, acts as a check against insurance fraud.

MLR Abbreviation of minimum lending rate. *See* **rate, minimum lending**.

model code Stock Exchange code of conduct that sets out guidelines for share dealings by company directors. It specifies, broadly, that directors should not engage in questionable dealings with company stock, and in particular forbids share dealings in the two months preceding a company announcement of profit, loss, dividend, a proposed merger, takeover, sale of assets and so on.

modern portfolio theory Theory of stock valuation developed in the early 1980s. Modern portfolio theory values stocks by estimating their future earnings discounted back to the present.

momentum In finance, the rate at which a **price** increases or decreases.

monetarism Group of economic theories which state in general that the level of prices and wages in an economy is ultimately determined by the amount of money in circulation (the **money supply**); that variations in the amount of money (monetary growth) have no long-term effect on the level of real activity (*e.g.* output and hence unemployment); and that monetary growth can be controlled by government in order to control price inflation.

money Medium of exchange; any generally accepted token that may be exchanged for goods or services.

active money Money in circulation.

broad money Alternative term for M3. *See* **money supply**.

cheap money Alternative term for easy money. *See* **money, easy**.

danger money Extra money that is paid as **wages** to employees carrying out dangerous work. In the USA also informally known as combat pay.

dear money Money is said to be dear when it is difficult to find investment or loans and the interest rate is thus high.

earnest money US *Either* part payment (**deposit**) made on goods or services, showing that the buyer is serious about buying; *or* the **margin** on a futures market.

easy money Money borrowed at a low rate of **interest**, usually consisting of funds made available by authorities wishing to encourage economic activity. Also known as cheap money. *See also* **money, tight**.

front money Alternative term for seed money. *See* **money, seed**.

hot money Informal term for stolen money. In business, however, it is money that is moved rapidly and at short notice from one country to another to take advantage of changes in short-term interest rates or to avoid the imminent devaluation of a currency.

money at call Loans that may be called in at short notice, and which therefore attract only low rates of **interest**.

money had and received In law, money in the possession of one person which belongs to another. The term is applied whether or not the possessor obtained the money in good faith.

moneylender Person licensed by the government to lend funds to others. The term is, however, used informally to describe any person lending money independently of banks and other financial institutions, often at high rates of interest; and as such carries certain negative connotations.

money runner US Informal term for a person who invests in markets throughout the world, probably creating hot money in the process. *See* **money, hot**.

money supply Total amount of money available at short notice in a given country. There are several categories of money supply: M0, M1, M2 and M3.

M0 is defined as notes and coin in circulation and in bank tills, plus the operational balances that banks place with the **Bank of England**. M0 is the narrowest category and is sometimes called narrow money.

M1 is defined as notes and coin in circulation and deposited in bank current accounts. It is the best gauge of money immediately available for exchange.

M2 is an obsolete definition of the money supply. It includes notes and coin in circulation and in bank current accounts, together with funds saved in deposit accounts maintained with the clearing banks, National Giro Bank, Bank of England banking department, and discount houses.

M3 is defined as M2 plus interest-bearing non-sterling deposit accounts held by British residents, and other certificates of deposit. M3 is the broadest definition of the money supply and may also be known as broad money. A subsidiary measure, £M3, excludes non-sterling deposit accounts.

narrow money Alternative term for M0. *See* **money supply**.

paper money Paper tokens issued by a bank, representing a sum of money, which it 'promises to pay the bearer on demand'. Usually applied to banknotes, but sometimes extended to **cheques and bills of exchange**.

seed money Money leant as venture capital to a company that is very young. *See* **capital, venture**.

tight money Money available only at a high rate of **interest**. Tight money is created when the authorities reduce the **money supply** in an attempt to curtail the level of activity in the economy; funds therefore become scarce and thus attract high interest rates.

See also **broker, money; fund, money market**.

monopoly Strictly, an industry with only one supplier. Also applied more widely to an industry controlled ('monopolized') by one company, which produces a sufficient proportion of the total output of that industry to effectively control **supply** and therefore **price**. In the UK monopolies, and mergers or takeovers that might lead to the creation of a monopoly, are subject to the scrutiny of the Monopolies and Mergers Commission.

absolute monopoly Total monopoly, occurring where there is only one manufacturer of a product or supplier of a service and therefore no competition for the commodity or service in question.

discriminating monopoly Monopoly situation in which the monopolist sells its goods or services at two different prices to two or more different sectors. *E.g.* the electricity industry sells electricity at a cheaper rate to industrial users than to domestic users, thus preventing the movement of the larger industrial users to cheaper forms of power.

monopsony Industry in which there are many manufacturers but only one customer for the goods produced. By controlling demand the consumer can, in theory, set the price. Monopsonies generally evolve to serve nation states; the market for warships, for example, is a virtual monopsony in that the vessels produced are purchased only by the government of the nation concerned, or by other governments that have its approval.

moonlighting Informal term for the practice of having two jobs, one of them generally involving work in the evening or at night.

moral obligation Obligation, usually to perform some service or complete some transaction, which cannot be enforced in law but which is nevertheless met out of honour.

moratorium Grant of an extended period in which to repay a loan, or a period during which the repayment schedule is suspended.

mortgage Transfer of the deeds to a property as **security** for the repayment of a **debt**. *E.g.* building societies that provide a loan for the purchase of a house take legal possession of the property until the loan and interest have been repaid.

endowment mortgage Mortgage linked to a life **assurance** policy. The borrower pays interest only on the loan advanced, and takes out a life assurance policy (which expires at the end of the mortgage term) with an assured sum equal to the capital of the loan. The proceeds of the life assurance policy are used to repay the mortgage advance; any surplus is retained by the policyholder/borrower.

puisne mortgage Mortgage issued despite the failure of the lender to take possession of the title deeds to the property offered as security for the loan. The lender may instead register the property with the Land Register or the Land Charges Register; this ensures that any transactions concerning the property must have the approval of the lender.

top-up mortgage Alternative term for a margin loan. *See* **loan, margin**.

See also **debenture, mortgage**.

multilateralism Broadly, international trade. Multilateralism is the use of the proceeds of a sale in one country to fund purchases in another. Thus, a nation selling arms in Iran and using the proceeds to purchase weapons in Nicaragua is practising multilateralism.

multinational Concerning more than one nation.

multinational corporation **Corporation** that has operations and offices in more than one country.

multiple Term with three meanings.
   First, a chain store; a group of shops in numerous locations but selling the same stock and under one **management** group.
   Second, the factor by which one multiplies the cost of producing a unit of goods, to arrive at a satisfactory selling price.
   Third, manyfold.
"It would contravene the terms of the issue of British Gas shares if one person made multiple applications for the shares."

muster roll Register of the holders of a **security**.

N

NASDAQ Acronym for National Association of Securities Dealers Automated Quotations, the US equivalent of OTC, now beginning to trade in the UK.

national Concerning or administered by a nation state. *See also* **debt, national; insurance, national**.

nationalization Government policy whereby industries previously in private ownership are bought by the state and subsequently controlled by the government. *See also* **industry, nationalized; privatization**.

natural Used to qualify many terms, but in business generally indicating something that is not artificial.

natural increase Increase in population over a specified time, calculated by subtracting the number of deaths in that period from the number of births. A falling population is therefore subject to natural decrease.

natural justice Rules to be observed by an arbitrator when adjudicating a dispute. Broadly, he or she must act in good faith and demonstrate a lack of bias or personal involvement. All the documents pertaining to the case must be made available to both parties, and no evidence may be presented without each being present. Both parties must have an equal opportunity to state their case.

natural wastage Method of reducing the workforce of a firm without resorting to enforced redundancies. As far as possible, the employer will not replace employees who die, retire or resign.

See also **economy, natural; growth, natural rate of; interest, natural rate of**.

NAV Abbreviation of net asset value. *See* **value, net asset**.

near-term *US* Short term; in the near future. American securities markets have been criticized for near-termism, the practice of examining price performance over a period of days rather than years.

negative Wanting; lacking a positive attribute. *See also* **easement, negative; tax, negative income**.

negligence Breach of a duty to take reasonable care. Negligence may be displayed by a doctor failing to make an accurate diagnosis, by a lawyer who fails to advise his or her client of the law, by a company chairman who fails to consider the interests of his shareholders etc. Professional people frequently guard against actions brought for negligence by taking out professional indemnity insurance.

negotiable Transferable, or subject to adjustment by negotiation. "The company made a preliminary bid for the contract, but indicated that their terms were negotiable."

not negotiable Document that may not be freely exchanged, and to which the holder has no better claim than any previous bearer. Cheques, postal orders and bills of exchange may be crossed 'not negotiable' as a safeguard against theft. *See* **cross**.

See also **instrument, negotiable**.

net That which remains after all deductions and charges have been made. *See* **gross; product, net domestic; worth, net; ratio, net profit**.

NIC Acronym for newly industrializing country, a country which, although part of the Third World, has rapidly developed a substantial industrial base. Examples include South Korea and Taiwan.

niche Market or section of a market controlled by an operator who is catering for a well-defined and usually small group of customers.

nil paid New issue of shares for which the issuing company has yet to be paid. The term is most commonly applied to rights issues. *See* **issue, new**.

NIT Abbreviation of negative income tax. *See* **tax, negative income**.

NL Abbreviation of no liability, the Australian equivalent of a public limited company (plc). *See* **company, public limited**.

no-brainer *US* **Fund** that tracks the performance of a stock **index**. Its manager buys all the stocks listed on a major index, and hence no discretionary management is required. *See also* **management, passive**.

nominal Existing in name only. *See* **account, nominal**; **value, nominal**.

nominee Agent, frequently one who purchases shares on behalf of an undisclosed client. *See* **shareholder, nominee**.

non-domiciled Person regarded by the authorities as 'offshore', or non-resident, principally for **tax** purposes.

non-profit making (organization) (NPO) Company or institution that has a legal obligation to make no profit. The term is most usually applied to registered charities.

non-qualifying policy Pension scheme that does not qualify for tax relief.

non-qualified *US* Employee share option plan in which the gain made by the employee (*i.e.* the difference between the grant price and the market price) is taxed as **income** and not as a capital gain. *See* **tax, capital gains**.

non-resident Person who does not live in an area or state, or who lives there but does not meet the legal requirements for 'residence'.

non-union Describing a person who is not a member of a **trade union**, or a company that employs such people. Non-union labour often consists of workers brought in by an employer, generally to the exclusion of organized labour. In such instances the employer's purpose is usually to inhibit or destroy the power of an established trade union, or to replace workers who are on strike or working to rule. *See also* **scab**.

notary public Official licensed to attest the validity of documents and of the signatures on them by signing and/or sealing them. Dishonoured or protested bills also require the seal of a public notary.

note Token or proof of a transaction.

advice note Notice from a supplier giving details of goods ordered or delivered. It either accompanies or precedes the shipment, and precedes the invoice. *See also* **note, delivery**.

allotment note Means by which a sailor authorizes the master of his ship to pay his wages directly to his wife, family or bank.

bank note Paper currency produced by a bank of issue that carries a promise to pay the bearer on demand the sum specified on the note.

bond note Document indicating that imported goods held in bond may be released, because all import formalities have been completed.

credit note Document, often printed in red, issued to confirm the transfer of credit from one account to another.

debit note In **accounting**, notification sent to a customer that the supplier is about to **debit** the client's account with a certain sum. Debit notes are normally issued in unusual situations, *e.g.* when a client has been charged too little for goods received.

delivery note Broadly, a note advising a recipient of the intended delivery of goods. In the **securities** market, however, a delivery note requests the delivery of a security.

floating rate note Security issued by a borrower on the **Eurobonds** market, that has a variable rate of interest.

note circulation Area velocity of money, a measure of the speed at which cash circulates around the economy.

note of hand Alternative term for promissory note. *See* **note, promissory**.

promissory note Document that states that a person promises to pay a certain sum of money on a certain date. Also known as a note of hand.

sold contract note Alternative term for sold note. *See* **note, sold**.

sold note Document sent by a broker to his or her client, confirming that a sale has been made. Also known as a sold contract note.

notice Advice of a forthcoming action issued in advance, *e.g.* a notice to quit or notice of dismissal. The term is generally applied to the period that elapses between the moment when an employee is informed that his or her services are no longer required, and the day on which he or she leaves the firm.
"He had been considering handing in his notice for a long time."

"He attended several interviews during the time he was working out his notice."

exercise notice Notice issued when the holder of an **option** wishes to take up his or her right either to buy or sell the security for which the option has been agreed.

notice in lieu of distringas Notice issued by a shareholder and supported by a statutory declaration, that formally advises the issuing company of his or her holding. Such notices prevent any attempt by the company to transfer the shares in question to a third party.

notice of abandonment Formal notification that an owner is relinquishing all rights to a property (often a ship) to the insurer. Notice of abandonment is usually given in the event of a total loss. *See* **abandonment; loss, total**.

noting and protest First two stages in the dishonouring of a **bill of exchange**. The bill is first 'noted', or witnessed, by a **notary public**, who thereby testifies to its existence but not necessarily to its validity. It is then presented again, and if refused for a second time it is protested by being returned to the notary, who then testifies to its refusal. Noting must be completed within one working day of the bill's first being dishonoured.

notional Theoretical; supposed. *See* **income, notional; rent, notional**.

novation Discharge of one contract in favour of the creation of another. *E.g.* a builder may contract to start work on a certain day, and later notify the client that he will be unable to do so. In this case the client may discharge the contract and sign another on the same terms with a second builder.

NPO Abbreviation of **non-profit-making organization**.

NPV Abbreviation of no par value.

null and void Phrase used when a contract is invalidated. "The court ruled that the contract be made null and void."

number fudging Informal term for creative accountancy; the creation of a favourable account sheet without resort to actual fraud. Also known as window dressing.

NV Abbreviation of *Naamloze Venootschap*, the Dutch equivalent of the British public limited company (plc). *See* **company, public limited**.

NYMEX Acronym for New York Metals Exchange, which with the Chicago Metals Exchange conducts a significant part of the world's hard commodity trading. The two institutions are in fierce competition with each other.

NYSE Abbreviation of New York Stock Exchange, the largest security market in the United States. *See* **exchange, stock**.

O

obsolescence Loss of the value of something when it becomes out of date. In accounting, obsolescence refers to an asset that has to be written off, not through deterioration, but when its continued use becomes uneconomic. *E.g.* a piece of machinery may be superseded by a new, faster version. It is therefore uneconomic for the company to continue to use it, and the asset becomes obsolete. *See also* **wear and tear; write off**.

built-in obsolescence Practice of manufacturers who design a product so that it needs to be replaced by the consumer in a relatively short time, resulting either from fast deterioration or changes in fashion.

odd lot *US* Group of fewer than 100 shares or, if the stock is inactive, fewer than 10 shares that are dealt at a higher commission rate than larger quantities. *See also* **round lot**.

offer Statement that one party is willing to sell something, at a certain price and under certain conditions. If a particular buyer is unwilling to buy at the offer price or under the conditions of the offer, he may make a **bid** against the seller's offer.

general offer Offer made to the general public. *E.g.* a person may offer to pay a certain amount for a piece of information, and members of the public accept the offer by sending the information.

godfather offer An offer that cannot be refused. In a **takeover** situation, a godfather offer for the company's shares is made at such a good price that the management of the target company can only accept it.

offer by prospectus In contrast to an **offer for sale**, an offer by prospectus is the offer by a company to sell shares or **debentures** directly to the public by issuing a **prospectus**, instead of selling the shares to an **issuing house**.

offer by tender Alternative term for **tender offer**.

offer for sale One way a company may issue shares for sale is to sell them all to an **issuing house**, which then publishes a **prospectus** and sells the shares to the public. *See also* **tender offer**.

offer period During a **takeover**, the offer period is the length of time an offer of shares must remain open (at least 21 days).

offer to purchase Alternative term for **takeover bid**. *See also* **price, offer**.

offering *US* Offer.

offering circular *US* Document that contains information regarding offers of shares exempt from **SEC** regulations and registration.

minimum offering period Minimum period of time for which an offer to the public to purchase shares may be left open. In the UK this period of time is usually 14 days.

Official List Stock Exchange Daily Official List (SEDOL). Official publication of the London Stock Exchange, appearing daily at 5.30pm, that details price movements and dividend information for almost all securities quoted on the Exchange.

official quotations Figure quoted daily for almost all securities on the Stock Exchange Daily Official List. *See* **Official List**.

official receiver = receivership

offshore Describes a business that operates from a **tax haven** such as Liechtenstein.

offshore financing *US* Raising capital in countries other than one's own.

offshore fund Investment scheme operated from a **tax haven**, by which investors may benefit from the haven's taxation privileges without leaving their home country. *See* **shelter, tax**.

Old Lady of Threadneedle Street The Bank of England, situated in Threadneedle Street in the City of London. A popular term of endearment appearing to date from the early 19th century.

oligopoly Industry in which there are many buyers but few sellers. Such conditions give the producer or seller a certain amount of control over price, but leave him especially vulnerable to the actions of competitors. *See also* **monopoly**.

imperfect oligopoly Oligopoly in which the goods that are produced are slightly different from each other. This difference may allow the seller to alter the price in relation to other sellers without a significant affect on sales.

perfect oligopoly Oligopoly in which the goods being produced by each seller are of the same type.

oncost Another name for **overheads**.

on demand Bill of exchange that is payable to the bearer immediately on presentation, such as an uncrossed cheque.

one-man Business, company or operation involving only one person, rather like a one-man band.

on-floor Transactions that are conducted and concluded on the floor of an exchange in the usual manner.

on stream When an asset or investment begins to function, it is said to come on stream.

open Unrestricted or unlimited. Also, to open is to take out a futures position. *See* **cheque, open; contract, open; credit, open; fund, open-end; indent, open; market, open; policy, open; position, open**.

opening Action that begins something.

opening range On a financial **futures** market, the highest and lowest prices recorded at the opening.

The Opening Refers to the **call-over** at the start of each trading session on some exchanges. Otherwise, the term is used as shorthand for opening price. *See* **price, opening**. *See also* **bid, opening; sale, opening**.

operating Day-to-day running of something, such as a business or a machine. *See* **budget, operating; cost, operating; profit, operating**.

operation Another term for a business or the activities it undertakes. "She was called in to mastermind the company's new printing operation."

associated operation Operation that is in some way linked to another within a company. Associated operations within a company may, *e.g.*, manufacture similar products or use similar production methods.

operation of law If one party obtains a legal judgement on a contract under which the party's liabilities are discharged, the contract is said to be discharged by operation of law, in that the legal requirements of the contract become merged with the requirements of the judgement.

operational (operations) research Mathematical technique that can be applied, *e.g.* to discover how the various activities within an industry may be regulated to coexist with maximum efficiency.

option An investor may pay a **premium** in return for the option to buy or sell a certain number of securities at an agreed price (known as the exercise price), on or before a particular date. The dealer may exercise his option at any time within the specified period and normally does so at an advantageous time depending on market prices. Otherwise he may allow the option to lapse.

at-the-money option Call or put option where the price of the security on the market is the same as the exercise price. *See* **price, exercise**.

call option Option to buy shares, commodities or financial futures at an agreed price on or before an agreed future date.

conventional option Alternative term for traditional option. *See* **option, traditional**.

double option Option either to buy or sell.

in-the-money option Term with two meanings.
   First, it is an option to buy shares (call option) for which the price on the open market has risen above the price fixed (called the option's exercise price).
   Second, it is an option to sell (put option) for which the market price has fallen in relation to the exercise price. An in-the money option is said to carry intrinsic value. *See* **price, exercise**; **value, intrinsic**.

lock-up option US In a situation in which a company is being threatened with an unwanted **takeover**, defensive tactic whereby the target company promises to sell its most attractive **assets** to a **white knight**. *See also* **crown jewel tactic**.

naked option Option to buy shares in which the seller of the option (the option writer) does not already own the shares. In this instance, the option writer hopes to buy back the option before it is exercised and so avoid having to supply the shares. If the option is exercised and the market price of the shares has risen, then the option writer makes a loss. An option writer who sells naked options is known as a naked writer.

option money Premium paid in return for an option.

option writer Someone who sells call options, thereby agreeing to supply shares, *or* someone who sells put options, agreeing to buy shares.

out-of-the-money option Option to buy shares (call option) for which the market price has fallen since the price was fixed.
Equally, it is an option to sell (put option) for which the price on the market has risen above the agreed exercise price. In either case, the dealer makes a loss if he or she decides to exercise the option. *See* **price, exercise**.

put option Option to sell shares, commodities or financial futures at an agreed price on or before an agreed future date.

seller's option US On the New York Stock Exchange, option that enables the seller to deliver the relevant **security** at any time within a period of 6–60 days.

share option UK scheme that gives employees the option to buy shares in their company at attractive prices (normally well below market price) at a specific future date. *See also* **capitalism, popular**.

traded option Unlike traditional options, traded options are transferable and the terms of the option are fixed. Thus, it has been possible to form a market for trading the options themselves, as well as the underlying security commodity or future.

traditional option Non-transferable option that has been available on a market for over a century, written on a variety of shares listed on the exchange. Each time a dealer wishes to buy a traditional option, the terms are re-written.

order Either a demand from someone in authority that a particular action be taken (or that a person refrains from a particular action), or a equest made to a supplier for a particular quantity of a certain product or for his or her services.

adjudication order Order of court, declaring someone bankrupt. Also known as adjudication of bankruptcy. *See also* **bankrupt**.

banker's order Alternative term for a standing order. *See* **order, standing**.

cash with order Terms of an agreement by which goods are supplied only if payment is made in cash at the time the order is placed.

charging order Court order that allows a debtor's goods to be 'earmarked' for the creditor. If the debt is not repaid, the goods become the property of the creditor.

garnishee order In bankruptcy, an order may be made by the court to holders of a bankrupt's funds (third parties such as banks etc.) that no payments are to be made to the bankrupt until the court authorizes them. The third party is known as the garnishee and the court order is known as a garnishee order. The purpose of the garnishee order is to protect the interests of the bankrupt's creditors. *See also* **bankrupt**.

money order Method of transmitting money overseas via the UK Post Office, which avoids the need to send cash or cheques through the post.

open order Alternative term for an order **good-till-cancelled**.

order and disposition In bankruptcy, order and disposition is a means whereby a bankrupt's creditors may seize property to which the bankrupt has no title. Order and disposition comes into effect only if title is not obviously someone else's and if the bankrupt has led a third party into believing the goods are his in order to receive credit. *See also* **bankrupt; owner, reputed**.

order driven Describes an economy, industry or trading on a stock market that reacts in relation to the flow of incoming orders. *See also* **quote driven**.

resting order Alternative term for an order **good-till-cancelled**.

standing order Also known as a banker's order, an order to a bank to make (usually) a series of payments on the customer's behalf. Used to pay bills that are due at regular intervals.

stop order Instructions given by a client to a **stockbroker**, to sell securities should they fall below a certain price.

ordinary Normal, usual. *See* **shares, ordinary**.

organogram Chart that shows the organization of a company, its hierarchy and the relationships between departments.

OTC Abbreviation of over-the-counter, usually referring to the over-the-counter market. *See* **market, over-the-counter**.

outcry market = market, outcry

outgoer Farmer who accepts financial inducements to turn his or her agricultural land to another function, *e.g.* for leisure pursuits or a caravan site.

outlay Money paid for something; expenditure.

capital outlay Expenditure on fixed assets such as machinery. *See* **asset, fixed; capital**.

output Amount produced by a company, single person or machine. *See also* **tax, output**.

outwork Work done by a worker, normally at home. It often pays a company to employ unskilled workers to work at home, normally producing goods at a low rate of pay.

overbought If there are many buyers on a market, prices, (*e.g.* of shares) are pushed to artificially high levels and the market is said to be overbought. *See also* **oversold**.

over-capitalization = capitalization

overdraft When a bank customer withdraws more money from a bank account than is actually deposited with the bank, the excess is known as a bank overdraft. An overdraft must normally be agreed with the bank i question and interest on the overdraft is charged on a day-to-day basis. Normally only used as short-term borrowing. *See also* **account, current**.

daylight overdraft US Occurs when a bank allows a customer's account to go into the **red**, on the understanding that the debt will be repaid by the end of the day. *See also* **float**.

overexposure = **exposure**

overheads (**overhead** *US*) Costs incurred during the everyday running of a business and not variable according to output. Also known as indirect costs, fixed costs or supplementary costs, overheads include heating, lighting and energy costs, administration, insurance, rent and rates.

over-insurance Practice of insuring property for a sum above its actual value. Over-insurance is futile, because an insurer does not normally pay more than the true value of the property. *See also* **insurance, double**.

overshoot When the price trends on a currency market continue to rise above levels anticipated by analysts, they are said to overshoot.

oversold Market in which there are too many sellers and so the price falls to an artificially low point, too rapidly. *See also* **overbought**.

oversubscription A sale of shares by **application and allotment** is said to be oversubscribed if the number of shares applied for exceeds the number of shares available. The situation is often remedied by a **ballot**. *See also* **allotment**.

over-the-counter market = **market, over-the-counter**

over-trading Potentially dangerous situation in which a company tries to take on more business than its working capital will allow.

ownership Basic right to possess something. Not to be confused with possession, for whereas a person may own something, he or she may still lose possession of it, *e.g.* to a bailee or to a thief. *See* **bailment**.

beneficial owner When a shareholding is held by a **nominee** such as a stockbroker, the nominee's name appears on the register of shareholders. The real owner is known as the beneficial owner. *See* **shareholder, nominee**.

reputed owner Person who acts as the owner of a property, even if he or she is not. If the reputed owner becomes bankrupt, the property is divided among the creditors. *See also* **bailment; estoppel; order and disposition**.

social ownership Ownership of some or all of a country's industries by the government (on behalf of society in general). *See also* **nationalization; privatization**.

P

pa Abbreviation of **per annum**.

PA Abbreviation of personal account or personal assistant. *See* **account, personal**.

packaging Container or wrapping of a product, generally designed to protect the contents, facilitate handling, identify the product and encourage its purchase.

packing *US* Adding to the payments on a loan charges for services, such as insurance, etc., without the borrower requesting them, or indeed fully understanding what he or she is buying. This practice is illegal.

pacman defence Method of defending against a hostile **takeover**, whereby the target company makes a tender **offer** for the shares of the aggressor.

paid up Used either as a verb or an adjective to mean that a person has paid the money he or she owes, or, more specifically, that he or she has paid a subscription. Also used to distinguish fully-paid from **partly-paid** shares.
"After we chased them for two weeks, they finally paid up."
"He is a paid-up member of the union."
See also **capital, paid-up**.

painting the tape *US* Method of creating an impression of activity around a share, by reporting fictitious transactions. Painting the tape is illegal.

paper Describing any form of **loan**, but particularly a short-term loan such as a Treasury bill. It refers to the paper on which a pledge to repay money at a specified time is recorded. Most paper is negotiable and can be bought or sold like any other commodity. *See* **bill, Treasury**.

commercial paper Corporate debt in a tradeable form. In the USA, the commercial paper market is a short-term, non-bank market in which firms lend money to each other without the intervention of a financial intermediary.

third class paper Corporate debt issued by companies with a low credit rating. Third class paper is a hazardous investment. *See* **rating, credit**

See also **money, paper**.

par = parity

parcel Block of shares that changes hands during a **bargain**.

pari passu Latin for with equal step, indicating simultaneous effect, often applied to new share issues. In this context, it means that the designated share will rank equally for **dividends** with comparable existing shares.

Paris Club = Group of Ten

parity Equality.
"It is unlikely that the US dollar will reach parity with sterling."

at par Equal, indicating a share price equal to the paid-up or nominal value.

below par Share price that has fallen below the nominal value at which the share was issued.

par The nominal or face value of stocks and shares. *See* **value, nominal**.

Parkinson's Law Work expands to fill the time allotted, a principle originally propounded by Professor C. Northcote Parkinson in 1957.

partly-paid Describing securities and shares for which the full nominal value has not been paid and on which the holder is liable to pay the balance either on demand or upon specified dates. Formerly, it was common for a company to **call up** only a part of the nominal value of each share, retaining the right to demand the balance when it became necessary to increase its **capital**. This gave the company access to capital without the need for new share issues. The term also applies to new issues in which the issue price is to be paid in instalments. *See* **value, nominal**.

partner Person engaged in a business enterprise jointly, and generally with the same status and responsibility as, another or others. *See also* **partnership**.

active partner Partner working for a firm. *See also* **partner, nominal; partner, sleeping**.

general partner Partner whose liability for the debts of the partnership is unlimited.

limited partner Partner whose liability for the debts of the partnership is limited in law to the sum that he or she invested in it. A limited partner does not generally share in the management of the firm. He or she may, however, offer advice and examine the books of account.

nominal partner Partner who lends his or her name to a firm, but who has invested no capital and does not take an active part in the company. He or she remains liable for the partnership's debts.

sleeping partner Partner who invests capital in a firm but takes no active part in its management. He or she remains liable for the partnership's debts.

partnership Business association, in the UK formed by between two to twenty partners.

deed of partnership Agreement that forms the basis of a partnership between two or more people.

general partnership Formal partnership in which each partner shares equally in the running of the firm and accepts liability for an equal share of its debts, although his or her share of the profits is usually proportional to the capital that he or she has invested.

limited partnership Partnership in which one or more partners have only limited liability for the firm's debts. In each limited partnership there must be one general partner with unlimited liability. A limited partnership is therefore unpopular and a public limited company preferred, because all shareholders in such a company have only limited liability. *See* **company, public limited; liability, limited; partnership, general**.

partnership at will Partners are normally bound by a formal agreement; if not, the partnership is called a partnership at will, and may be broken at any time by any partner.

passing a name Provision to a seller of the name of a potential buyer. A broker often 'passes a name' in this way, but rarely guarantees the buyer's solvency when so doing.

On the London Stock Exchange it is practice to pass the names of buyers in advance of **account day** so that accounts may be prepared in good time.

pass-through *US* Certificate representing an interest in a pool of mortgages held by private members. The principle and the interest are passed through the pool from the mortgagee to the investor.

patent Authorization that grants the addressee the sole right to make, use or sell an invention for a specified period of time. Applicants for a patent must establish the novelty of their invention.

pawnbroker Person who lends money secured against goods called a **pledge**. Loans are normally made for a period of six months and seven days and, if not repaid within that time, the pawnbroker is entitled to sell the pawned goods.

pay Money, specifically salary or wages. Also used as a verb to describe the payment or transfer of funds.
"They gave him his pay in cash."
"Please pay the above amount by the end of June."

pay day Term with two meanings.
First, it is generally, used for the day on which employees receive their wages.
Second, it is an alternative term for settlement day. *See* **day, settlement**.

severance pay Sum of money given to an employee when he or she is made redundant.

payable That which must be paid.

payable to bearer **Bill of exchange** on which neither the **payee** nor the **endorsee** is named. The bill therefore becomes payable to the bearer.

payable to order **Bill of exchange** on which the payee is named but the endorsee is not. The bill may be paid to any endorsee.

payables Informal term for a company's short-term **debts** (debtors).

pay-as-you-earn (PAYE) System of income tax collection whereby tax is deducted from current earnings at source. The employer is responsible for collecting the tax, and the employee receives only **net** wages. *See* **tax, income**.

PAYE Abbreviation of **pay-as-you-earn**.

payee Person or people to whom money is to be paid. On a cheque, the payee is the person to whom the cheque is made payable.

account payee Words added to a crossed cheque that ensure that the cheque is paid only into the account of the person or people named.

payment Remuneration of someone in money or kind.

part payment Interim payment or instalment.

payment in kind Payment, generally of wages, made in goods or services rather than in money. Payment of total wages in kind was made illegal in the UK in the nineteenth century, but part payment in kind is still common. For example, workers who receive luncheon vouchers or the use of a company car are receiving payment in kind. *See also* **perk**.

payment on account Part payment of an outstanding debt, usually coupled with an agreement to repay the balance on a specified date.

payout Issue of **payment**, *e.g.* the money paid to the insured on an article lost, damaged or destroyed.
"He was disappointed that the payout on his insurance claim was a mere pittance."

payroll List of people employed (usually full-time) by a firm and of the amount that each is due to be paid.
"After only two years from start-up, they had 100 employees on the payroll".
See also **tax, payroll**.

peculation Embezzlement, particularly the appropriation of public money or goods by an official.

pegging the exchanges Maintenance of a fixed currency **exchange rate**, by government intervention in the markets. Pegging the exchanges is generally resorted to in order to prevent an unfavourable rise or fall in the value of a currency.

penny One-hundredth of a pound sterling (also called a new penny) or, colloquially, a US cent. Before the introduction of decimal currency in Britain in 1971, a penny was a two hundred and fortieth of a pound. *See also* **share, penny**.

pennyweight Measure of weight, equivalent to one two hundred and fortieth of a pound **Troy**. Often now used to mean anything of small weight.

pension Regular payment, made after retirement, generally for the remainder of the pensioner's life.

deferred pension Occupational pension that is paid to an employee who leaves employment before retirement. Also known as preserved pension.

disability pension State pension paid in the UK to a person who is disabled in some way.

earnings-related pension State pension scheme in the UK that provides a pension in relation to the level at which a person was being paid during his or her working life, rather than a flat-rate pension.

executive pension In addition to a group pension plan organized by a company for its employees, a company may also take out individual pensions for its senior executives. In such a case, the company would make tax-deductible contributions in order to increase the real **value** of the pension.

ex gratia pension Free pension sometimes awarded to an outstanding employee by a company.

graduated pension scheme Form of state pension operated in the UK between April 1961 and April 1975. Persons earning more than £9 per week paid additional contributions which entitled them to a graduated pension in addition to the basic state pension, the amount due being proportional to contributions and, therefore, to their income during that period.

guaranteed minimum pension (GMP) The minimum pension that an occupational or personal pension plan must guarantee a person who has contracted out of the state pension scheme.

loanback pension Loan made by a pension fund to a contributor (generally self-employed) to that fund. Loanback pensions are secured not against the total value of contributions to date, but against some other asset. However, the maximum available loan is usually equal to the total value of accumulated units. The loan becomes an asset of the borrower's pension plan and interest payments are part of the income of the plan. *See* **fund, pension**.

non-contributory pension Occupational pension scheme in which no contribution is levied from the employee. The employer generally offers it as a **perk** and himself benefits financially because the scheme can be treated as a fringe benefit for tax purposes. *See* **benefit, fringe**.

occupational pension scheme Pension plan operated by an employer who opts out of the state scheme in the UK. The employer pays no National Insurance contributions on behalf of the employees, and, instead, provides them with an approved alternative scheme.

old-age pension State pension paid in the UK to those over the age of 80 years. The term is commonly used also for **retirement pension**.

preserved pension Alternative term for deferred pension. *See* **pension, deferred**.

private pension Investment plan outside any state scheme by which people provide a pension for themselves or pay into a pension plan provided by others.

retirement pension Pension paid in the UK by the state to those men over 65 and women over 60 who are no longer in regular employment and who have made the necessary contributions to the National Insurance scheme during their working life. *See* **insurance, national**.

self-administered pension plan US Also known as the Keogh Plan, pension scheme taken out and administered by the contributor himself, and suitable for people who frequently change jobs. By maintaining a scheme independent of any employer, the contributor does not risk the loss of benefit sometimes suffered by those who have contributed to an occupational pension scheme.

self-employed pension Self-employed people do not automatically qualify for a state pension. Many choose to pay National Insurance at the self-employed rate, and this qualifies them for the basic state retirement pension. They cannot, however, qualify for an earnings-related pension, and therefore often take out private pension plans, which must at least guarantee to pay the contributor the equivalent of a basic state pension.

state pension Pension paid by the government in the UK to those who have paid the appropriate National Insurance contributions during their working lives. State pensions fall into two categories: the retirement pension and the old-age pension. *See also* **pension, private**.

widow's pension Pension paid in the UK to a married woman after her husband's death.

PEP Abbreviation of personal **equity** plan.

P/E ratio Abbreviation of price/earnings ratio. *See* **ratio, price/earnings**.

per capita Latin for by the head. Usually an indication that a sum will be divided equally among a group. Thus per capita income is calculated by dividing the total income received by a group by the number of people in that group.

per contra Latin for by the opposite side. In accounting, an entry on the opposite side of an account or balance sheet. Therefore, a self-balancing item.

per diem Latin for by the day. Usually applied to an allowance, rental or charge made on a daily basis.

perfecting the sight Supplying the full details demanded on a **bill of sight**.

performance Earnings or losses made on a security or by a company. "This year, the company's performance was poor – it made substantial losses in most areas."

specific performance Order made by a court to one party to a contract to fulfil the obligations to which that party is contracted. A specific performance order may be made, for example in place of **damages**.

See also **bond, performance**.

perk Abbreviation of perquisite, a casual **benefit**. In general terms a **payment in kind,** but more specifically applicable to informal rather than formally agreed benefits.

period Unit of time.

base period Time period selected as the base for an **index** number series. The index for a base period is usually 100, and changes in prior or subsequent periods are expressed relative to it.

See also **bill, period**.

permission to deal Authorization issued by a stock exchange that permits dealings in the shares of a company. Permission to deal must be sought three days after the issue of a **prospectus**.

perpetual Eternal; valid for an indefinite time.

perpetual succession Continuation of a company after the departure or death of its directors. A company is an individual legal entity which exists irrespective of its personnel, and which ceases to exist in law only after its **liquidation**.

See also **debenture, perpetual; inventory, perpetual; note, perpetual**.

personal Pertaining to an individual, or private as opposed to public. *See also* **account, personal; allowance, personal; loan, personal**.

PERT Acronym for **programme evaluation and review technique**.

PET Acronym for property enterprise trust, a form of mutual fund which invests solely in **enterprise zone** properties in order to gain tax advantages for its investors. *See* **fund, mutual**.

petrocurrency Money (usually US dollars) paid to the exporters of petroleum in exchange for their product. After the OPEC countries quadrupled petrol prices in 1973, the amount of petrocurrency in circulation rose sharply and exceeded the capacity of the oil- exporting countries' economies to absorb it. Much of it was therefore invested in the world's financial markets, where it helped to offset the trade deficits caused by the OPEC price rise.

petrodollar **Petrocurrency** denominated in dollars.

petties Abbreviation of petty cash, used most commonly on an invoice to denote charges made for various small items not separately enumerated. *See* **cash, petty**.

PHI Abbreviation of permanent health insurance. *See* **insurance, permanent health**.

piecework Work that is paid per unit of output (*i.e.*, instead of per hour of time worked). By linking earnings to output, the worker is provided with an incentive to increase productivity. *See also* **rate, piece**.

PIN Abbreviation of personal identification number, the confidential number issued to holders of cash and credit cards that prevents their unauthorized use at an **ATM**.

pit Used on a commodity exchange to denote the equivalent of a stock exchange trading floor. It derives from the local nickname for the floor of the Chicago Commodities Exchange. Now, a pit is the floor of any open outcry exchange. *See* **market, outcry**.

pitch Area in which a trader operates.

jobber's pitch On the London Stock Exchange, trading position on the floor of the exchange from which jobbers operate.

placement Process of issuing shares through an intermediary, usually a stockbroker or **syndicate**. The intermediary 'places' the shares with clients, frequently institutional investors, or with members of the public. A certain proportion of any share issue quoted on the London Stock Exchange must be made available to the public through the Exchange.

pre-placement Activity that takes place before a share issue has been placed.

placing Security issued to raise new capital in a **placement**. Stockbrokers acting on behalf of the company concerned 'place' shares by selling them to financial institutions and to the public. Also used as a synonym for **placement**.

private placing Sale of the whole of a new issue of shares to a financial institution.

plant Fixtures or machinery used in an industrial process or a general term for a factory or industrial complex. *See* **hire, plant; register, plant.**

plastic Nickname for **ATM** cards, or credit cards. *See* **card, credit**.

PLC Abbreviation of public limited company, also expressed as plc. *See* **company, public limited**.

pledge Transfer of personal property from a debtor to a creditor as security for a **debt**. Legal ownership of the property concerned remains with the pledger. *See also* **pawnbroker**.

point Unit of price in which stocks are traded. One point generally equals £1 or $1.

basis point Unit used to measure the rate of change of investment payments for bonds or notes. Each basis point is equal to 0.01 per cent.

poison pill Technique used by companies facing a hostile **takeover** bid to make their stock as unattractive or inaccessible as possible. Stock may be diluted by new issues and company articles changed to require the approval of a greater proportion of the shareholders for the takeover. Expensive subsidiaries may be purchased to reduce the attractiveness of the company balance sheet, and provision is often made for **greenmail** payments and for **golden parachutes**.

policy Term with two meanings.
First, it is an agreement that a group of people (*e.g.* a company) will, in certain circumstances, act in a certain way.
"It was the store's policy not to give refunds on any goods."

Second, in **insurance**, a policy is a document setting out exactly the terms of an insurance contract.

"She met with her insurance company to decide which was the best policy to take out."

all-risks policy In the UK, insurance policy that covers personal possessions against loss or damage, usually anywhere in the country. All-risks policies are frequently extended to cover possessions in other parts of the world, and are therefore popularly used to insure small movable items.

beggar-my-neighbour policy Economic policy that improves a nation's economic standing at the expense of its trading partners. *See also* **dumping**.

blanket policy Insurance policy that covers either all the property at a specific location, or all examples of a specified property or possession at several locations.

business interruption policy Insurance policy whereby the holder is compensated for interruption of business activity caused by a mishap such as a fire.

buyout policy Occupational pension scheme whereby the subscriber (the employee of the company offering the scheme) may buy out of the scheme if he or she wishes to leave the company.

dividend policy Company policy, agreed by the **board** of directors regarding the allocation of profits between shareholders (in the form of dividends) and **reserves**.

floating policy Insurance policy that covers goods of different values and located in different places.

franchise policy Insurance policy under which the insured party makes no claims for loss or damage up to a specified sum, known as the franchise. Claims for amounts exceeding the franchise are met in full by the insurer. The purpose of a franchise policy is to eliminate the insurer's obligation to deal with small but time-consuming claims.

honour policy Another term for **policy proof of interest**.

non-qualifying policy Pension scheme that does not qualify for **tax relief**.

open policy Marine insurance policy that provides cover for a fixed period of time, usually twelve months, rather than for a specified voyage. The nature and value of each cargo must be declared to the insurers. *See* **insurance, marine**.

policy proof of interest (PPI) Insurance policy, most common in commerce. In the event of the contingency insured against actually occurring, the holder of a PPI need not suffer material loss in order to claim against the policy; possession of the policy itself is regarded as sufficient proof of interest.

valued policy Insurance policy usually issued to cover articles of fixed value. In the event of a total loss, the insurer undertakes to pay the total of the sum insured, irrespective of the actual current value of the article insured. *See* **loss, total**.

whole-of-life policy Insurance policy protecting the holder's life at a fixed or level **premium**, paid either for life or until retirement, the policy being payable only on death.

poll List of names.

opinion poll Survey of opinion carried out by interviewing a number of people, in person or by telephone, and detailing their preferences and opinions, usually in statistical form. Opinion polls are most commonly associated with politics, but are widely used by manufacturers and advertisers to assess public taste and preferences.

ponzi scheme *US* Scheme in which investors are paid off by using capital from the investments of later investors. A ponzi scheme is fraudulent.

porcupine provision Provision written into a company's **articles of association,** or into a corporate charter or byelaw, designed to act as a deterrent to hostile **takeovers**. An example of a porcupine provision is the **poison pill** defence.

portfolio Selection of securities held by a person or institution. Portfolios generally include a wide variety of stocks and bonds to spread the **risk** of investment, and the contents of a portfolio are managed − that is, continually changed in order to maximize income or growth.

indexed portfolio Portfolio linked to a stock **index**, such as the FT-100 share index.

portfolio analysis Technique of strategic analysis used to distinguish the characteristics of different business units in a multi-business corporation.

position In general terms, the place of an investor in a fluctuating market.

bear position Position of an investor whose sales exceed his or her purchases, and who therefore stands to gain in a falling or bear market. *See* **bear**.

bull position Position of an investor whose purchases exceed his or her sales, and who therefore stands to gain in a rising or bull market. *See* **bull**.

open position Position of a speculator who has bought or sold without making any hedging transactions, and who therefore gambles that the market will rise or fall as he or she has predicted.

post Latin for after.

post-bang Events or developments on the UK Stock Exchange that occurred after the **Big Bang** (October 1986).

post-entry Events or developments that occur after a company's entry into a stock market.

postdate To affix some future date to a document, most commonly a cheque, thereby preventing the occurrence of actions or transactions concerning that document before the specified date.

poste restante Postal service that enables items to be sent to a person uncertain of his or her precise future whereabouts. Letters and packages are addressed care of a specific post office (a poste restante address) and collected by the addressee.

pot is clean *US* Indicates that all shares allocated during an issue for offer to institutional investors have been taken up.

power lunch Substantial lunch, over which large deals are often finalized.

PPI Abbreviation of **policy proof of interest**.

pre-emption Right to purchase shares before they become generally available, usually offered in the case of new issues to existing shareholders. Rights of pre-emption are often proportional to the value of an existing holding.

preference Prior right; the superiority one person or thing over another.

time preference Theory of interest that suggests that interest is the price paid by a borrower for immediate consumption, and a compensation to the lender, who loses the opportunity to use the articles or money lent for his or her own purposes. Therefore, time perefence is a person's preference for current rather than future consumption, or vice versa.

See also **shares, preference**.

premium Very broadly, a price, payment or bonus valued higher than the norm. The term has a number of specific meanings.

First, it is most often used to describe the payments, usually annual, made to an insurance company to maintain a **policy**.

Second, the premium is the difference between the offer price of a new share issue and the price at which it begins trading, if the latter exceeds the former. The term is also used to describe the positive difference between the face value and redemption value of any stock or bond.

Third, it is the amount by which a currency stands above its par value.

premium bond Ticket, costing £1, in a lottery run by the UK government. Prizewinners retain their bonds, which may win again. A premium bond can be redeemed for its face value at any time.

premium brand Brand of a product that sells at a higher price than most others, usually because of higher perceived quality.

share premium On a new issue of shares, premium charged on the nominal value of the shares if it seems that the real value is likely to be much higher. *See* **value, nominal; value, real**.

single premium Life assurance scheme in which the investor pays a lump sum as a single premium, as opposed to making a series of smaller, regular payments. *See* **assurance, life**.

See also **bond, premium savings**.

prepayment Payment made in advance. When applied to a **bill of exchange**, prepayment is the payment before the bill matures, and in the context of mortgages it is the repayment of the debt before its maturity.

pre-refunding *US* Practice of issuing shares to re-fund (*i.e.* pay for debts that are about to mature), not immediately before maturity of the old issue, but in advance of it, in order to take advantage of good **interest rates**. *See also* **refinancing**.

president *US* Chief executive of an American company, equivalent to a managing director in the UK.

price Cost of purchasing a unit of goods or services. Very broadly, prices are generally set by the manufacturer and retailer, taking into account all fixed and variable costs and allowing for a **profit** margin. *See* **cost, fixed; cost, variable**.

administered price Price set and partly controlled by the seller, and based on his or her knowledge of the costs of production and estimates of **demand** and **competition**. An administered price lies between **monopoly** and free market prices, and characterizes a state of imperfect competition. *See also* **market, free**.

average price Alternative term for target price. *See* **price, target**.

bid price Price a market maker is prepared to pay to buy securities. *See also* **spread, bid-offer; price, offer**.

cash price Price at which goods may be bought using cash. The price paid in cash is usually different from the **hire purchase** price in that the latter usually includes interest.

choice price On futures markets, refers to a situation which, when comparing different market-makers' bid-offer spreads, one finds identical bid and offer price. This price is known as the choice price. *See also* **backwardation**.

closing price Price of shares at the close of trading each day on a stock exchange.

exercise price Alternative term for striking price. *See* **price, striking**.

fine price Price of a security on a market in which the difference between the buying and selling prices is very fine.

firm price Guaranteed price, usually offered only if the cost of providing a good or service can be assessed accurately.

forward price Price quoted for goods not immediately available or not yet manufactured. The forward price is usually lower than the eventual retail price because it takes into account only the estimated costs of manufacture at some future date. More specifically, it is the price quoted in a **futures** deal.

grant price Price at which an employee is able to exercise an option on his or her company's stock.

hidden price increase Decline in the real value of a good or service occasioned by a decrease in its quality or quantity rather than by a rise in its price. *See* **value, real**.

intervention price Price slightly below the threshold price at which the European Commission intervenes to purchase agricultural surpluses, thus supporting home markets and helping to achieve the target or average price. *See* **price, target; price, threshold**.

middle-market price Price mid-way between the bid and offer prices on the open market. It is the price which the Inland Revenue takes into account when calculating capital gains tax on share dealings. *See* **price, bid; price, offer; Revenue, Inland; tax, capital gains**.

offer price Price at which a market maker is prepared to sell a security. *See also* **spread, bid-offer; price, bid**.

opening price Price of a share at the beginning of a day's business on a stock exchange. This may differ from the previous evening's closing price, generally because the price has been adjusted to take into account events that occurred overnight and the performance of other exchanges.

price control Method of controlling **inflation** or allocation of resources in a centrally-planned economy by pegging prices within specified limits. Market forces make it difficult to control prices in this way in the long term, and the method is normally used only for short-term crisis management.

prices and incomes policy Government policy for controlling wages and prices as a means of checking **inflation**. Five prices and incomes policies have been operated in the UK since World War II, all but one of them by Labour governments acting with the sometimes reluctant co-operation of the trade unions.

probate price In finance, a share price calculated for tax purposes by taking the lower of the bid and offer prices and adding to it one-quarter of the difference between the two. This process is known as quartering up.

recommended retail price (RRP) Price at which a manufacturer suggests his goods should retail. The RRP is often specified on the **packaging** to indicate to the customer that the retailer is not over-charging him and to allow a comparison to be made between the prices of competing brands. *See also* **retail**.

redemption price Price at which forms of indebtedness (*e.g.* bills of exchange or bonds) are redeemed by the institution or government that issued them.

retail price Price at which a good or service is actually sold through a retailer.

sell price Alternative term for cash price. *See* **price, cash**.

spot price Price quoted for goods available for immediate delivery, usually higher than the forward price because it takes into account all costs except delivery.

striking price Also known as the exercise price, the price at which an **option** for the purchase or sale of a security is exercised.

target price Average price for commodities fixed by the Common Agricultural Policy of the EEC and achieved by purchasing goods at the intervention price. *See* **price, intervention**.

threshold price Price fixed under the Common Agricultural Policy by the European Commmission, below which the price of agricultural imports from non-member states is not allowed to fall.

See also **pricing; ratio, price/earnings**.

pricing Method used to set a **price**, specifically by equating supply with demand.

average cost pricing Determination of a price in accordance with the average cost of producing a good. The manufacturer makes neither a profit nor a loss.

delivered pricing Practice of calculating a price of goods for sale that includes the cost of delivery.

double pricing Practice of displaying two prices on goods, usually to show the prospective customer that the price has been reduced.

primary First, initial. *See* **capital, primary; dealer, primary; distribution, primary**.

prime Of high quality. In finance, most often used to describe the debts incurred by a person or firm with a good credit rating.

prime entry In international trade, imported goods on which customs **duty** is levied as soon as they enter the country, and which are impounded until the duty is paid.

See also **books of prime entry; rate, prime**.

principal Person who gives instructions to an **agent**. In finance, the original sum invested or lent, as distinct from any profits or interest it may earn.

undisclosed principal Person represented in a business transaction by an agent or broker, and whose identity is therefore unknown to the person with whom the intermediary is conducting business.

private Person or institution independent of the government sector.

going private Removing a company from stock exchange listing, a process achieved by the company purchasing its own shares. Going private is usually the result of a decision by the principal shareholders that they require more direct control of the company. Its primary purpose is to reduce interference by outside investors and to render the company considerably less vulnerable to takeover bids.

privately held Capital, company or other possessions in the hands of a person or group of people.

See also **bank, private; company, private; enterprise, private; placing, private**.

privatization Practice of offering shares in previously national industries, for sale to the general public. During the 1980s Britain's Conservative government privatized several national industries including: British Aerospace, British Gas, and British Telecom.

probate Acceptance of the validity of a will by a proper authority. A will that has not been probated has no legal force. *See* **price, probate**.

produce As a noun, goods that are grown (agricultural produce); as a verb, to manufacture or grow goods. *See* **exchange, produce**.

product That which is produced, either in terms of goods, or in terms of income.

gross national product (GNP) Value of all goods and services produced by a nation over a specified time period, both within the country, and overseas. *See also* **product, gross domestic**.

gross domestic product (GDP) Value of goods and service produced within a nation. GDP does not take into account the value of goods and services generated overseas. Sometimes also known as gross value added. *See also* **product, gross national**.

net domestic product Value of gross domestic product after a figure for capital consumption has been subtracted. *See* **product, gross domestic**.

per capita gross national product Value of gross national product divided by the number of people in the nation's population.

production Broadly, practice of manufacturing goods for sale.

direct production System of production that does not use machinery or division of labour. In a true system of direct production, each person makes the things that he or she requires, rather than making them to sell for profit. *See also* **production, indirect**.

factor of production Collective term for those things necessary for production to take place. Factors of production are most usually divided into the following categories: capital, labour and land.

indirect production Production of goods for sale by employing labour and machinery and using a system of divided labour in order to make a profit. *See also* **production, direct**.

primary production Production of raw materials and foods. *See also* **production, secondary**.

roundabout production Alternative term for indirect production. *See* **production, indirect**.

secondary production Production of goods that have been manufactured, as opposed to raw materials or foodstuffs. *See also* **production, primary**.

productivity Output of any of the factors of production (land, labour and capital) per unit of input. Productivity may be enhanced by the improvement of any one of the three factors, most usually by the introduction of new technology or an incentive schemes. Productivity of land is generally measured in output per acre or hectare, that of labour in output per working hour, and that of capital as a percentage per annum.

productivity bargaining Bargaining process that results in a **productivity deal**.

productivity bonus Alternative term for incentive bonus. *See* **bonus, incentive**.

productivity deal Agreemement between management and labour, designed to enhance productivity, generally in return for bonuses in the form of increased wages or profit-sharing, or in return for changed working practices.

professional Originally, a member of one of the professions (*e.g.* medicine, law, accountancy). Increasingly the term used to describe someone paid to do a job or perform a duty, particularly one requiring special skills or long training, or merely someone who takes his or her job seriously. *See also* **indemnity, professional**.

profit Surplus money, after all expenses have been met, generated by a firm or enterprise in the course of one accounting period.

after-tax profit Profit calculated after all tax deductions have been made.

capital profit Profit generated by selling capital goods (fixed assets), rather than by trading. *See* **asset, fixed**.

economic profit Profit as calculated in **accounting** as the difference between **income** and **cost**. In economics, however, economic profit also takes into account opportunity cost. *See* **cost, opportunity**.

operating profit Earnings from normal business transactions. Operating profits do not include interest on loans or return on other investments.

pre-tax profit Profit calculated before allowance has been made for tax.

profit-sharing Distribution of some or all of a firm's profits to its employees as a **bonus**. The distribution may be in the form of cash or shares.

profit-taking Selling stock and taking the profit on the transaction, instead of waiting for a better price. Profit-taking occurs when dealers believe that the market will not improve much more.

retained profit Profit remaining to a firm after the distribution of dividends and profit-sharing bonuses. Retained profit is generally used for the long-term expansion of the business, and is sometimes referred to as undistributed profit.

undistributed profit Alternative term for retained profit. *See* **profit, retained**.

windfall profit Unexpected profit, usually sizeable, such as that caused by a rise in stock prices or by an inheritance.

See also **account, profit and loss; margin, profit; tax, profit**.

projection Estimate of future developments made on the basis of, or projected from, a knowledge of past and present events.

promoter Entrepreneur, especially a person involved in the organization or launch of a business.

property Legally, property is divided into real and personal property. Real property may be defined as land and buildings held freehold. Personal property consists of other personal possessions. More specifically, property is sometimes defined as something appreciating in value or yielding income.

pro rata Latin for in proportion to. *See also* **pari passu**.

prospectus Document that describes a proposal, *e.g.* issued to prospective shareholders by a company intending to make a public issue of shares, giving details of past and current performance and of prospects. *See also* **red herring**.

protected bear = bear, covered

protectionism Policy based on self-interest, *e.g.* one that shields an industry from overseas competition, usually by the imposition of selective or general **quotas** and tariffs. *See also* **barrier, tariff; dumping**.

provision Allowance for some eventuality. In accounting it is a sum written off to provide for depreciation of **assets**.

fair-price provisions Price controls, generally instituted by a government, that guarantee fair prices to the consumer by ensuring that the manufacturer and retailer make reasonable rather than excessive profits.

loan-loss provisions Reserves held by a bank or other lending institution against loans that are not repaid by the borrower.

See also **porcupine provisions**.

proxy Authorization given by a voter to another person to allow that person to vote on his or her behalf, *e.g.* a shareholder may give someone proxy to vote at a company meeting which he or she is for some reason unable to attend.

prudence concept In accounting, the prudence concept calls for the exclusion on the **balance sheet** of all monies or goods owed but not yet received, and the inclusion of all liabilities, whether or not they must be met immediately. It therefore postulates a **worst-moment** scenario. *See also* **accounting principles**.

PSBR Abbreviation of public sector borrowing requirement.

PSL1 Abbreviation of private sector liquidity 1, an obsolete measure of the **money supply**. It is equal to the private sector's holding of **£M3**, money-market instruments, and certificates of tax deposit.

PSL2 Abbreviation of private sector liquidity 2, an obsolete measure of the **money supply**. It is equal to the private sector's holding of **£M3**, money-market instruments, and certificates of tax deposit excluding the holdings of building societies.

psychographics Division of demographic groups for marketing purposes into categories related to psychology. *E.g.* lifestyle, usage-rate, sensitivity to quality or price, etc.

public That which is in the hands of the people and, as such, managed or controlled by the government; or that which is open to anyone.

going public To offer shares to financial institutions and the general public, and thereby receive a listing on the stock exchange. *See also* **company, public; sector, public; trustee, public**.

pull Colloquial for to withdraw, *e.g.* to cancel a deal just as it reaches the final stages of negotiation.

pullback After a period when market prices have been fluctuating erratically, the pullback is the movement of return to more recognizable and predictable trends.

purchase To buy something, or the thing that has been bought.
"After considering the high price of the goods, Anthony decided not to purchase them after all."
"At the end of a long day spent shopping, David came home laden down with the weight of his purchases."

cash purchase Purchase that has been made in cash. *See also* **hire purchase**.

central purchasing Practice of making all purchases required by a company through one department.

closing purchase Purchase of an option that closes an open **position**.

forward purchase Buying of **securities** or **commodities** made in **advance** of delivery. *See* **futures**.

put = option, put

put band Period for which a put option is valid. *See* **option, put**.

put-through Stock exchange dealing procedure used in cases of very large orders, whereby a stockbroker finds both a seller and a buyer and is therefore able to 'put the shares through' the market in a single quick transaction.

pyramid selling Practice of selling distributorships, or the right to sell distributorships. The pyramid seller makes his or her profit from the sale of **franchises** and leaves the franchisee to dispose of goods. In a typical system, each franchisee must guarantee to purchase a certain quantity of goods, which he or she then disposes of by recruiting sub-distributors. Those at the bottom of the pyramid generally sell to family and friends.

Q

quality control On a production line, the process of checking the standard of a product (or sample of it).

quango Acronym for quasi-autonomous non-governmental organization, which in the UK covers many semi-permanent public bodies set up to investigate certain cases or to deal with special problems. Examples of quangos are the Advisory Conciliation and Arbitration Service (ACAS) and the National Economic Development Council (NEDC).

quantity Amount of something, or numbers of an item. *See* **discount, quantity; rebate, quantity; surveyor, quantity**.

quantum meruit If a supplier only half-completes the work he has been contracted to do, he may in some cases claim payment in proportion to the work he has done, known as payment quantum meruit (as much as he has earned).

quarter day Four days that are generally taken to mark the quarters of the year. Traditionally these are days upon which payments such as rent are made. In England and Wales, the quarter days are Lady Day (25 March), Midsummer Day (24 June), Michaelmas (29 September) and Christmas Day (25 December).

quartering up = price, probate

quasi-autonomous non-governmental organization = quango

queue (queuing) theory Mathematical theory that can be used to analyse the problems involved in the physical provision of services, taking into account the arrival of customers, the time they have to wait to be served, how they queue, how long the service takes to be rendered and the length of time a service unit remains idle. It is especially useful in the design of such establishments as airports, banks, etc.

quid pro quo Literally, this for that. The principle of quid pro quo underlies all contracts in that a contract is an agreement to exchange something such as services for something else, such as cash.

quintal *US* Term used in the US and sometimes in the north of England for 100lb **avoirdupois**.

quorum Minimum number of people who have to be present at a meeting for it to go ahead and the decisions made by it to be valid. In the UK, the quorum for a member's meeting is noted in a company's **articles of association**.

quota Amount of something (*e.g.* goods) allowed to one person, or company, normally fixed by a body in authority.

import quota Amount of a certain type of goods that is allowed to be imported, fixed by the government.

quotation (quote) Term with two meanings.
First, it is an estimate of how much something will cost.
"I have asked our suppliers to quote on the job in hand."
Second, it refers to the **official list** of the stock exchange. Appearance of a company's shares on this list is known as a quotation.

quotation spread US The difference between the **offer price** and the **bid price** on a security. Also known as the bid-offer spread.

quoted company Company whose shares are listed on a stock exchange, with the implication that its shares may be dealt on that exchange.

quoted investment In accounting, an investment in shares or debentures that are quoted on an official exchange.

quoted price Price of a security as it is quoted on an exchange. The quoted price may fluctuate from day to day, or minute to minute.

quote driven Stock market that reacts (in terms of prices) to the quotations of market makers rather than to the number and flow of incoming orders. *See also* **order driven**.

quote machine US Computer that allows a broker access to up-to-the-minute information on quoted prices.

QWL *US* Abbreviation of quality of work-life. Concept that is at the basis of pushes towards improving working conditions.

R

R & D Abbreviation of **research and development**.

raid To buy significant numbers of a company's shares sometimes as a prelude to a takeover bid.

dawn raid Buying of a significant number of a target company's shares at the start of the day's trading, or before the market becomes aware of what is happening, often at a price higher than normal. The purpose of a dawn raid is to give the buyer a strategic stake in the **target** company, from which the buyer may launch a **takeover** bid.

raider Person or group initiating a hostile **takeover** by buying quantities of the **target** company's shares.

rally Rise in market prices after a period when prices have stagnated or consistently fallen. *See also* **reaction**.

random walk theory Theory of stock movements developed in the 1950s and 1960s, which states that share prices move in a random way, and so their movements up or down cannot be predicted. Later this theory was developed into the Efficient Market Hypothesis. *See* **EMH; growth, higgledy-piggledy**.

rate Amount of money charged or paid, calculated according to a certain rule or ratio.

bank rate Official rate of interest charged by the central banks as **lender of the last resort**. The term has fallen out of use in the UK, to be replaced by **minimum lending rate**. *See* **MLR**.

base rate Minimum amount of interest a bank charges on a loan. The base rate is normally augmented in actual circumstances, according to current market pressures and the risk involved in the loan.

bill rate Rate at which a **bill of exchange** is discounted. *See* **discounting**.

blanket rate Fixed charge that covers a series of transactions or services, and unchanging.

burn rate When a new company begins trading on venture capital, the burn rate is the rate at which the company consumes capital in financing fixed overheads. *See* **capital, venture; overheads, fixed**.

cross rate Rate at which one currency may be exchanged for a second, expressed in terms of a third currency.

discount rate Term with two meanings.
First, in the UK it is the rate at which a **bill of exchange** is discounted. *See* **discounting**.
Second, in the USA it is an alternative term for minimum lending rate. *See* **rate, minimum lending**.

fixed rate Charge that does not change.

London inter-bank offered rate (LIBOR) Rate of interest that commercial banks offer to loan money for on the London inter-bank market. Along with the minimum lending rate, LIBOR has a significant effect on bank interest rates. *See* **rate, minimum lending**.

minimum lending rate (MLR) Minimum rate at which the Bank of England, acting in its capacity of **lender of the last resort** is willing to discount **bills of exchange** and at which it offers short-term loans. The MLR has a direct effect on bank interest rates.

piece rate Payment to a worker based on his or her level of output. *See also* **rate, time**.

prime rate US Preferential interest rate charged for short-term loans made to people or organizations with a high credit rating. Approximately equivalent to the minimum lending rate in the UK. *See* **rate, minimum lending**.

rate of exchange (*exchange rate*) Rate at which the various currencies are exchanged for each other.

rate of interest (*interest rate*) Amount charged for loan services, normally expressed as a percentage of the loan.

rate of return Amount of money made on an investment (in the form of interest or a dividend), normally expressed as a percentage of the amount invested.

red-circle rate US Rate of pay that is higher than usual for the job undertaken.

time rate Payment for work done based on the amount of time the job takes. *See also* **rate, piece**.

rates In the UK, a local government tax levied on householders and occupiers of commercial premises to pay for local works, expressed as a certain amount in the pound of the rateable value. *See* **value, rateable**.

rate support grant Payment made by the UK government to local authorities to support council services that are neither self-financing nor receive any other form of **grant**.

ratification Official approval, giving something (*e.g.* a document) validity.
"After the proposal had been finalized, we had to put it before the Board of Directors for ratification."

rating Grade assigned to *e.g.* bonds or preferred stocks by an official agency such as Standard & Poor's or Moody's, in order to guide investors. *See also* **beta; triple A rating**.

credit rating Rating assigned to a person or company in order to indicate creditworthiness.

ratio Way of comparing quantities using proportions.
"The ratio of men of marriageable age to women of marriageable age will shortly become two to one."

accounting ratio One of several ratios that are considered important in assessing the financial viability of a project or company.

acid-test ratio Ratio of a company's assets (not including stock) to its current liabilities.

assets-to-equity ratio Value of assets owned by a company compared to the value of investment.

capital/labour ratio Proportion of capital to labour used in an economy.

cash ratio Amount of reserves that a bank considers it necessary to maintain, calculated with reference to the bank's turnover.

current assets ratio Slightly different to the acid-test ratio, the current assets ratio is the ratio of a company's assets, including its stock-in-trade, to its current liabilities.

debt-to-equity ratio A company may finance itself through borrowing or through shareholder investment, depending on current interest rates. The proportions of each is known as the debt-to-equity ratio, or **gearing**.

liquid assets ratio Ratio of the value of total assets held to the value of assets that may be converted into cash without loss.

net profit ratio Ratio of net **profit** to sales.

price/earnings ratio (P/E ratio) Market price of the shares of a company compared to the dividends those shares produce.

reaction Fall in market prices after a period of continuous price rises. *See also* **rally**.

real Actual or true. *See* **accounts, real; value, real**.

realize To put a plan into action or sell assets for cash. The act of doing so is realization.
"He had to realize his assets in order to pay his creditors."
  See also **account, realization**.

rebate Sum of money returned to a payee because he or she has paid too much, or a discount on the price of something.
"At the end of the year you will receive a tax rebate."

quantity rebate Reduction in the price per unit of a product in return for bulk buying.

receipt Note stating that money has been paid or that goods have been received, such as a wharfinger receipt. *See* **warrant**.
"If you leave your watch with the jeweller to be repaired, make sure you get a receipt."

receipts Payments received.

receivership A receiver is an official into whose hands a company with financial difficulties is placed, to ensure that, as far as possible, the creditors are paid. Thus, receivership is the company's state when a receiver is called in.

"After several attempts at solving their financial problems, the company went into receivership."

interim receiver Person appointed by a court to act as receiver, until a receiver proper is appointed.

receiving order Court order placing a company into the hands of a receiver.

recession Stage in a trade cycle during which the decline in economic activity accelerates, causing investment values to fall, companies to have to deal with adverse trading conditions, unemployment to rise and so income and expenditure to fall. A recession may end in a **depression** unless there is a **recovery**.

recognizance Contract between a court and a person by which the person is bound to perform a certain act, such as to appear in court on a certain date, to be of good behaviour so as not to cause a breach of the peace, or to stand bail for someone else.

recommendation Normally refers to financial advice, *e.g.* the recommendation of a market analyst to a broker or of a stockbroker to a client.

buy recommendation Recommendation to buy.

"Two market analysts today changed their recommendations on A & G shares from attractive to outright buy."

reconciliation Act of making two accounts, statements or people agree.

bank reconciliation At any time a bank statement is unlikely to agree with the balance in a firm's cash book, because cheques received or paid may not have been banked. A reconciliation is thus prepared to prove that a true record is being kept by the company. This is done by taking the balance in the cash book, and taking into account transactions not detailed on the statement. At the end of the exercise, the two balances should be the same.

reconciliation statement Report that explains why two accounts do not agree.

distributable reserves Reserves that a company is planning to distribute (usually as **dividends**) among its shareholders.

recovery Upturn in the economy, the financial position of a company or in share prices. *See also* **boom; depression; recession; share, recovery**.

rectification of register If a court believes that an official list (*e.g.* a company's list of its shareholders) is incorrect it may make an order, known as a rectification of register, to have the list amended.

red To be in the red is to be in **debt**.
"At the end of last quarter, the company went into the red."

redemption Repayment of an outstanding loan or debenture stock by the borrower. *See* **date, redemption; fee, redemption; price, redemption**.

red herring *US* On Wall Street, an initial prospectus for a share issue, circulated before the price has been fixed and the issue has been ratified by the appropriate regulatory authority.

red ink *US* Appearing on a balance sheet, red ink shows that a company is making a loss, has debts or has greater liabilities than assets.

red-lining *US* Practice among lenders, illegal in some states, whereby declining neighbourhoods and Third World countries are blacklisted for mortgages and loans.

re-export To import goods from one country and to then export them to another.

refinancing Taking out a loan to pay back other borrowing. Also known in the United States as refunding.

reflation Government action that attempts to boost a country's economy. This is done by increasing the money supply, usually by reducing interest rates and taxation. *See also* **deflation; inflation**.

refunding = refinancing

register Official list, normally of names.

Lloyd's register List showing details of all the registered merchant ships in the world.

plant register Register that details the **plant** owned by company. Record is kept of purchase cost, running costs, current worth and annual **depreciation**.

register of charges List of charges payable by a company on its property, such as mortgages. A copy of this list must be filed by all UK companies at Companies House in London.

register of companies List of UK companies kept at Companies House in London, detailing registered addresses and the names of directors.

register of debentures List drawn up by a company of those people who hold debentures. *See* **debenture**.

registered office Address of a company as listed on the register of companies at Companies House. This need not be the actual working address of the company.

share register Register of shareholders that is held by a company, giving names, addresses, and details of shareholding, etc.

reinsurance Practice of dividing an insurance transaction between two companies or more to spread the risk involved. Each company receives a part of the **premium**.

relative strength Usually expressed as a **ratio**, the relative strength of a share, commodity or anything else traded on the markets or elsewhere, is the performance of the particular investment compared to the performance of its market **index**. *See also* **beta**.

relief Help; normally refers to allowances made to certain taxpayers for various reasons.

marginal relief Tax relief granted to a taxpayer whose **income** only marginally exceeds a specified level or tax **bracket**. He or she receives a portion of the relief available to those in the lower bracket.

rendu Form of contract by which an exporter pays to have goods delivered to a buyer's warehouse. Also known as a franco or a free contract. *See also* **FAS; FOB; CIF**.

rent Money paid for the occupation or use of something for a period of time (*e.g.* a building, office, factory, car or television set).

ground rent Payment made, normally annually, by the occupier of a building to the owner of the land on which the building stands (the freeholder). Ground rent is paid only if the building is occupied **leasehold**.

notional rent **Peppercorn** or minimal rent paid to establish a landlord-tenant relationship.

peppercorn rent Very small ground rent on a property, that normally only serves to establish the fact that the property is leasehold and not **freehold**. *See* **rent, ground**.

rack rent Extremely high rent, which probably stretches a tenant to his or her financial limits.

rent roll List of rents payable to a particular estate.

rent back To sell one's property (offices, factory space, etc) on the understanding that the new owner will lease back the property to its original owner. It is a good way to raise capital by realizing property assets without having to vacate the premises.

renunciation Act of giving up ownership of shares.

repatriation Act of transferring capital from overseas to the home market.

replevin In a case of **distraint**, the return of goods to their owner while the court is deciding whether the distraint was lawful.

repo *US* Abbreviation of reposession, or of repurchase agreement, a transaction between a **bond** dealer and a bank. The dealer sells government **securities** while at the same time agreeing to buy them back at a specified time at a price high enough to allow the bank a profit margin. In this way, the repo may be looked upon as a form of loan.

reverse repo Similar transaction to a **repo** whereby the dealer buys the bonds instead of selling them, so that in essence they are acting as **security** on the loan.

report Verbal account or document that describes and explains a state of affairs or an incident that has taken place.

annual report Document required by law to be released annually by public companies, describing the company's activities during the previous year. It usually also includes the company's balance sheet for the year.

interim report Short statement published at the end of the first half of a public company's financial year, detailing results for the previous six months and declaring any interim dividend. *See also* **dividend, interim**.

repudiation Act of informing the other party in a **contract** that one does not intend to honour the contract. Repudiation may also refer to the repayment of a debt, or to the termination of any form of agreement.

repurchase Situation that occurs when an issuer buys its own securities. It is most frequent in **unit trust** holdings.

reputed owner = ownership

resale price maintenance Practice whereby a supplier refuses to sell goods to a retailer unless the retailer agrees to sell them at a certain price, or above a minimum price. Resale price maintenance may be applied to prevent retailers from using the product as a **loss leader**. Resale price maintenance is allowable under the Resale Prices Act (1976) if the supplier can prove that it is in the interests of the consumer, as in the case of books and some pharmaceuticals.

research and development (R & D) Activity that aims to discover or invent new products or services. It covers pure scientific and technical research, applied research, product improvement and technological innovation.

reserves That part of a company's profits that are put aside for a particular purpose.

capital reserves Profits from a company's trading that represent part of the company's capital and so may not be repaid to shareholders until the company is wound up.

general reserves Sometimes also known as revenue reserves, profits not distributed to the company's shareholders.

hidden reserves Reserves not declared on a company's balance sheet.

official reserves Gold and currency reserves kept by the government. *See* **gold and foreign exchange reserves**.

reserve for bad debts Money put aside against the possibility of unpaid debts.

reserve for obsolescence Money put aside to cushion a company against the possibility of its fixed assets becoming obsolescent or uneconomic. *See* **asset, fixed**.

secret reserves Alternative term for hidden reserves. *See* **reserves, hidden**.

See also **currency, reserve**.

resolution When a motion put before a meeting has been agreed upon, it becomes a resolution.

special resolution **Resolution** to change the articles of association of a company which usually must be passed with a three-quarters majority. *See* **association, articles of**.

resting order = good-till-cancelled

restitution Either the giving back of something to someone or a compensatory payment.
"The court ordered the restitution of the property to its owner."
"The court ordered the vandal to make restitution for the damage he caused to the building."

export restitution **EEC** term for subsidies paid to member food exporters.

restrictive Something that sets limits on something else.

restrictive (trade) *practice* Agreement made between companies, that aims to makes restrictions regarding the supply of their goods, on such things as price, quantities, processes, geographical area, etc. On the whole, restrictive practices are assumed by the law to be against the public interest.

See also **covenant, restricted; endorsement, restrictive**.

retail Sale of goods or services to the general public. *See* **banking, retail; index, retail price; price, retail**.

retention Holding back money to be used for a particular purpose.

retention money A buyer may hold back some of the payment due on completion of a contract, for a certain period of time, to allow him or her to check for possible defects in the work. This sum of money is known as retention money.

retentions Shortened form of either retained earnings or retained profits. *See* **earnings, retained; profits, retained**.

retiral *US* Retirement.

retirement Act of ceasing to work at an occupation.

retire a bill To withdraw a **bill** from circulation by having the acceptor pay it, either on or before the due date.

return The comeback: profits and income from transactions or investments. It may also be a document (usually describing a financial situation) sent to an authority.

annual return Document that in the UK must be submitted to Companies House every year by every company with share capital, detailing such items as the address of the registered office, a list of current members, charges on the company, etc.

tax return Document submitted to the **Inland Revenue** annually, stating an individual's earnings and expenses for the year and used to calculate that person's tax liabilities. *See* **revenue, inland**.

See also **rate of return**.

revaluation Practice whereby a company puts a new value on its fixed assets, because nominal and real values of such assets as property and machines have changed. *See* **assets, fixed; value, nominal; value, real**.

revenue Money received from any transaction or sale, or money received by the government in the form of taxation.

average revenue Total amount of money received divided by the number of units of a product sold.

Inland Revenue UK government department whose major responsibility is the collection of various taxes, such as income tax, capital gains tax and corporation tax. *See* **tax**.

Internal Revenue Service (IRS) *US* Equivalent to the Inland Revenue in the UK.

revenue account Accounts of a business that state the amount of money received from sales, commission etc.

reversal Change in a company's fortunes (from being profitable to being unprofitable, or vice versa).

reverse Either upside-down or back-to-front. *See* **repo, reverse; takeover, reverse; yield gap, reverse**.

reversion Return of property, goods or rights to their original owner. "The reversion of the property to the freeholder is imminent."

reversionary bonus Holders of a with-profits assurance policy may receive a reversionary bonus from time to time, depending upon the performance of the company in the previous year and the size of the sum assured.

revolver *US* = **credit, revolving**

RIE Abbreviation of recognised investment exchange, a market for securities recognized by the UK Securities and Exchange Commission. *See* **securities; SEC**.

rigging the market Action that influences a market, by overriding market forces. *E.g.*, it may be done by one dealer buying a substantial number of shares or a significant quantity of a commodity, thus pushing the market price up.

right of resale A seller may, in certain circumstances, reclaim goods from a buyer and resell them, *e.g.* if a stoppage in transitu or a **lien** occurs and the goods are likely to perish as a consequence. In this case, the seller may sell to another buyer and give a lawful title to the goods.

rim country *US* One of the newly-industrializing countries in the eastern Pacific, *e.g.* Singapore and Malaysia, at present concentrating on assembly-based industries.

ring In general, a group of people who get together in order to illegally rig the market, *e.g.* by acting in concert to push prices up or down. *See also* **bidding ring; concert party; rigging the market**.

A ring is also a method of trading on the London **futures** market or metals exchange.

risk Amount one potentially stands to lose by a transaction.

market risk Part of the total risk inherent in buying a stock, which depends on market movements as a whole rather than on the particular characteristics of the stock itself. *E.g.* during a market **crash**, the share prices of many sound companies whose earning prospects remain unchanged, may fall in line with less sound stock. This illustrates the market risk, rather than the specific risk inherent in stock market dealing.

See also **arbitrage, risk; capital, risk**.

rollover *US* Movement of an investment from one institution to the owner of another institution.

roll-over relief Capital gains tax on the sale of a company's fixed assets may be relieved if the company is buying other assets in order to replace the first ones. *See also* **taxation, deferred**.

rotation of directors Process whereby at each annual general meeting of a public company, a certain proportion of the directors retire (normally one third), although they may then be re-elected to the board. This enables shareholders to change a director without having to dismiss him or her. *See* **AGM**.

round lot *US* Number of shares or bonds traded at the same time, as a lot. The **commission** charged on a round lot is usually slightly less than on an **odd lot**.

round trip On the futures market, the practice of buying and then selling the same investment or *vice versa*.

round turn An entire **futures** transaction from start to finish.

roup Term used in Scotland for a mean **auction**.

Royal Mint UK government department with the sole responsibility for the minting of coins, under the direction of the Chancellor of the Exchequer. The US equivalent is the Bureau of the Mint.

royalty Sum paid to an inventor, originator or author, or owner of something from which a product may be made (such as an oilfield), and calculated as a proportion of the income received from the sale of the product.
"She is still receiving royalties on a song she wrote ten years ago."

RPI Abbreviation of retail price index. *See* **index, retail price**.

Rule 535 Stock Exchange rule concerned with permitted dealings. Clause (i) lists the items that can be dealt. Clause (ii) permits dealings in shares not listed, but with certain restrictions. Clauses (iii) and (iv) apply to overseas companies and exploration companies respectively.

rummage Preventative search of a ship for contraband by Customs officers, often undertaken without warning.

running yield = **yield, flat**

running the books *US* The job of a **lead manager**, at the head of a **syndicate**.

rustbelt *US* Also known as the rustbowl, the area in the midwest and northeast regions of the United States where there is a high proportion of declining industries, such as iron- and steel-making.

rustbowl *US* Alternative term for **rustbelt**.

S

SA Abbreviation of **société anonyme**.

safe custody Service sometimes provided by banks, by which customers deposit valuables in safe deposit boxes in the bank's care.

salary Money paid to an employee, normally expressed as so much per year, but *usually* paid by cheque or directly into the employee's bank account on a monthly basis. *See also* **wage**.

sale Formally, the act of transferring goods (or services) from one person to another, accompanied by the exchange of money.

closing sale On an **options** market, transaction in which an option is sold in order to close a **position**.

closing the sale Persuading a customer or client to commit to a purchase.

opening sale Sale of an **option** contract where the seller becomes in effect the writer of the option by assuming responsibility for its performance.

sale and lease-back (**leaseback**) Sale of a property where the buyer agrees to lease the property back to its original owner. In this way, the seller is able to turn the property into liquid capital while at the same time remaining *in situ*.

sale or return Agreement whereby a distributor or retailer takes goods from a manufacturer or wholesaler on the understanding that he or she may return them if they are not sold within a specified period of time.

sales Colloquial name for a department within a company that deals with the sale of its goods or services.
 An alternative meaning makes sales an abbreviation of sales revenue, synonymous with **turnover**, as represented on a company's profit and loss account (especially in the USA). *See* **account, profit and loss**.

domestic sales Goods sold within the country of origin, as opposed to foreign sales, which are goods sold as **export**.

See also **audit, sales; journal, sales**.

sample Product or part of a product that is sent to a prospective buyer so that he or she may decide whether or not to buy.

check sample Sample taken from a consignment of goods and examined to determine whether or not the consignment is acceptable.

sandbag Defensive tactics for a **takeover** situation, by which the **target company** agrees to negotiate a takeover, but lengthens talks in the hope that a **white knight** may ride by in the meantime.

sans recours = without recourse

saturation Situation in which something is completely full.

capital saturation Situation in a company or industry, in which there is such a proportion of capital to labour, that any increase in capital would have no significant positive effect on output.

market saturation Situation in which a **market** has as much of a product as it can sell.

save as you earn (SAYE) UK government savings system, whereby a proportion of a person's income is deducted at source and transferred to a National Savings account. *See* **savings, National**.

savings Money put aside by individuals, often in a way that pays **interest**.
"Andrew used his savings to buy a motor boat."

National Savings UK government savings scheme, operated by the Post Office, into which savers may deposit money and invest in government savings certificates etc.

savings and loan US US equivalent of a UK **building society**. Also known as a **building and loan association**.

See also **bank, savings**.

SAYE Abbreviation of **save as you earn**.

scab Informal term for a person who continues to work during a strike. Scab is also used for people brought in by management to continue the business of the company while its regular workers are on strike.

science park Area, usually located near a university, that is set aside for industries with a technological or research base.

scorched earth Defensive tactics for a hostile **takeover** situation in which the **target** company sells its most attractive assets, or initiates adverse publicity about itself in an effort to make it seem a less than desirable acquisition.

SCOUT Acronym for shared currency option under tender. In situations where a foreign currency contract is under tender from several companies, SCOUT allows them to share a single **hedge** in the form of a currency **option**.

screw you money *US* Informal phrase for investments made by an entrepreneur as a cushion against the possibility of his or her main business failing. Also, money that enables an employee to leave his or her job without serious financial problems.

scrip issue Practice of issuing extra shares to existing shareholders free of charge. This is done by transferring reserves into the company's share account. In this way, the company increases its capitalization while at the same time reducing its share price and increasing the number of shares on the market. Also known as a bonus issue, a capitalization issue or a free issue.

SDR Abbreviation of **Special Drawing Rights**.

SEAF Acronym for **Stock Exchange Automatic Exchange Facility**.

seasonal variations Statistical variations that occur during a particular season. These variations are often taken into account when calculating *e.g.* unemployment figures and trends. In these cases the figures are said to be adjusted.

SEAQ Acronym for **Stock Exchange Automated Quotations**.

SEC *US* Abbreviation of Securities and Exchange Commission, the New York-based financial watchdog and rulemaker for the New York Stock Exchange, set up in 1934.

second via Second (duplicate) document in a bill of exchange in a set, that is sent by a different route to avoid loss. *See* **bills in a set**.

secretary In broad terms, somebody who prepares correspondence, keeps files and records and arranges appointments.

company secretary Someone who is responsible for ensuring that his or her company complies with company law.

honorary secretary Someone who takes on the running of a society or charity in the same way as a company secretary but without payment. *See* **secretary, company**.

sector Economic term for a part of the national economy or business activity.

private sector That part of the business activity of a country that is financed and controlled by individuals or private companies (*e.g.* shareholders or investment institutions). *See also* **privatization**.

public sector That part of the business activity of a country that is financed and controlled by government. Public sector industries, *e.g.* British Rail, are often known as nationalized industries.

securities = security

security Term with two meanings.

First, it is anything (usually property) pledged as **collateral** against a loan, or the document that sets out the terms of such collateral.

Second, it is any financial **instrument** that is traded on a stock exchange and that yields an income. Securities represent a loan that will be repaid at some time in the future. In this sense the word is most often used in the plural, and securities include **bills of exchange, bonds,** convertible **assurance** policies, **debentures, gilt-edged securities, options, shares** and **stocks**.

bearer securities Securities that are payable to the bearer and thus easily transferable.

fixed-interest securities Securities where the income is fixed and does not vary. Fixed-interest securities include **bonds, debentures and gilt-edged securities**.

government securities Alternative term for **gilt-edged securities**.

negotiable security Security that is easily passed from one owner to another by delivery. In the UK, very few instruments are negotiable in this way.

non-marketable securities That part of a national debt not traded on the stock market. Non-marketable securities include National Savings Certificates, Premium Savings Bonds, certificates of deposit, official funds in perpetual or terminable annuities, and the whole of the external national debt. About one-third of the total national debt is currently in the form of non-marketable securities. *See* **annuity; bond, Premium Savings; debt, national; deposit, certificate of; savings, National**.

securities swill US Informal term for securities that are worth virtually nothing.

short-dated securities Fixed-interest securities that have a redemption date of less than five years. *See* **securities, fixed-interest**.

underlying security Security that is the subject of an **options contract.**

unlisted securities Those securities not listed on the stock exchange. *See* **market, unlisted securities**.

unquoted securities Alternative term for unlisted securities. *See* **securities, unlisted**.

See also **gilt-edged securities**.

SEDOL Acronym for **Stock Exchange Daily Official List**. *See* **Official List**.

Securities and Investment Board (SIB) UK financial watchdog, set up in 1986 by the DTI to oversee the UK's deregulated financial markets. The US equivalent is the Securities and Exchange Commission (**SEC**). *See also* **deregulation; Big Bang**.

self-employment Working for oneself rather than for someone else or a company.

self-liquidating = **liquidation**

self-regulatory organization (SRO) In the UK a non-governmental organization that governs a particular area of business activity, laying down codes of practice and protecting consumers and investors.

sell Act of providing goods or services in exchange for money.

sell at best Instruction to a broker to sell shares or commodities at the best price possible. *I.e.*, if the broker is selling, he or she must find the highest selling price. If the broker is buying, he or she must find the lowest price.

selling out If a person who has agreed to buy shares cannot close the deal, the seller is entitled to sell the shares for the best price possible and then charge the person who made the original tender the difference between the selling price and the original tender price, and any costs.

selling short Practice of making a bargain to sell securities or commodities the seller does not own. The seller does this in the hope that before settlement is due, the price of the item will go down and he or she will be able to buy enough to cover the bargain at a lower price, thereby making a profit. The practice is also known as shorting or short selling. *See also* **bear; short**.

sell-side US Those people who are on the market to sell, rather than to buy.

See also **cost, selling; price, sell**.

seller Person who exchanges goods or services for money.

sellers over Market in which there are more sellers than buyers.

See also **market, seller's; option, seller's**.

SEPON Acronym for stock exchange pool nominees, a company that acts as a central pool for shares while they are being transferred from buyer to seller. Sold stock is deposited into SEPON and buy orders are fulfilled from it, through the **TALISMAN** system.

sequestration Act of seizure of property or other assets by the courts until a dispute has been settled.

SERPS Acronym for state earnings related pension.

service Something provided, usually for a fee, that may not be classed as manufacturing or production in any form (such as legal advice, brokerage, agency services, etc.).

service a debt To pay the interest on a **debt**.

See also **after-sales service; economy, service; industry, service; unpaid services**.

Servicetill Popular term for an automatic telling machine. *See* **ATM**.

set of bills Alternative term for **bills in a set**.

set-off In accounting, two parties that have indebtedness of the same standing to each other may set off both debts against each other by assuming that one debt has paid off the other and *vice versa*. This is known as a set-off.

settlement Act of paying in full for goods or services received. *See* **date, settlement; discount, settlement**.

sever To terminate a contract, especially a contract of employment. *See* **pay, severance**.

shakeout *US* When a market cannot support the number of suppliers it has attracted, many of the less profitable suppliers leave the market, with only the more healthy operators remaining. This process of 'natural selection' is known as a shakeout.

A shakeout may also be the reorganization of a company, *e.g.* after a **takeover**, when employee numbers are reduced and operations are streamlined.

shareholder Person who holds **shares** in a company.

dissident shareholder *US* One of a group of shareholders that have expressed their discontent with present management performance, and are determined to replace current managers.

minority shareholder Person who holds a minority interest in a company. *See* **interest, minority**.

nominee shareholder Usually an institution that acquires shares in a company on behalf of somebody else (the beneficial owner). This enables the true shareholder's identity to be concealed and is often used when a person wishes to build up his or her shareholding prior to a takeover bid.

shareholder democracy Either the notion that each shareholder is entitled to a vote, or the principle that as many people as possible hold shares in public companies and thus have a say in their management.

shareholder derivative suit US Legal action taken against the directors of a company for mismanagement or breaches of responsibility, by a shareholder or group of shareholders.

shareholder relations US Department within a company, rather like customer relations, that concentrates on keeping shareholders up-to-date with company performance etc.

shares Form of security that represents the shareholder's stake in a business. Income on shares is in the form of a dividend rather than interest and is declared depending on the company's performance over the year. In the USA, shares are known as common stock.

A-shares Shares with rights different from those legally attached to **ordinary shares**. There are also B-shares, C-shares, etc. The term is frequently used to describe non-voting shares. *See* **share, non-voting**.

deferred ordinary shares Category of shares, usually issued to a company's founders, entitling them to special dividend rights.

founder's shares Alternative term for deferred ordinary shares. *See* **shares, deferred ordinary**.

fully-paid shares Shares that have been fully paid for by the shareholder. A company may not **call** upon holders of such shares to make any further contribution to share capital. Most shares are traded in this fully-paid form. The major exception is that of large new issues, in which trading sometimes begins while they are still partly-paid. *See* **capital, share; shares, partly-paid**.

gold (golden) share Single share in a company that has special voting rights such that it can outvote all other shares in certain circumstances.

heavy shares Shares that command a relatively high price on the stock market.

non-voting shares Shares that carry no voting rights. Non-voting shares are issued to raise additional capital for the company, while permitting existing shareholders to retain control of the company. Such shares are often known as A-shares and generally rank *pari passu* with voting shares in respect of other rights.

ordinary shares Holders of ordinary shares are the owners of a company. They are entitled to a dividend after other preferential payments have been made (although payment of the dividend is at the discretion of the directors). Ordinary shares are sometimes classed as voting or non-voting shares and are sometimes also known as equities.

participating preference shares Preference shares that entitle the shareholder to additional dividends or bonuses from the remaining profits of a company if the dividend on ordinary shares exceeds a specified amount. *See also* **share, preference**.

partly-paid shares Shares that have not yet been fully-paid for by the shareholder. Many large new issues are paid for in two stages, to avoid **liquidity** problems for investors. *See also* **shares, fully-paid**.

penny shares Shares in a company that are traded in low denominations (usually under 50p). Penny shares are often highly volatile.

preference shares Also known as preferred stock, preference shares offer the shareholder preferential claims to dividends, usually at a fixed rate, and a prior claim to ordinary shareholders on the company's assets in the event of **liquidation**. The market price for preference shares tends to be more stable than that of ordinary shares. Preference shareholders may not vote at meetings of ordinary shareholders. Preference shares fall into five categories: cumulative, non-cumulative, redeemable, participating and convertible. *See also* **share, participating preference**.

preferred ordinary shares Ordinary shares that carry additional rights, usually in respect of payment of dividend.

qualifying shares Fixed number of shares a person must hold before he or she is entitled to a position on the board of directors or a bonus issue.

recovery shares When a company's performance is improving after a period of difficulty, its share price is likely to go up. Shares in such a company are known as recovery shares.

redeemable preference shares Preference shares that the issuing company has the right to redeem, *i.e.* buy back under special circumstances. *See* **share, preference**.

share pushing Hard selling of shares that may be worthless to investors.

share split If the market price of a share is thought to be too high, a company may decide to issue extra shares to its holders (known as a bonus issue), increasing the number of shares on the market, and thus decreasing the price of each share. This process is known as a share split. *See* **issue, bonus**.

See also **alpha; beta broker, share; capital, share; certificate, share; delta; economy, share; exchange, share; gamma; index, share; issue, share; option, share; premium, share; register, share; warrant, share.**

shark Informal term for a person or company that may be preparing to make a **takeover** bid.

shark repellants US Informal term for **defensive tactics** in the event of a takeover bid.

shark watcher Consultant who studies the buyers of a company's shares in an effort to identify possible sharks.

shell company = company, shell

shelter *US* Investment instrument that enables the investor to reduce his or her income tax liability (*i.e.* avoid **taxation**) through statutory allowances.

abusive shelter Investment instrument that gives little in the way of return but allows the investor to reduce income tax liabilities.

short covering When a person is **selling short**, short covering is the purchase of the security concerned in order to cover the bargain.

short end That part of the market that deals with securities with relatively little time to go before repayment is due. The amount of time varies from a few days to up to five years, depending on which security is being traded.

shorting Alternative term for **selling short**.

shorts Alternative term for short-dated securities. *See* **securities, short-dated**.

short selling Alternative term for **selling short**.

short-term Loosely, something (in the finance world, a security) with only a short time left before maturity. In the USA, short-term generally means something with less than a year to run. A US alternative is near-term. *See also* **capital, short-term**.

show stopper Informal term for a court injunction initiated by the **target** company and served against the **raider** in a **takeover**, stopping the hostile company party taking action any further.

SIB Abbreviation of **Securities and Investment Board**.

SIC Abbreviation of **standard industrial classification**.

sight draft Bill of exchange that is payable on sight.

silver wheelchair Terms sometimes written into the employment contract of a company's top management or directors, whereby the employee receives a large sum in compensation if he or she loses his or her position as a result of a takeover. If the terms are generous enough, the silver wheelchair may act as a disincentive to raiders. *See also* **golden parachute**.

single capacity System that operated on the UK Stock Market before the **Big Bang**, whereby the functions of **jobber** and **stockbroker** were kept separate. A jobber was not allowed to deal with the general public and a stockbroker could not trade in shares except through a jobber. Since Big Bang, the two functions may be amalgamated (**dual capacity**) and the people who perform these combined functions are known as **market maker**s. *See also* **Chinese Wall**.

skinny bid Alternative term for thin bid. *See* **bid, thin**.

skittish *US* Popular term describing a market that is extremely volatile.

slice (of the action) Informal way of saying that a person is entitled to a share in the profits of a company by being a shareholder, or of a transaction by taking a commission.

sliding scale Scale of charges that is based on the value of the thing upon which the charges are to be made. *See* **ad valorem**.

slippage Under-performance of a **start-up** company. Slippage may lead to the need for additional capital.
   Alternatively, it is the fluctuation in the price of a contract on a futures exchange.

maximum slippage Also known as maximum fluctuation, the amount by which the price of a contract may fluctuate during a given period, laid down by the governing body of the exchange on which the contract is made.

slump Period of time during which the economy is poor, with high levels of unemployment and reduced economic activity.

snake Popular term for the European system that links the following currencies: the Belgian and French francs; the Danish kroner; the Irish punt; the Dutch guilder; the German deutschmark; the Italian lira.

société anonyme (SA) French equivalent of the UK public limited company (plc). *See* **company, public limited**.

société responsibilité limité (SRL) French equivalent of the UK private company. *See* **company, private**.

society Originally, a group of people who come together because they have the same interest or goal.

friendly society Society (first coming into existence in the seventeenth century, to help provide working people with some form of security) that provides mutual benefits to its members, such as life assurance and pensions in return for a yearly subscription. There are various kinds of friendly society, including:

1. **accumulative society**, which operates by keeping a float to cover claims.

2. **affiliated society**, which has centralized administration.

3. **collecting society**, so-called after the method of collecting subscriptions house-to-house.

4. **deposit society**, which adds part of the funds remaining after claims have been met to members' accounts, thus providing them not only with a form of insurance cover but also a method of saving.

5. **dividing society**, which periodically divides the funds remaining after all claims have been met between its members.

See also **building society**.

socks and stocks *US* Because of Federal Reserve regulations that do not permit branch banking, some banks (popularly known as socks and stocks) have been set up to deal with either current account facilities or commercial lending, but not both.

softs Popular name given to traded **commodities** other than metals. *E.g.* foodstuffs such as wheat and coffee.

sola **Bill of exchange** that does not have a duplicate as in **bills in a set**.

solicitor In the UK, a professional person who gives legal advice and initiates legal proceedings on a client's behalf.

South Sea Bubble = bubble

spaghetti war Trade war between the USA and Italy over Italian imports of pasta to the USA. Also known as the pasta war.

special Something that is out of the ordinary. *See* **resolution, special**.

Special Drawing Rights (SDR) Form of **credit** extended by the International Monetary Fund to its member countries, as an addition to the credit they already hold. SDRs do not represent actual money, they are simply a form of credit, but they do not have to be repaid to the IMF and thus form a permanent addition to the reserves of each member country. Originally, they were allocated to member countries in proportion to their subscription to the IMF, but since then additional allocations have been made. At first SDRs were valued in relation to the value of gold, but have since been valued in relation to the member country's own currency. SDRs may be exchanged between member countries or between those countries and the IMF.

specie Coins, rather than banknotes or gold bullion.

speculation Discussion about a possible future event. Broadly in finance, it is the practice of making investments or going into a business that involves risk. The term is sometimes used with pejorative undertones to apply to investment for short-term gain. In certain markets, such as **commodities** and financial **futures**, speculation is clearly distinguished from transactions undertaken in the normal course of trading (physical buying or selling) or **hedging** (where the specific purpose is to minimize overall gains and losses arising from price movements).

spin-off A term with three meanings.

First, it is a company that has been formed from part of or separated from the ownership of a larger company.

Second, it is merchandise that is produced to take advantage of one high-profile product. *E.g.* a television programme may have many spin-offs: a book; a recording of the theme tune; T-shirts; badges; etc.

Third, it is a technology or product that arose as a by-product of another.

split Marketing exercise in which a company issues more shares to existing holders in order to reduce the price per share. *See also* **issue, bonus**.

spot Something that is carried out at once, on the spot. Most often used on **futures** markets, where its opposite is **forward** or highest (as in highest prices). *See* **goods, spot; market, spot; price, spot**.

spread Broadly, the difference between two (or sometimes more) prices or values.

alligator spread Profit made on an **option** that is instantly snapped up by the broker as commission, leaving nothing for the investor.

285

bid-offer spread Difference between the bid price and the offer price offered by a **market maker**. *See* **price, bid;** price, offer.

Ted spread US Difference between the price of a treasury bill and the price of the Eurodollar. *See* **bill, treasury; Eurodollar**.

squeeze = bear squeeze

SRA Abbreviation of **self-regulatory agency**.

SRL Abbreviation of **société responsibilité limité**.

SRO Abbreviation of **self-regulating organization**.

stabilizer Something that acts to keep *e.g.* the economy or prices stable.
  automatic stabilizer Also known as a built-in stabilizer, part of a system that stabilizes it to keep fluctuations to a minimum without direct intervention.

stag Person who buys new issues of shares in the hope that he or she will be able to make a fast profit by selling them soon after trading on the exchange opens. With the UK government privatization programme of the later 1980s, the number of stags has risen. Not to be confused with **STAGS**. *See also* **dolphin**.

stagflation *US* Combination of high inflation and economic stagnation.

STAGS Acronym for sterling transferable accruing government securities, form of zero coupon bond, denominated in sterling and backed by Treasury stock. Not to be confused with a **stag**. *See* **bond, zero coupon**.

stakeholder Person who holds a stake (normally shares) in a company and thus has a piece of the action.

standard Broadly, a norm against which other things are measured.

standard industrial classification (SIC) Method of classifying business, manufacturing and all commercial activity for statistical purposes.

standby LC *US* Abbreviation of standby letter of credit.

start-up Normally used of a company that is beginning from scratch. A start-up often needs venture capital financing to help it on its way. *See* **capital, venture**.

statement Written report often taken as an official or legal document.

bank statement Document from a bank giving details of all financial transactions on the particular account over a given period, usually a month.

statement in lieu of prospectus If a company proposes to make a new issue of **share**s or **debenture**s and does not issue a **prospectus**, it must pass a statement in lieu of prospectus to the registrar of companies at least three days before the issue is to take place.

See also **reconciliation statement**.

status inquiry Inquiry (often by a credit card agency) to determine the creditworthiness of one of its customers.

sterling UK standard currency.

sterling area = **territory, scheduled**.

stipend Alternative term for **salary**.

stock Term with four meanings.

First, a fixed-interest security that is denominated in units of £100. *See* **security, fixed interest**.

Second, in the USA an alternative term for ordinary shares. *See* **share, ordinary**.

Third, sometimes also used in the UK to mean some types of ordinary share. *See* **share, ordinary**.

Fourth, collection of raw materials or goods held by a manufacturer, wholesaler, retailer or end-user. Often known as stock-in-trade or inventory.

active stock Shares that are frequently traded on the exchange.

ambulance stock Securities recommended to a client whose investment portfolio has done badly. The practice is especially common in Japan.

attractive stock US Ordinary shares that promise a good return.

bearer stocks Like bearer bonds, securities that are payable to the bearer, not to a named holder.

capital stock Value of all capital goods owned by a company, industry or nation, after **depreciation** has been taken into account.

dated stock As opposed to undated stock, stock that has a fixed maturity date.

debenture stock **Debentures** may be divided into units and traded on the exchange. These securities are known as debenture stocks.

defensive stock US Shares in companies that are not effected by economic cycles, because they produce necessities, *e.g.* food.

high technology stock Shares in a company involved in high technology.

inscribed stock Now discontinued method of registering the name of a stockholder, by which the holder was issued with a slip indicating that the holder's name had been registered. This slip did not have the status of a certificate. Also known as registered stock.

junior stock US Shares offered to a company's executives at below the market price. Initially, junior stock has a low dividend rate, but may be converted to ordinary shares to provide a capital gain.

loan stock Security issued by a company in respect of loan funds made available by investors. Similar to a **debenture**, although loan stock is often unsecured.

outright buy stock (WSJ) Stock that is recommended unreservedly by market analysts.

preferred stock Alternative term for preference shares. *See* **share, preference**.

registered stock Alternative term for inscribed stock.

takeover stock Shares that are bought by a raider during a takeover battle.

undated stocks Fixed interest security with no redemption date attached.

utility stock Share in a company providing utilities such as water, electricity and gas.

watered stock Stock that has become a smaller percentage of a company's total share capital because of subsequent share issues.

See also **exchange, stock**.

stockbroker Someone who gives advice and buys and sells stocks and shares on an exchange on behalf of clients.

Stock Exchange Automated Quotations (SEAQ) Electronic system now in use on the London Stock Exchange that displays in the offices of brokers and others up-to-date prices and information for all quoted securities. Only market-makers are permitted to quote prices on SEAQ, accepting certain obligations in return for the increased business that SEAQ offers.

Stock Exchange Daily Official List (SEDOL) = **Official List**

Stock Exchange Automatic Exchange Facility (SEAF) Computerized system now in use on the London Stock Exchange, which allows buying and selling of securities to be done at terminals in the broker's office. *See also* **SEPON; Stock Exchange Automated Quotations; TALISMAN**.

stock-in-trade Alternative term for **stock** (fourth meaning).

stockjobber Alternative term for **jobber**.

stop loss order Alternative term for stop order. *See* **order, stop**.

story *US* Security that is being actively traded at the present time, but which may lack underlying value.

straddle Practice of simultaneously buying forward and selling forward a **futures** contract or **option** in the same security in order to make a profit if the price of the security moves in either direction.

straight line method In **accounting**, method of calculating **depreciation** by writing off the value of the **asset** in equal amounts in each year of the asset's lifetime.

strangle *US* Practice of buying out-of-the-money call and put **options** that are close to expiry at a relatively low **premium**. If the price of the underlying **future** rises or falls suddenly, the buyer makes a profit.

Street, The *US* Popular term for the New York stock exchange, referring to **Wall Street**.

strike To stop work in order to draw the attention of management to workers' grievances, or for political ends.

general strike Strike by many of the workers in a country.

official strike Strike action that is agreed upon by the elected officials or members of a trade union according to its rules.

unofficial strike Strike action that has not been agreed upon by a trade union executive according to its rules and so is not officially backed by the union.

wildcat strike Strike organized by some local workers without the knowledge or sanction of a trade union. Such strikes often occur at a moment's notice.

strip *US* Practice of taking US Treasury bonds, stripping the interest-bearing **coupon** and selling that and the principal separately. Such securities are said to have been stripped.

subscriber On the formation of a company, a person who signs the **articles of association** and memorandum of agreement.
See also **capital, subscribed**.

subscription Sum paid to a company for shares in a new issue.

subsidiary Company that is wholly owned by a (usually larger) parent company.

subsidy Sum paid to companies in certain industries to enable them to sell their goods or services at a price close to the prevailing market price. Also to provide financial support to a commercial or quasi-commercial activity that would otherwise not be viable in narrow profit and loss terms, usually in order to sustain broader economic or social benefits.

subvention In the UK, a payment made from one company to another (related) company in order to give a better picture of the group's performance.
In the USA, a grant made by the government, a company or other institution, to a non-profit-making organization.

suicide pill Defensive tactics in the event of a takeover. If the raider manages to acquire a certain percentage of the **target** company's shares, the remaining shareholders are automatically entitled to exchange their shares for **debt** securities, thus exchanging the company's **equity** to debt and making it seem less attractive to the raider.

sunlighting *US* Practice of having two full-time jobs at once. *See also* **moonlighting**.

superannuation Alternative term for company pension, paid to the employee during retirement.

supermajority Between 70-80 per cent of the voters. It is usual to demand a supermajority decision when deciding on such points as **mergers** or **takeovers**.

superstock *US* Share issue that gives the existing holders a large number of votes per share. Normally used as a defensive tactic during a hostile **takeover,** superstock must be held for a certain period of time before the extra votes are credited to the holder.

supplementary costs = overheads

supply Provision of goods and services.

supply and demand Two market forces that in microeconomic theory determine the price of goods, services or investment instruments. If supply is low and demand high, the price increases. Conversely, if demand is low and supply high, the price falls (unless price controls are in operation).
See also **money supply**.

support Practice of actively buying securities or foreign exchange by an 'official' in order to stop their market value from falling. This most often happens when the central bank buys its own securities to stop the price falling and thus forestall a rise in interest rates. *See* **bank, central**.

SUPSI Acronym for specific unpublished price-sensitive information. *See* **insider dealing**.

surety Alternative term for **guarantee**.

surveyor Person whose job is to examine buildings etc. and report on their condition.

marine surveyor Surveyor who specializes in ships.

quantity surveyor Surveyor who specializes in calculating quantities of raw materials (and sometimes labour) needed for a construction project.

swap *US* Alternative term for a **bed-and-breakfast deal**.

switching Practice of transfering investment from one security to another (in a comparable class) in order to take advantage of price fluctuations or to improve a tax position.

equity switching Practice of moving investment funds from one share issue to another, usually of a company in the same industry.

gilt switching Switching between **gilt-edged securities**.

syndicate Group of people that come together to work for a common aim, *e.g.* in underwriting large risks for **Lloyds**. *See also* **consortium**.

syndication Practice of dividing investment risk between several people in order to minimize individual risk.
   Syndication is also the practice of distributing information (especially news information and newspaper and magazine articles) to several outlets.

synergy Additional benefits to be gained by the combination of hitherto separate activities. Often colloquially expressed as '2+2=5', and cited to justify the takeover or merger of companies with complementary or mutually reinforcing activities or resources.

T

tail-gating *US* Act of a broker who recommends purchase of a stock to one customer on the basis of another customer having just expressed faith in the stock by making a purchase.

tailspin *US* Describes a sudden plunge in market prices.
"This week's crash sent equity prices on several European markets into a tailspin."

take back *US* When a company is sold, the take back is a situation in which the owner must accept payment in something other than cash.

takeover Buying of a proportion of a company's shares so that the purchaser gains control of the company or its assets. *See also* **merger**.

friendly takeover Purchase of control of a company that is welcomed by the **target** company's board and shareholders.

hostile takeover Attempt to purchase control of a company that is unwelcome to some of the target's shareholders and board. Unwelcome takeovers may be resisted by a gamut of **defensive tactics**. *See* **crown jewel tactic; golden parachute; Jonestown defence; knight; poison pill; shark repellent; shark watcher; suicide pill**.

reverse takeover Purchase of control of a public company by a smaller, private company. This is often done in order that the private company may obtain listing on the Stock Exchange.

takeover bid Offer made to a company's shareholders to buy their shares at a certain price, in order to gain control of the company.

takeover panel UK Stock Exchange body responsible for seeing that the City Code on Takeovers and Mergers is observed by parties wishing to make a takeover bid.

See also **stock, takeover**.

taker-in Person who is willing to take up a commitment made by a **bull** dealer, in the event of the dealer being unable or unwilling to pay for it at that time.

TALISMAN Acronym for Transfer Accounting, Lodgement for Investors, Stock Management for Jobbers. It is a central computerized system for settlement of equities. TALISMAN also facilitates the transfer of stock from the central Stock Exchange pool and the issue of new certificates. *See* **SEPON**.

TALISMAN bought transfer (TBT) Method by which stocks are transferred from **SEPON** to a buyer.

TALISMAN sold transfer (TST) Method by which stocks are transferred to **SEPON** from a seller.

tally Originally a notch made on a piece of wood as a record of a debt or payment, now most often referring to a distinguishing mark on an item of merchandise.

tallyman Term with three possible meanings.
   First, it may be an accountant (*e.g.* working for a bookie on a racecourse).
   Second, it is a person who gives credit to be repaid in instalments.
   Third, it is a person responsible for checking merchandise as it is loaded and unloaded from a vessel.

talon Slip that accompanies a sheet of coupons of bearer bonds, which may be sent to the issuing company when more coupons are required. *See* **bond, bearer; bond, coupon**.

tangibles = assets, tangible

tap When the government makes a new issue on the gilt market, it is very rarely fully subscribed. The remaining gilts in the issue are gradually released by the government broker and this action is known as a tap. *See* **gilt-edged security; broker, government**.

tap buying In certain circumstances, the government will buy back gilts before they have matured. This is known as tap buying.

tap issue Issue of government securities direct to government departments rather than onto the open market.

tap stock Gilt-edged stock released onto the market in a tap.

tape dancing *US* Unethical method of manipulating share prices whereby a dealer reports a deal inclusive of his commission. This makes the share price seem to rise.

tare When the weight of goods is being established, the tare is the weight allowed for the packaging. Tare is also the weight of a (goods) vehicle without fuel; its unladen weight.

target Objective towards which somebody or an organization is working. In corporate finance, it is a company that is the object of a **takeover bid**.
"All the sales representatives met their sales targets for this year."
"Having been made aware of the imminence of a hostile takeover bid, the board of the target company met to discuss defensive tactics."
See also **price, target**.

tariff List of charges made in return for goods or services. There are two more particular meanings.
    First, the tariff is the list of dutiable goods and duty payable, issued by Customs.
    Second, the term may refer to a system of charges in which a certain rate is payable up to a certain point (*e.g.* a certain quantity of goods) and then the rate changes beyond that point.

common external tariff (CET) Import tariff charged by all members of a trading community (*e.g.* the EEC) on goods being imported from non-member countries.

tariff office Insurance company that is bound with respect to the level of its premiums by membership of an organization (*e.g.* the Accident Offices Association).

two-part tariff System of charges comprising two elements. In some cases, a fixed sum is supplemented with a variable sum (*e.g.* a taxi driver makes a fixed charge and then adds a certain amount depending upon the time of day and the time the journey has taken, or upon the distance travelled).

See also **barrier, tariff**.

TAURUS Acronym for transfer and automated registration of uncertified stock, a computer system, (as yet not totally operational) that will enable stocks and shares to be transferred by computer, making contract notes and certificates unnecessary.

tax Money paid to central or local government to cover its expenditure. Various kinds of taxes are collected by the Inland Revenue (the Internal Revenue Service in the USA), HM Customs and Excise (in which case the tax is known as a duty) and local government authorities. *See also* **duty; rates**.

advance corporation tax (ACT) Corporation tax is levied in two parts. The first part is levied on the distribution of profits and is known as advance corporation tax. The second half of the tax is estimated on the company's earnings. *See* **tax, corporation**.

back tax Also known as back duty, payment of tax on income that was not paid at the time it was earned or first claimed. *See also* **tax evasion**.

capital gains tax (CGT) Tax paid on capital gains.

capital transfer tax (CTT) Tax paid on the transfer of capital, *e.g.* in the form of a gift or bequest. Capital transfer tax covers the old form of inheritance tax.

cascade tax Tax imposed at each stage of production. *E.g.* a product may pass from one country to the next as each stage of production is carried out, and would thus attract several taxation stages, and the price of the finished product would be higher than if it had been produced entirely in one country.

corporation tax Tax levied on a company's profits. *See also* **tax, advance corporation**.

dividend tax Form of income tax on share **dividends**. When in operation, dividend tax is deducted by the company at source.

excess profits tax Tax paid on a company's profits over and above a level that is thought to be normal.

hidden tax Tax included in the price of a goods so that it is not obvious to the consumer. Most forms of indirect taxation are hidden in this way, *e.g.* tax (duty) on tobacco and alcohol.

income tax Tax paid on income such as salaries or wages.

inflation tax Extra revenue brought into the government because inflation has brought new taxpayers on stream or pushed taxpayers or taxable items into higher brackets. *See also* **bracket creep**.

inheritance tax Tax paid on inheritances by heirs, often calculated in relation to the closeness of the relationship between the heir and the dead person. In the UK at the present time, capital gains tax covers income from inheritances. *See* **tax, capital gains**.

input tax In the value-added tax system, the tax that is collected from the seller of goods by the **Customs and Excise**. *See* **tax, value-added**. *See also* **tax, output**.

land tax Tax on the ownership of land, normally paid in the form of **rates**.

negative income tax (NIT) System of taxation by which those earning less than a specified income receive tax credits to bring their income in line with a guaranteed minimum income.

output tax In the value-added tax system, the tax that is charged by a supplier to a customer. *See* **tax, value-added**. *See also* **tax, input**.

payroll tax Tax on business undertakings, levied in relation to the number of people employed or as a percentage of the total wage bill. Payroll tax is often used to control the relative elasticities of the supply of and demand for labour. Its imposition deters companies from employing more workers than they currently require.

profits tax Tax levied on a company's profits.

tax abatement Reduction in the rate of tax. It should not be confused with a tax rebate. *See* **rebate**.

tax avoidance Use of loopholes in tax legislation to minimize tax liability. Unlike tax evasion, tax avoidance is legal. *See also* **tax evasion**.

tax base The form of income upon which tax is calculated. *E.g.* the tax base for income tax is a person's taxable income.

tax bracket The percentage of one's income that one pays in tax depends on the level of income. Incomes are divided into brackets for the purpose of calculating tax.

tax concession Allowances made against a person's income, etc., for tax purposes.

tax deduction card In **pay as you earn** (PAYE) income tax, a record of all deductions made by the employer at source, submitted for each employee to the Inland Revenue annually.

tax deductions Money removed from a person's salary to cover tax. In the USA, however, tax deductions are expenses that are deductible against tax.

tax evasion Evasion of tax liabilities by providing false information to the Inland Revenue. Tax evasion is a criminal offence in the UK. *See also* **Revenue, Inland; tax avoidance**.

tax exemption Not having to pay tax. In the USA, however, it is the proportion of income upon which tax is not payable.

tax exile Person who lives abroad in order to minimize liability for tax.

tax gap US Difference between the amount somebody owes the Inland Revenue (the Inland Revenue Service (IRS), in the USA), and the amount they actually pay.

tax haven Country with liberal tax and banking regulations. In some instances it benefits companies to set up their registered offices in such a country, to avoid paying taxes in their own country.

tax holiday Period during which a start-up company need not pay taxes.

tax point Point at which **value added tax** (VAT) is payable. *See* **tax, value added**.

tax relief Concessions made to taxpayers in respect of certain liabilities. "He expected to get tax relief on his mortgage."

tax return Document circulated by the Inland Revenue to every tax-paying adult, on which he or she declares annual income and makes any claims for tax relief.

tax shelter Investment instrument that does not attract tax.

value added tax (VAT) Form of indirect taxation by which the producer, seller and consumer pay a percentage of the excess value of the product or service. *E.g.* if a manufacturer buys his raw materials at £10 per unit and sells each unit for £20, the added value is £10. The manufacturer is required to pay a percentage of the £20 in VAT, and can claim back the VAT paid on the £10 worth of materials. VAT currently stands at 15% in the UK, although some goods and services are exempt and some **zero-rated**. *See also* **ad valorem; value, added**.

See also **income, taxable; loss, tax; year, tax**.

taxation Imposition and subsequent collection of a tax.

ability-to-pay taxation Theory of taxation whereby those who are able to pay more are taxed at a higher rate. Ability-to-pay taxation may be applied to luxury goods, which therefore attract a high rate of tax.

benefit taxation Theory of taxation by which taxes to cover public services are paid by those who use them, rather than by the general public at large.

deferred taxation Tax for which a person or company is liable, but which has not yet been considered or demanded by the Inland Revenue.

direct taxation System of taxation, whereby companies and individuals pay tax on income directly to the Inland Revenue (or through and employer), as opposed to indirect taxation, in which tax is added to the price of goods and services. *See also* **taxation, indirect**.

indirect taxation Tax paid to one person, who then pays it to the government. Value added tax is a form of indirect taxation. *See* **tax, value added**.

taxation schedule One of six categories into which income is divided for the purposes of calculating taxes.

T-bill *US* Abbreviation of treasury bill. *See* **bill, treasury**.

TBT Abbreviation of TALISMAN bought transfer. *See* **TALISMAN**.

TCV Abbreviation of **total contract value**.

teaser *US* Initial low rate of interest offered on an adjustable rate mortgage (**ARM**), which may seem very attractive at the time of arrangement, but which inevitably rises.

technical office protocol (TOP) Scheme aimed at standardizing computer systems that link design and engineering functions within manufacturing companies. *See also* **MAP**.

technopole Derived from technopolis, meaning a society dependent on high technology, a technopole is a place where businesses dealing with high technology products have congregated.

telebanking Method by which bank customers may make financial transactions from their homes or offices, using a computer linked by a modem to the bank's computer.

telecommuting Increasingly common practice whereby people work at home, 'commuting' by computer link-up rather than by car or public transport. *See also* **electronic cottage**.

telemarketing Advertising, selling and conducting market research over the telephone, person to person.

telemarketing system Computer system that canvasses people in their homes over the telephone. Dialling is done electronically and a voice-activated audio-tape carries on the 'conversation'.

telesales Selling a product over the telephone. A branch of **telemarketing**.

teleshopping Service whereby a store's customers may order goods for delivery, either over the telephone or, increasingly, using a home or personal computer.

teletext output price information computer (TOPIC) Computerized system that provides stock dealers with up-to-the-minute information on market prices. *See also* **quote machine**.

teller Bank employee whose function is to take and pass out money over the counter. *See also* **ATM**.

tenancy Either an agreement whereby a person is entitled to occupy a property, usually in return for **rent**, *or* the length of time agreed for such occupancy.

joint tenancy Situation in which two or more people have equal rights to tenancy of a property. The difference between a joint tenancy and **tenancy in common** is that if a joint tenant dies, the property reverts to the other tenants, and so on until only one tenant remains, with sole tenancy rights.

tenancy in common In principle, a situation in which two people are entitled to tenancy of the same property and may do as each wishes with their part of it. If one tenant dies, his share of the property is passed on to his heir, rather than to the other tenant(s). Now, however, tenancy in common applies only to groups of four or more people. *See also* **tenancy, joint**.

tender Generally, an offer to supply goods or services at a certain price and under certain conditions. A tender is usually submitted in response to an invitation to do so and is normally made in competition with other suppliers.

issue by tender Stocks and shares may be issued by the process of inviting tenders above a stated minimum price and then selling to the highest bidder. *See also* **application and allotment**.

legal tender Currency; coins or notes that may be offered as a medium of exchange.

tender bills Treasury bills, issued by the government each week to cover short-term finance. Tenders for these bills are made by discount houses and financial institutions. *See also* **bill, treasury; tap**.

tender offer UK Offer for sale by tender.

tender offer US Offer made to the shareholders of a public company to buy their holding at a certain price, normally above the current market price. This may be done by a company in order to effect a **takeover**.

tender pool One of a series of groups into which an acquisitive company may divide its target company's shareholders, in order more successfully to persuade them to take up a **tender offer**. A form of divide and conquer.

tenor Period of time before a **bill of exchange** has to be paid. In effect, the 'life' of the bill.

term Period of time during which something is valid. *See* **assurance, term; loan, term**.

terminal The end of something. *See* **bonus, terminal**.

terminate To finish something, often used in regard of a contract or agreement.
"They terminated his contract of employment after he was caught trying to defraud the company."

terms Conditions attached to an agreement or contract.

terms of trade Indication of a country's trading position, based on a comparison of its imports and exports.

trade terms Special conditions (usually discount prices) available to people working in the same industry or trade.

territory Geographical area covered by a sales representative or by a company's operations.

scheduled territory Official name for those countries that have tied their currencies to sterling by keeping it as their reserve currency. Also known as the sterling area. *See* **currency, reserve**.

three-six-three *US* Late-lamented lifestyle of the banker: pay interest at 3 per cent; lend at 6 per cent; be on the golf course by 3pm.

threshold Limit or point at which something changes. *See* **agreement, threshold; company, threshold; price, threshold**.

thrift *US* Shorthand for **thrifts and loans**.

thrifts and loans *US* Financial institutions that are backed by an insurance fund and oriented toward the consumer. Also known as industrial banks. *See also* **savings and loan**.

tick Minimum price movement on a financial futures contract. *See also* **uptick**.

tied outlet Retail outlet that is financially backed by a manufacturer on the condition that the outlet sells only the manufacturer's brands. *E.g.* most public houses are tied outlets.

tie-up Arrangement whereby a large company helps to finance a smaller company, thus gaining rights in some or all of its developments. Tie-ups most often occur where the receiving company is developing in high-technology areas. *See also* **accord**.

tiger = **TIGRs**

TIGRs *US* Pronounced as tigers, acronym for treasury investment growth receipts, a form of zero coupon bond in dollar denominations. *See* **bond, zero coupon**.

time *See* **bargain, time; deposit, time; preference, time; rate, time**.

double time Rate of overtime payments to workers that is double the normal hourly rate.

"It does not worry me that I sometimes have to work on Sundays and Bank Holidays, because I am paid double time."

new time On the London Stock Exchange, the last two days of an **account**. Transactions conducted in new time are settled at the end of the next account; therefore, new time is effectively part of the next account period.

time and motion Study of the way in which a particular job is carried out, in an effort to streamline the physical actions involved and so save time.

time server Worker who has lost sight of any promotional ambitions and has no motivation to work with any interest or initiative. The time server freewheels until he or she retires.

time sharing Has slightly different meanings in the fields of computing, property and employment.

In computing, time sharing is the use of data and facilities of a mainframe computer by several different users at the same time.

In property, a time-share is an arrangement whereby people buy time during which they are entitled to use a property. *E.g.* it is becoming increasingly common to buy a two-week time-share in a holiday villa abroad.

In employment, a time-share job is a full-time job shared by two or more people, each performing the same function, but working at different times. Also known as a job-share.

time value of money US Theory by which one's money is more valuable now than at any time in the future, whether it be in an hour's time, next week or next year.

tip Cash given to someone who has rendered a service, over and above the payment agreed. Tipping customs vary from country to country, but those who are normally tipped include taxi-drivers, waiting staff, beauticians and hairdressers. Also known as a gratuity.

A tip may also be a piece of information passed to someone to whom it may be of advantage.

tithe Literally meaning 'one-tenth', a tithe was originally a payment of that proportion of one's income to the Church. Now, tithe has come to mean payment of a fixed sum at regular intervals.

title A person's right to own something.

title deed Also known as a deed of title, a legal document proving a person's title in a property and detailing the property itself and the changes of **ownership** in the property over the years.

token coin Coin whose exchange value is more than the value of the metal from which it is made.

tolerance In manufacturing, the degree to which a product differs from the ideal specification, without giving grounds for it to be rejected.

toll Payment made for the use of a facility such as a bridge or tunnel. In some countries there are also tolls payable for the use of motorways. The toll is normally charged to cover the cost of maintaining the service.

toll call US Long-distance telephone call, charged to the caller.

tombstone *US* Informal term for an advertisement, placed in the press, giving details of those involved in a securities issue. A tombstone is not normally an offer to buy.

TOP Acronym for **technical office protocol**.

TOPIC Acronym for **teletext output price information computer**.

top hat Pension plan offered to a company's senior managers.

top slicing Method of calculating tax payable on gains from a life **assurance** policy.

top up To improve the benefits gained from an existing arrangement *e.g.* by increasing contributions to a pension or assurance scheme. *See also* **mortgage, top-up**.

total contract value (TCV) Applied to futures markets and calculated by multiplying the size of the contract (*e.g.* 10 tons of cocoa) by market price (*e.g.* £1,300/ton) to give the value of the contract (£13,000).

toxic waste *US* Informal term rating a security as a very bad investment. *See also* **bond, junk**.

TPI Abbreviation of tax and price index.

TQM Abbreviation of **total quality management**. *See* **management, total quality**.

trade Business of buying and selling in general. In the USA, a trade may also be another term for a **bargain** or deal.

aids to trade Activities (often services) that assist other businesses, such as advertising, banking, insurance and transport.

external trade Trade with countries other than one's own.

free trade Concept of international trading in which there are no tariff barriers between countries.

invisible trade Trade in services rather than tangible goods. *See* **invisibles**.

trade gap In an adverse **balance of trade**, the difference between the values for imports and exports.

trade mark Logo or name (trade name) used to distinguish one manufacturer's product from another's. Registered trade marks may not be used by another manufacturer in the country of registration.

tradeoff Exchanging one thing for another. Goods may be traded off against each other, but so may many other things such as the terms of an agreement.
  "After five hours at the negotiating table they decided on a tradeoff of terms to break the stalemate."

trade references List of trading partners to whom a company may refer if they wish to confirm the creditworthiness of a potential customer.

trade union Association of workers (or other groups such as students) who have come together under a constitution in order to bargain more effectively with management and government. *See also* **non-union**.

visible trade Trading in visible goods between countries. *See also* **agreement, trade; balance of trade; bill, trade; creditor, trade; deficit, trade; discount, trade; investment, trade; option, traded**.

trader Person who concerns himself or herself in trade.

floor trader Someone who is authorized to trade on the floor of a stock or commodities exchange.

sole trader Person who trades on his or her own behalf and has not registered as a business.
   In the financial and stock exchange worlds, however, the term has three precise meanings.
   First, a trader is somebody involved in buying and selling securities short-term, for his or her own account.
   Second, it is somebody who specializes in buying and selling securities on behalf of a broker or dealer, usually working as an employee.
   Third, it is a person who buys and sells contracts in financial futures without a **hedge** in the appropriate cash market.

trading Activity of a **trader** in all its meanings.

horse trading Hard negotiations, normally ending in both parties making concessions to the other. *See also* **tradeoff**.

ring trading Method of trading adopted on the London Metal Exchange, whereby dealers sit in a ring and trade by open outcry. *See also* **market, outcry; ring**.

side-by-side trading US Prohibited practice of trading a share option at the same time as trading the underlying security, on the same exchange.

trading certificate Certificate handed to a new company by the Registrar of Companies to enable it to begin trading.

trading crowd Group of dealers interested in trading in a particular security.

trading estate Area of land, usually situated just outside a town or city, set aside for warehouse and light industrial units. Also known as an industrial estate or industrial park.

trading floor The area within an exchange building where trading takes place.
   "There was panic on the trading floor of the Exchange today as prices began to fall sharply."

trading halt Temporary stoppage in trading on a securities or options market.

trading post US On the **trading floor** of the New York Stock Exchange, an area where dealers congregate to trade.

trading stamps Discount given by a retailer to its customers in the form of stamps. The stamps only have a redemption value (in cash or goods) and the discount is represented by this value.

See also **account, trading; association, trading; bank, trading; day, trading; loss, trading**.

tranche Slice. In general, one of a series of payments which put together add up to the total amount agreed.
"The author received his advance as five tranches of £100 each."
   More specifically, a tranche is a block of a stock issued before or after (and sometimes at a different price to) another block of identical stock.

tranche funding Method of providing finance by which successive sums of money are forwarded, each dependent upon the financee attaining prearranged targets.

tranchette Small block of gilt-edged stock issued to the market, as an addition to stock already on the market. *See also* **tranche**.

transaction Act of carrying out a business deal.
"Considering the lengthy negotiations involved, they concluded the transaction surprisingly swiftly."

protected transaction Transaction, generally made in faith, that occurs after a company goes into liquidation or a person is declared bankrupt. A protected transaction cannot be nullified by the liquidator.

transaction charge Charge payable to the London International Financial Futures Exchange on each transaction made.

transaction costs Costs incurred in buying and selling securities, such as the brokers' commissions, taxes, etc.

transfer Legal movement of something (*e.g.* property, shares, etc.) from one owner to another.

blank transfer In the transfer of shares, a transfer form that is left blank as regards the name of the transferee. *E.g.* if the shares are to be put up as security to a mortgage, the transfer form will be left blank, as the mortgagor has the right to take possession of the shares if the mortgagee defaults.

certification of transfer Act of signing a transfer deed in order to transfer stocks from one owner to another. The transfer is further made official by reporting it to the registrar.

credit transfer Method of paying money into another person's bank account (usually by **giro).**

telegraphic transfer Method of transferring money to a transferee abroad. The transferor instructs his or her bank, who will then contact their agent in that country to pay the transferee.

transfer deed Document proving the sale of a property or registered stock. To make the transfer official, the seller must sign the deed. In the case of a registered stock the document is also known as a stock transfer deed or a transfer form. *See also* **TALISMAN**.

transfer payment Payment made by the UK government that is not in return for goods or services. *E.g.* state pensions, unemployment benefit.

unrequited transfer US Gift of finance made by one country to another.

See also **duty, transfer stamp**.

treasury Government department that deals with national finance and government funding, and is responsible for the execution of the government's economic policy. Some large companies also have treasury departments. *See also* **bill, treasury; bond, treasury**.

trend Direction of a price movement, which may be measured over various periods of time.

Trial of the Pyx Annual test made at the Royal Mint in the UK, to check that coins contain the correct quantities of the relevant metals.

tribunal Special court set up to make a judgement on specific problems.

trickle-down theory Theory whereby the money put into the pockets of those who are already rich by government policy, is thought to seep down into the hands of those who are less well off. Trickle-down is thought to be a more efficient method of re-distributing wealth than **transfer payments**.

triple-A *US* In the rating of stocks and bonds, a triple-A rating is the highest rating a stock may achieve.
  "Turnover was light in most bonds, but triple-A rated issues continued in demand."

triple-witching hour *US* The last hour before quarterly futures and options expire, during which turnover increases considerably, causing drastic changes in market prices.

troy weights System of weights most commonly used to weigh precious metals and gemstones. *See also* **avoirdupois**.

true and fair Describes the ratification of an **account** in auditing. *See* **audit**.

trust Three meanings are possible.
  First, it is a group of companies that join forces to form a **cartel** or in some cases a **monopoly**, for their mutual benefit. In this sense, the term is more commonly used in the United States, *e.g.* in the term **anti-trust law**.
  Second, it is a sum of money or property placed into the care of a group of trustees, to be managed (although not necessarily invested) for the benefit of an individual or organization such as a charity.
  In the securities industry, a trust is an investment operation that is managed by a group of trustees on behalf of other people, such as a unit trust.

fixed trust Unit trust in which investors' money is invested in a set portfolio.

flexible trust Unit trust in which investors' money is not invested in a set portfolio, but is moved from one investment to another in order to increase earnings.

investment trust Investment scheme, similar to a unit trust, whereby the small investor is able to invest in a range of shares through the agency of the schemes managers. *See* **trust, unit**.

trust deed Legal document that transfers property into the hands of trustees and sets out the terms of the trust.

trustbusting *US* United States government action taken to prevent trusts (in the US sense) forming, and to break them up if they are already in operation in an apparent effort to stimulate competition.

trustee Person managing a **trust**.

public trustee Person appointed by the state who undertakes to act as a trustee, executor, or investment advisor to any member of the general public.

TSA Abbreviation of The Securities Association, a recognised **SRO**.

TST Abbreviation of TALISMAN sold transfer. *See* **TALISMAN**.

turn Difference between the price at which a security is bought and the price at which it is sold. The turn is the profit on the transaction.

jobber's turn Profit made by a **jobber** on a deal.

turnkey Situation, especially in the computer and construction industries, in which a supplier provides a complete customized package to a customer.

turnover Gross value of all sales made by a company during the accounting period. On the Stock Exchange, the turnover is the total number of shares changing hands during a certain period of time.

turnover rate Rate at which something moves, *e.g.* goods in a retail outlet. More specifically it is the number of shares that change hands on the Stock Exchange in a year, compared to the number of shares in issue.

tycoon Someone who has amassed a large fortune and a great deal of personal and professional power through business or inheritance.

U

uberrima fides Sometimes also quoted as **uberrimae fidei**, meaning the **utmost good faith**. The phrase refers to contracts of **insurance** in which both parties must disclose all facts that may influence the other's decision to enter into the **contract**, whether they are asked to do so or not. If either party has not acted in the utmost good faith, then the contract may become void.

UCITS Abbreviation of undertakings for collective investments in transferable securities, which are **unit trusts** that may be traded in any of the EEC countries.

ullage Potentially a confusing term which may be used in three different senses.

First, ullage is the difference between the capacity of a cask and the volume of its current contents.

Second, ullage is now used by Customs officials to refer to the actual contents of a cask. In this case the term **vacuity** is used to describe the difference between capacity and actual volume.

Third, ullage in marine insurance terms still refers to the difference between a vessel's capacity and the volume of its actual contents. Ullage is not considered to be a loss and so is not normally covered in an insurance policy. *See* **insurance, marine**.

ultimo Commercial Latin for 'of the previous month', sometimes abbreviated to 'ult'.

ultra vires Meaning 'beyond the power of', this phrase denotes an act that goes beyond or against the acting company's objectives as defined in its **articles of association**.

umpirage In cases of **arbitration**, there may be more than one arbitrator. A group of arbitrators are governed by an umpire and in the event that the arbitrators are unable to reach a unanimous decision the umpire's decision is final. The act of referring to the umpire in this way is known as umpirage.

unbundling *US* Separation of a broker's prices from his services. Also a term in the computer industry that deonotes sales of parts (often software) separtely from the main machine.

uncertificated units = unit trust

undercapitalization Term that describes a company that does not have enough capital to take it through the initial burn-out period immediately after **start-up**. *See also* **capitalization; rate, burn**.

underpin To strengthen something, *e.g.* the current trend in market prices, a current way of thinking, etc.
"This month's government deficit data is expected to help underpin the gilt market."

undertaking Agreement or promise to do something.
"They have given us a written undertaking to supply the goods within ten days."
"They have undertaken the new brief for the job."

commercial undertaking Another name for a firm or business.

underwater *US* Describes share prices that drop in value after the initial public offering. *See also* **IPO; value, discounted**.

underwater option US Stock option offered to employees. The shares are normally offered at a discount on the market rate, but when the market price falls below the grant price, the option goes underwater. *See* **option; price, grant**.

underwriter Person or institution that agrees to take up a proportion of the risk of something. *E.g.* an underwriter may take up the shares of an issue that are not taken up by the public, in return for a commission (known as an **underwriting commission**). For the issuer, the underwriter represents a guarantee that the whole issue will be subscribed.
A second form of underwriter is an **underwriter at Lloyds,** a firm that deals in marine insurance. A Lloyds underwriter agrees to take liability for a certain proportion of the insurance required.

undisclosed Describes an action performed for various reasons without others knowing about it or without knowing the reasons behind it. *See* **principal, undisclosed**.

undue influence If a party to a **contract** can be shown to have been influenced by a third party, such as a relative or close friend, so that the third party has some benefit from the contract (say, as the beneficiary of a **will**), then undue influence may be declared and the contract made void.

unemployment Situation in which a person is without work. Definitions of people who are regarded as unemployed vary, but they are generally taken to include people who cannot find work, those who are not actively seeking work (*e.g.* someone who has been made redundant shortly before he or she is due to retire and has decided not to seek another position), those who have turned down unsuitable or badly-paid work, and those who do not want to work.

In the USA, unemployment is calculated by taking a poll of about 60,000 households, whereas in the UK unemployment figures are based on the number of people registered for unemployment benefit.

concealed unemployment Another term for disguised unemployment. *See* **unemployment, disguised**.

cyclical unemployment Unemployment cause by movements in the trade cycle, *e.g.* during a **recession**.

disguised unemployment Also known as **concealed unemployment**, unemployment of those who are not earning and are not searching for work. *E.g.* during times of high unemployment, a housewife may wish to work but decide it is not worth trying to find a suitable job. This form of unemployment is 'disguised' by the method of calculating unemployment figures in the UK. It can be said not to exist in the US, where calculation methods enable the authorities to take such cases into account.

frictional unemployment Unemployment caused by the movement of people between jobs. Thus, there may be enough jobs to go round, but some people may still experience periods of unemployment between the finish date of one job and the start date of the next.

hidden unemployment Another term for disguised unemployment. *See* **unemployment, disguised**.

seasonal unemployment Unemployment caused by seasonal fall-off in demand for workers because of the nature of the occupation. *E.g.* the agriculture industry needs crop pickers only at harvest time. Even skilled workers are affected if their work cannot take place at certain times, but in this case wages must be high enough to carry skilled workers through times of unemployment, otherwise the industry would have difficulty in attracting such workers. It has been argued that the term does not apply in this instance.

structural unemployment Usually high level of unemployment, caused by the change from a labour-intensive to a capital-intensive economy.

unfair dismissal The removal of a person from his or her job for reasons that are unfair. To discover whether these reasons are indeed unfair, the case may be brought before an industrial tribunal.

unit Term with three meanings.
First, a unit is one single item produced for sale. *See also* **cost, unit**.
Second, a unit is the name given to a single area of factory or retail space, especially on industrial estates.
Third, in finance, a unit is a share (in the everyday sense) in an investment or series of investments. *See* **unit trust**.

accumulation units In **unit trusts** or life assurance, an accumulation unit is one for which the **dividend** is ploughed back into the investment to produce higher earnings. *See* **assurance, life**.

capital units Another name for initial units.

initial units In life assurance or a pension policy for which there is a regular investment, initial units may be allocated for a specified period of time, which provides the investor with a lower income than accumulation units, the difference covering the initial administration costs of the plan. *See* **units, accumulation**.

uncertificated units In **unit trusts**, the dividends from the trust may be reinvested, to form new units. In most cases the dividends are too small to justify the issuing of a new certificate and so uncertificated units are held on behalf of the investor until the units are surrendered.

See also **unit trust**.

unit trust Trust into which small investors may buy by acquiring units.

The capital thus collected is invested in various securities in a wide range of markets. Contributors to unit trusts benefit from the diverse nature of the **portfolio** built up, and from the expertise of a manager.

unlawful The formal difference between an act that is unlawful and an act that is illegal is that an illegal act is forbidden by law, whereas an unlawful act is not protected by law. *E.g.* most forms of wagering are unlawful.

unlisted securities = **USM**

unloading Practice of putting on the market large quantities of a certain product (or certain shares) at a low price. *See also* **dumping**.

unpaid services In calculating the national product, unpaid services are not taken into account. Such services include those provided by people who do work for themselves, such as gardening and DIY, wives who look after children and manage households, and 'carers' who provide nursing care for relatives who are ill.

unquoted Adjective that normally describes shares or debentures traded unofficially and not quoted on the Stock Market. *See also* **investments, unquoted; securities, unquoted**.

unsecured If something (normally a loan of some kind) is unsecured, perhaps because there are no assets to act as collateral, there is no guarantee it will be repaid. *See* **creditor, unsecured; debentures, unsecured; security**.

up or out (position) *US* High-pressure job or position. In such a job an executive is either promoted very quickly or is replaced equally speedily. "The job of brand manager is an up or out position."

upside *US* The bright side – the possibility of things getting better. "Trade figures will have to be very bad indeed to affect the dollar. Upside potential in this case is far greater than downside potential."

upstream Movement, *e.g.* of funds, from a subsidiary company to its parent. *See also* **downstream**.

upstream activity Activity within an industry or company that extends beyond basic manufacturing and marketing. Upstream activities are generally more expensive than these **downstream** activities, but are important in that they help to expand activities in general. Two examples of upstream activities are research and development in any industry, and exploration in the oil industry.

"Higher crude oil prices bolstered earnings for upstream activities, such as oil exploration and production, while downstream activities showed steep declines."

uptick (up tick *US*) Describes a transaction (such as a sale of shares) that is made at a higher price than the one obtained immediately before. Also known as a plus tick. Uptick is also used to denote a (short-lived) rise in a price or value.

"There was a small drop in sterling late in the day, which seemed to be caused by a slight uptick in the dollar."
See also **down tick; tick**.

uptrend Improvement of some general kind, *e.g.* in market prices.
"The company's executives expected a small setback in profits in the short term, but were optimistic that the uptrend would continue."

usance Term with three meanings.
First, usance is the rate of interest charged on a loan.
Second, usance is unearned income derived from the ownership of wealth or capital. *See* **income, unearned**.
Third, usance is the amount of time customarily allowed for payment of short-term **bills of exchange** between two foreign countries. The usual period is 60 days.

USM Abbreviation of **unlisted securities market**.

usufruct The right to the use of property belonging to someone else, but not the right to diminish its value in such use.

utmost good faith = **uberrima fides**.

V

valium picnic *US* Popular term for a quiet day on the New York Stock Exchange.

valuation Estimate of what something is worth. More particularly, however, the term can be used to mean a summary of the value of a **portfolio** of investments at a given time.

value Term that is not as precise as it might seem. The value of something is the price a buyer is prepared to pay for it, but this can fluctuate according to all sorts of variables, *e.g.* whether it is a buyer's or a seller's market, to what use the buyer will be putting the goods, etc. *See* **buyer's market; market, seller's; market, open**.
 Normally, the term is qualified, so that confusion as to its meaning is minimized.

annual value Income that accrues annually from the possession of, say, property or a portfolio of shares. A distinction is normally made between **net annual value** and **gross annual value**, the former being the annual income from a possession after expenses of ownership have been deducted, and the latter being the income before expenses have been taken into account. *See also* **value, rateable**.

asset value Value of the assets of a company.

asset value per share Value of the assets of a company, minus its liabilities, divided by the number of shares.

book value Alternative term for written down value. *See* **write down**.

break-up value Value of a share or company on the assumption that the company is being disbanded or broken up. The break-up value of a share is calculated by dividing the probable net proceeds from the sale of the company's assets by the number of shares. Sometimes, the term is used as a loose synonym for asset value per share.

discounted value If a share price falls below its par value, then the lower price is known as its discounted value.

extrinsic value Constituent part of the value of a traded **option** not calculated by difference in market price to exercise price. Extrinsic value is governed by such factors as time left to run and the volatility of the market concerned. *See* **price, exercise; price, market; value, intrinsic**.

face value Another name for nominal value. *See* **value, nominal**.

intrinsic value Value of the materials from which an object is made rather than its market or face value. E.g. a coin may be said to be worth so much and is exchanged on the basis of that stated value, but the metal used in minting it may be worth much less. Intrinsic value is also the value (if any) of a traded **option** that is in-the-money, brought about by a favourable difference between market price and exercise price. *See* **price, exercise; price, market; value, extrinsic**.

market value Price at which something is traded on the open market.

net asset value (NAV) Value of a company's assets after the company's **liabilities** have been deducted.

nominal value Also known as face value, the nominal value of something is the value or price written on it. *E.g.* the denomination of a bank note or the par value of a share.

present value Assessment of the current net **cost** or value of future expenditure or benefit. Most frequently used to measure return on **capital** investment.

rateable value Value of a property for the purposes of calculating the **rates,** based on the estimated amount of **rent** the property would fetch (the **annual value**) on the open market and with vacant possession.

real value Value of something when compared to fluctuations in price indexes, *i.e.* during times of **inflation** or **deflation**. *E.g.* the real value of a 10% wage increase at a time of 5% inflation is only 5%, because the cash represented by the 10% increase will buy only 5% more goods. *See* **index, retail price**.

surrender value Value (realized upon surrender) that certain kinds of **assurance** policies may acquire after they have been in force for a certain period of time.

value added Difference between the price a company or industry pays for its materials and the price at which it sells its product. *E.g.* a used car dealer may acquire a car, recondition the engine and respray the body. When he sells it, the added value is the value of these operations as reflected in the new (higher) selling price of the car. *See also* **tax, value added.**

value in exchange Value of something as a form of exchange, rather than as an object of use. *E.g.* precious stones are worth virtually nothing in terms of value in use but because they are desirable, they fetch a high price. *See also* **value in use; value paradox.**

value in use Value of something to the person using it. This value may be different to the sale value of the object. *E.g.* a machine may be valuable to its owner because it produces goods for sale, whereas it may be valueless in itself perhaps because it cannot be moved. *See also* **value in exchange; value paradox.**

value paradox An object or commodity may be valuable in terms of exchange, but totally worthless in terms of use. Equally, a thing may be extremely valuable in use but is inexpensive to acquire. *E.g.* Salt or water are very useful commodities, but are fairly cheap. Most precious stones may be said to be totally useless, but are expensive to buy because they are rare. The value paradox is this apparently illogical assignment of value. *See* **value in exchange; value in use.**

See also **broker, value; write down.**

valued policy = policy, valued

VAT Abbreviation of value added tax. *See* **tax, value added.**

vendor Person who sells goods or services

street vendor Someone who sells small items at retail in the street, sometimes without a licence to do so.

VER Abbreviation of **voluntary export restraint**, the limiting of certain types of exports from one country to another (or group of countries) in order to forestall the imposition of import quotas or other restrictions by importing countries. It is often preceeded by a voluntary restraint agreement, stating that this is what the exporting country intends to do.

verba chartarum fortuis accipiuntur contra proferentem Maxim used in legal circles, meaning that where the wording of a contract is imprecise and open to misinterpretation, it will be taken in the sense that goes against the party that drew up the contract. Also known as the contra proferentem rule.

verification Checking that a statement is accurate. More particularly, the term refers to the checking of statements made by a company in a **prospectus**. Verification is undertaken by the company's solicitors in order to protect the company's directors. When a prospectus is sent for verification, it is often accompanied by **verification notes**, clarifying each statement.

viability Ability of a person or a country to support itself, or of a product to survive in a market and generate a profit.

vicarious performance This occurs when a party who has contracted to supply something passes the work on to someone else to be done. In this case, legal responsibility under the contract still lies with the supplying party. *See* **assignment of contract; delegatus non potest delegare**.

vigilantibus non dormientibus jura subveniunt Maxim meaning that if people think they have a claim to make, they should go ahead and make the claim, as soon as possible. *See also* **laches**.

visible Describing something that can be seen, identified or counted. *See* **balance of trade; exports, visible; imports, visible**.

visibles A country's income from the sale of tangible goods as opposed to the sale of services. *See also* **invisibles**.

volatility Measure of the stability of a particular instrument. If, say, a share price or a market index moves often and vacillates widely, then it is said to be volatile.

volume Term very often confused with **turnover**, although in some instances they may be used to mean the same thing. Strictly, volume is the number of units traded whereas turnover refers to the value of the units traded.

"The stock exchange today saw the third largest drop in terms of points, but volume was moderate at about 650 million shares."

On the commodities market, however, volume refers to the quantity of **soft commodities** traded, and turnover refers to the **tonnage** of metals traded over a particular period of time (normally over a day of trading). *See also* **turnover**.

voting rights Right of a shareholder to vote at a company's annual general meeting. This right depends upon what type of shares are held; generally, ordinary shares carry voting rights whereas **debentures** do not. The **articles of association** and the company's **prospectus** detail which shares carry voting rights and which do not. *See also* **AGM; share, ordinary**.

voucher Generally, a paper given in place of money, such as a gift voucher or a luncheon voucher.

In **accounting**, a voucher is more precisely a document (such as a **receipt**) that supports or proves entries in books of prime entry. *See* **prime entry, books of**.

VRA Abbreviation of **voluntary restraint agreement**. *See* **VER**.

vulture capitalism View of venture capitalism, whereby investors lure talented people away from established companies, encourage them to set up on their own, work hard and be ingenious and then face a demand for a high return on the investment. *See also* **capital, venture**.

W

wage Payment made to a worker, normally fixed as a rate per hour, day or week. *See* **economy, wage; freeze, wage.**

minimum wage Lowest amount a company may pay a worker, often fixed by legislation or trade union agreements.

wage differential Differences between levels of wages, caused by many variables, *e.g.* occupation, industry, gender of the employee, geographical location, experience and qualifications of the employee, etc.

wage freeze Situation in which wages are fixed for a certain period of time, either by government authority on a national level or by agreement within a single company or industry.

wage-price spiral Form of **inflation**. If a producer is forced to increase wages, he must increase the price of his product to cover the increased wage costs, which in turn leads to new wage demands.

wager Essentially, a wager is a contract between two parties, that one will give the other something of value depending upon the outcome of some future event.

waiter Person on the London Stock Exchange or at Lloyds who runs errands, takes messages and looks after the day-to-day running of the exchange. Historically, the first waiters were those in the coffee houses where dealings first took place.

waiting time Time an employee spends not working *i.e.* waiting for a machine to warm up or be repaired, or waiting for another employee to finish the previous stage of a job.

waive To give up a right or to remove or overule conditions of an agreement.

Wall Street *US* Another name for the New York Stock Exchange (Wall Street is the street in Manhattan on which the exchange is located). Sometimes the name is further abbreviated to The Street.

wall, the *US* Popular name for the problem encountered by some bankers when trying to persuade customers to make use of automatic telling machines. *See* **ATM**.

warehousing With reference to shipping, warehousing is the business of storing, examining and sorting goods which takes place in a warehouse before they are released into the country in question.

bonded warehouse Type of warehouse for goods on which excise duties need not be paid until goods are removed.

warrant Term with three meanings.
First, a warrant is a receipt that describes goods held in a warehouse, transferable by endorsement. In this sense a **wharfinger warrant** (also known as a wharfinger receipt) is a similar receipt describing goods on a wharf. *See also* **wharfage**.
Second, it is a long-dated **option**.
Third, a warrant is a security of a specific market value that may be exchanged for a certain share at a predetermined price. The warrant's value lies in the difference between the predetermined conversion price and the market price of the share.

exploding warrant US Warrant introduced in order to dilute the shareholding of a company **raider** during a **takeover bid**. Also known as a springing warrant.

share warrant Certificate of ownership of shares, presented after shares are fully-paid.

springing warrant US Alternative term for exploding warrant.

warranty Term with three meanings.
First, a warranty is a statement or guarantee that goods are in working order or that workmanship is not faulty.
Second, in a **contract**, a warranty is an implicit or explicit guarantee that the premises upon which the contract is based are factual or true. If the warranty turns out to be false, the contract is not void, but the injured party may seek damages.
Third, in **marine insurance**, a warranty is the insuree's statement that certain things are true, *e.g.* that a vessel is seaworthy.

floating warranty Guarantee given by one party that induces a second to enter into a contract with a third party.

"Before using the mortgage broker, the home buyer sought a floating warranty from the estate agent."

warranty of authority Power given to an **agent** to act under the instructions of a principal.

watering stock = stock, watered

waybill Document, normally drawn up by a carrier of goods, describing the goods, naming the sender and addressee and the conditions of carriage.

air waybill Document that accompanies goods being shipped by air, itemizing the goods and constituting evidence of the existence of a **contract** to make the shipment.

wealth Total of a person's or country's **assets**, both tangible and intangible.

wear and tear Popular and legal term for **depreciation**. Wear and tear is the decrease in value of an item due to deterioration through normal use rather than through accident or negligence.

weekend effect *US* Theory that prices of stocks and shares do better on a Friday than on a Monday, due to such influences as the way in which dealers time their settlement of purchases etc.

weighted ballot = ballot, weighted

wharfage Payment made for placing goods on a wharf during loading or unloading of a vessel.

wharfinger Someone who is responsible for the running of a wharf, similar to a warehouseman. *See also* **warrant, wharfinger**.

whipsaw *US* Violent movement (or series of such) in prices on any market.

"Today's whipsaw action reflects nervousness in the foreign-exchange market."

"Whipsawed by the dollar, blue-chip stocks managed to end another volatile session yesterday little changed, but many other stocks fell."

white collar Employee who does office rather than factory work. *See also* **blue collar**.

white knight When a company finds itself the target of a **takeover bid**, it may seek an alternative company or person to whom it offers to sell itself in preference to being taken over by the original bidder. This friendly company is known as a white knight and the tactic is known as a white knight defence. *See also* **grey knight; white squire defence**.

white squire defence In a **takeover** situation, a **target** company may place a significant number of its shares with a friendly party in order to prevent the **raider** from acquiring them. *See also* **white knight**.

wholesaler Person who buys goods in bulk from a producer and then sells them in smaller quantities to retailers or other wholesalers, earning a profit either by charging a commission to the retailer or by adding to the manufacturer's price.

wife's earnings election In personal **taxation** in the UK, it may be advantageous for a wife to have her earned **income** taxed separately from that of her husband. The husband, however, continues to pay tax on her unearned income although they are essentially paying tax as single people. There have been moves recently to have all married couples taxed separately and to abolish the wife's earnings election.

will Legal document drawn up by a person (usually under the advice of a solicitor) giving instructions as to how the person's estate is to be distributed after his or her death. The signature of a will has to be witnessed by two people, neither of whom is a beneficiary. *See also* **intestacy**.

windbill Alternative term for **accommodation bill**.

winding-up Cessation of business activity on the part of a company and the start of that company's **liquidation**.

windmill Alternative term for **accommodation bill**.

window-dressing In **accounting**, a (legal) method of making a set of accounts seem better than they are by presenting them in such a way as to make the usual comparisons between figures difficult.

withdrawal of labour Slightly formal term for an official **strike**.
"At a mass meeting yesterday union officials called for immediate withdrawal of labour."

without recourse Note on a **bill of exchange** indicating that in the event of non-payment of the bill, the current holder may not blame the person from whom he or she bought it. Also written in French as sans recours.

with profits Assurance policy whereby the policyholder receives a share of the company's profits during the term of the policy.

work in progress In accounting, the value of goods currently under manufacture or services being supplied, but not completed at the end of the accounting period.

work study Study carried out to minimize effort put into a particular task; similar to a time-and-motion study.

work to rule Form of industrial action during which the workers abide strictly by the employment agreement negotiated between them or their trade union and the management, such as refusing to cover work for absent colleagues, or to work particularly fast.

working Active or producing. *See* **assets, working; capital, working; director, working**.

worst moment concept In preparing financial projections and budgets, the worst moment concept takes into account the worst times in **cash-flow**, *e.g.* periods when large bills must be paid, as well as the easier times.

writ Notice served by a High Court, normally signalling the beginning of a court action, informing a person that he or she is either to appear in court at a certain date or that he or she must perform (or refrain from performing) a certain action. Failure to comply with a writ is punishable by the court.

write down In accounting, to take the cost of an **asset** and deduct the amount by which the asset has depreciated in capital terms. This is the written-down or **book value** of the asset.

write off (**charge off** *US*) To delete an **asset** from the accounts because it has depreciated (or been written-down) so far that it no longer has any book value. *See also* **write down**.

writer to the signet In the Scottish legal system, a person who performs the same function as a **solicitor** in England and Wales.

WT *US* Abbreviation of **warrant**.

X

XA Abbreviation of ex all, denoting shares that have been bought minus rights to any benefits currently being offered, *e.g.* participation in a rights issue, rights to **dividends, etc.** *See* **issue, rights**.

XC Abbreviation of ex capitalization, denoting a share that has been bought minus the right to participate in a forthcoming **scrip** issue.

XD Abbreviation of ex dividend, denoting a share that has been sold without the right to receive the next **dividend**.

XR Abbreviation of ex rights, denoting a **share** that has been sold, but does not entitle the new holder to participation in a forthcoming rights issue. *See* **issue, rights**.

Y

yankee Slang term used on the London Stock Exchange, that refers to US **securities**.

yard Slang term for a **billion**.

year Period of twelve calendar months.

base year Sometimes also known as the **base date**, the time from which an index (*e.g.* the Financial Times All Share Index) is calculated. *See* **index**.

financial year Period of twelve months, beginning anywhere in the calendar year, used for company accounting purposes.

fiscal year Period of twelve months for the purposes of tax calculation. In the UK the fiscal year runs from 6 April to the following 5 April.

tax year Period of twelve months, specified to start at any calendar month, for tax and accounting purposes. Also known as financial year. *See also* **year, fiscal**.

year-earlier US Jargon meaning the previous year.
" A & G Electronics posted a pre-tax profit up 20% on year-earlier pre-tax profits of $20 million.

year-later US The next year.

year's purchase Method of calculating the **value** of a purchase (say, of a company) by relating it to the anticipated year's **income** from the purchase. *I.e.* the price of a business in relation to its average annual profits *or* the price of a building in relation to the average annual rent. The price is in this way said to be *x* year's purchase of the profit.

Yellow book Issued by the Stock Exchange Council, a book entitled *Admission of Securities to Listing*, which sets out the regulations of admission to the **Official List**.

yield Return on an investment, taking into account the annual income and the capital value of the investment, usually expressed as a percentage.

current yield **Dividend** calculated as a percentage of the price paid for each share.

dividend yield Yield calculated in relation to the current market price of the investment. *See* **dividend; value, nominal**.

earnings yield Hypothetical figure that provides a good measurement of the worth of an investment. It is reached by relating a company's divisible net earnings to the market price of the investment. Sometimes, with reference to fixed interest **securities**, the term is used interchangeably with **flat yield**.

effective yield Yield calculated as a percentage of the price of the investment.

flat yield Yield on a fixed interest security shown by relating the income from the security to the present market price. Also know as the **running yield**.

gross yield Return on an investment calculated before tax is deducted.

redemption yield Refers to **bonds** with a fixed **redemption** date. Redemption yield takes into account capital gain upon redemption plus the dividend, and relates them to the market price of the bond.

fixed yield Return that remains the same.

running yield Alternative term for flat yield. *See* **yield, running**.

yield gap Difference in average yield between investments in ordinary **shares** and in gilt-edged **securities**.

York-Antwerp rules Voluntary code, drawn up in 1877, for those involved in shipping cargo by sea.

Z

zai-tech Japanese and US Stock market practice of borrowing money in order to invest in stocks and bonds.

zebra Form of zero coupon bond. *See* **bond, zero coupon**.

zero Shorthand for zero coupon bond. *See* **bond, zero coupon**

zero-base budgeting Method of **budget** management whereby each manager assigns a priority rating to each budget request. Zero-base budgeting forces each manager to justify every request.

zero-rated In the UK, item attracting no **VAT**.
"For the time being, books continue to be zero-rated."

zip-code *US* Post code comprised of state abbreviation and five figures, used in much the same way as a post code in the UK.
"The company's zip-code is NY 10016."

Appendices

Business Schools

The following is a list of UK business schools and unversities which offer courses in business-related fields. Information about specific courses should be obtained in the first instance from these addresses.

University of Aston Management Centre
Nelson Building
Gosta Green
Birmingham B4 7ET   021-359-3011

University of Bath School of Management
Claverton Down
Bath BA2 7AY   0225-61244

Queen's University of Belfast
Department of Business Studies
University Road
Belfast B17 1NN   0232-245133

University of Bradford Management Centre
Emm Lane
Bradford BD9 4JL   0274-42299

City University Business School
Frobisher Crescent
Barbican Centre
London EC2Y 8HB   01-920-0111

Cranfield Institute of Technology
Cranfield School of Management
Cranfield MK43 0AL   0234-752728

Durham University Business School
Mill Hill Lane
Durham DH1 3LB   0385-41919

University of Glasgow
Scottish Business School
The University
Glasgow G12 8LS   041-339-8855

Henley Management College
Greenlands
Henley-on-Thames RG9 3AU   0491-66454

University of Hull
Department of Management Systems and Sciences
Hull HU6X 7RX   0482-46311

University of Lancaster
Gillow House
Bailrigg
Lancaster LA1 4YX   0524-65201

University of Leeds
Department of Management Studies
Leeds LS2 9JT   0532-31751

London Graduate School of Business Studies
Sussex Place
Regent's Park
London NW1 4SA   01-262-5050

London School of Economics
Houghton Street
London WC2A 2AE   01-405-7686

University of London Imperial College
Management Science Department
London SW7 2BX   01-589-5111

Loughborough University of Technology
Department of Management Studies
Loughborough LE11 3TU   0509-263171

University of Manchester
Manchester Business School
Booth Street West
Manchester M15 6PB   061-275-6333

**University of Manchester Institute of Science
    & Technology**
Department of Management Sciences
PO Box 88
Sackville Street
Manchester M60 1QD   061-236-3311

University of Oxford Templeton College
Oxford Centre for Management Studies
Kennington Road
Kennington
Oxford OX1 5NY   0865-735422

University of Salford
Department of Business and Administration
Salford M5 4WT   061-736-5843

University of Sheffield
Division of Economic Studies
Sheffield S10 2TN   0742-768555

University of Strathclyde Business School
130 Rottenrow
Glasgow G4 0GE   041-552-7141

University of Wales Institute of Science & Technology
Aberconway Building
Colum Drive
Cardiff CF1 3EU   0222-42588

University of Warwick
School of Industrial & Business Studies
Coventry CV4 7AL   0203-523523

Currencies of the World

Country	Currency	Division	Abbrev.
Afghanistan	Afghani	puli	Af or Afs
Albania	Lek	qindars	Lk
Algeria	Algerian dinar	centimes	AD or DA
Andorra	French franc	centimes	Fr or F
Angola	Kwanza	cents	KW
Antigua	East Carribean dollar	cents	ECar$ or EC$
Argentina	Austral	centavos	
Australia	Australian dollar	cents	A$
Austria	Schilling	groschen	Sch or ASch
Bahamas	Bahamian dollar	cents	Ba$
Bahrein	Bahreini dinar	fils	BD
Bangladesh	Taka	poisha	Tk
Barbados	Barbados dollar	cents	Bds$ or BD$
Belgium	Belgian franc	centimes	BFr or Bf or FB
Belize	Belize dollar	cents	B$ or $B
Benin	CFA franc	centimes	CFA Fr
Bermuda	Bermuda dollar	cents	Bda$
Bhutan	Ngultrum	tikchung	N
Bolivia	Bolivian peso	centavos	B$ or $B
Botswana	Pula	cents	Pu or P
Brazil	Cruzeiro	centavos	Cr or Cr$
Brunei	Brunei dollar	cents	Br$ or B$
Bulgaria	Lev	stotinki	Lv
Burkina Faso	CFA franc	centimes	CFA Fr
Burma	Kyat	pyas	Kt
Burundi	Burundi franc	centimes	Bur Fr or FrBr
Cameroon	CFA franc	centimes	CFA Fr
Canada	Canadian dollar	cents	Can$ or C$
Cape Verde Islands	Escudo caboverdianos	centavos	CV esc

Country	Currency	Division	Abbrev.
Cayman Islands	Cayman Island dollar	cents	CayI$
Central African Republic	CFA franc	centimes	CFA Fr
Chad	CFA franc	centimes	CFA Fr
Chile	Chilean peso	centavos	Ch$
Colombia	Colombian peso	centavos	Col$
Comoros	CFA Franc	centimes	CFA Fr
Congo	CFA Franc	centimes	CFA Fr
Costa Rica	Colón	centimos	CR¢ or ¢
Cuba	Cuban peso	centavos	Cub$
Cyprus	Cyprus pound	mils	£C or C£
Czechoslovakia	Crown or koruna	hellers	Kcs
Denmark	Krone	rer	DKr or DKK
Djibouti	Djibouti franc	centimes	DjFr
Dominica	East Caribbean dollar	cents	ECar$ or EC$
Dominican Republic	Dominican peso	centavos	DR$
Ecuador	Sucre	centavos	DR$
Egypt	Egyptian pound	piastres	£E or E£
El Salvador	Colón	centavos	ES¢ or ¢
Equatorial Guinea	Ekuele or ekpwele or peseta Guineana	centimos	E
Ethiopia	Birr or Ethiopian dollar	cents	Br
Fiji	Fijian dollar	cents	$F or F$
Finland	Marakka or Finnmark	pennia	Fmk
France	French franc	centimes	Fr or F or FF
French Guiana	French franc	centimes	Fr or F or FF
Gabon	CFA franc	centimes	CFA Fr
Gambia, The	Dalasi	butut	Di
Germany, East	Ostmark or DDR-mark	pfennig	M
Germany, West	Deutsche mark	pfennig	DM
Ghana	Cedi	pesewas	¢
Greece	Drachma	lepta	Dr
Grenada	East Caribbean dollar	cents	ECar$ or EC$
Guatemala	Quetzal	centavos	Q
Guinea	Syli	cauris	Sy
Guinea-Bissau	Guinea-Bissau peso	centavos	GB P
Guyana	Guyana dollar	cents	G$ or Guy$
Haiti	Gourde	centimes	Gde
Honduras	Lempira	centavos	La

Country	Currency	Division	Abbrev.
Hong Kong	Hong Kong dollar	cents	HK$
Hungary	Forint	filler	Ft
Iceland	Króna	aurar	IKr
India	Rupee	paise	R or Re or Rs
Indonesia	Rupiah	sen	Rp
Iran	Rial	dinars	RI
Iraq	Iraqui dinar	fils	ID
Irish Republic	Irish pund or punt	pence	IR$ or $
Israel	Shekel	agorot	IS
Italy	Lira	centesimi	L
Ivory Coast	CFA Franc	centimes	CFA Fr
Jamaica	Jamaican dollar	cents	J$ or Jam$
Japan	Yen	sen	Y or ¥
Jordan	Jordanian dinar	fils	JD
Kampuchea	Riel	sen	RI
Kenya	Kenyan shilling	cents	KSh or Sh
Korea, North	North Korean won	jon	NK W
Korea, South	South Korean won	chon	SK W
Kuwait	Kuwaiti dinar	fils	KD
Laos	Kip	at	K or Kp
Lebanon	Lebanese pound	piastres	£Leb or L£
Lesotho	Loti	lisente	L
Liberia	Liberian dollar	cents	L$
Libya	Libyan dinar	dirhams	LD
Liechtenstein	Swiss franc	centimes	SFr or FS
Luxembourg	Luxembourg franc	centimes	LFr
Macau	Pataca	avos	P or $
Madeira	Portuguese escudo	centavos	Esc
Malagasy Republic	Malagasy franc	centimes	FMG or Mal Fr
Malawi	Kwacha	tambala	
Malaysia	Ringgit or Malaysian dollar	cents	M$
Maldives	Maldivian rupee	paise	MvRe
Mali	Mali franc	centimes	MFr or MF
Malta	Maltese pound	cents	£M or M£
Mauritania	Ouguiya	khoums	U
Mauritius	Mauritian rupee	cents	Mau Rs or R
Mexico	Peso	centavos	Mex$

Country	Currency	Division	Abbrev.
Monaco	French franc	centimes	Fr or F or FF
Mongolian Republic	Tugrik	mngs	Tug
Montserrat	East Caribbean dollar	cents	ECar$ or EC$
Morocco	Dirham	centimes	Dh or DH
Mozambique	Metical	centavos	M
Namibia	South African rand	cents	R
Nauru	Australian dollar	cents	A$
Nepal	Nepalese rupee	paise	NR or NRe
Netherlands, The	Guilder or gulden or florin	cents	HFI or DFI or Gld or Fl
New Zealand	New Zealand dollar	cents	NZ$
Nicaragua	Cordoba	centavos	C$ or C
Niger	CFA franc	centimes	CFA Fr
Nigeria	Naira	kobo	N or N
Norway	Krone	rer	NKr
Oman	Omani Ryal or Rial	baizas	RO
Pakistan	Pakistan rupee	paise	R or Pak Re
Panama	Balboa	centesimos	Ba
Papua New Guinea	Kina	toea	Ka or K
Paraguay	Guarani	centimos	G
Peru	Sol	centavos	S
Philippines	Philippine peso	centavos	P or PP
Poland	Zloty	groszy	Zl
Portugal	Escudo	centavos	Esc
Puerto Rico	US dollar	cents	$ or US$
Qatar	Qatar riyal	dirhams	QR
Reunion	CFA franc	centimes	CFA Fr
Romania	Leu	bani	L or l
Rwanda	Rwanda franc	centimes	Rw Fr
St Lucia	East Caribbean dollar	cents	ECar$ or EC$
St Vincent	East Caribbean dollar	cents	ECar$ or EC$
Saudi Arabia	Saudi riyal or rial	halalah	SA R
Senegal	CFA franc	centimes	CFA Fr
Seychelles	Seychelles rupee	cents	SRe or R
Sierra Leone	Leone	cents	Le
Singapore	Singapore dollar	cents	S$ or Sing$
Solomon Islands	Solomon Island dollar	cents	SI$

Country	Currency	Division	Abbrev.
Somalia	Somali shilling	cents	Som SH or So Sh
South Africa	Rand	cents	R
Spain	Peseta	centimos	Pta
Sri Lanka	Sri Lanka rupee	cents	SC Re
Sudan	Sudanese pound	piastres	Sud£ or £5
Surinam	Surinam guilder	cents	S Gld
Swaziland	Lilangeni	cents	Li or E
Sweden	Krona	Hrer	SKr
Switzerland	Swiss franc	centimes	SFr or FS or SWFr
Syria	Syrian pound	piastres	£Syr or £
Taiwan	New Taiwan dollar	cents	T$ or NT$
Tanzania	Tanzanian shilling	cents	TSh
Thailand	Baht	satang	Bt
Tonga	Pa'anga	senik	
Togo	CFA franc	centimes	CFA Fr
Trinidad & Tobago	Trinidad & Tobago dollar	cents	TT$
Tunisia	Tunisian dollar	millimes	TD
Turkey	Turkish lira	kurus	TL
Tuvalu	Australian dollar	cents	$A
Uganda	Uganda shilling	cents	USh
Union of Soviet Socialist Republics	Rouble	kopecks	Rub
United Arab Emirates	UAE Dirham	fils	UAE Dh or UD
United Kingdom	Pound sterling	pence	£ or £Stg
United States of America	Dollar	cents	$ or US$
Uruguay	Uruguayan new peso	centesimos	N$
Venezuela		vatu	
Vietnam	Bol/var	centimos	B
Virgin Islands	Dong	xu	D
Yemen, South	South Yemen dollar	fils	YD
Yemen, North	Yemeni riyal	fils	YR
Yugoslavia	Dinar	paras	Din or DN
Zaire	Zaire	makata	Z
Zambia	Kwacha	ngwee	K
Zimbabwe	Zimbabwe dollar	cents	Z$

Major Stock Exchanges of the World

Australia

All six capital cities of the Australian states have a stock exchange, with the two largest – Sydney and Melbourne – accounting for over 90% of share-trading volume. With all exchanges now linked by computer, uniform prices are quoted, and a "national" stock exchange has resulted.

Dealing is by the trading post system, with brokers acting in dual capacity. All securities may be traded on the floor of the exchange, but there is no obligation to this effect.

Business hours local: 10.00am – 12.30pm, 2.15pm – 3.45pm
GMT: 12.00 midnight – 2.30am, 4.15am – 5.45 am

Settlement and delivery 5 days

France

The major exchange is the Paris Bourse, although there are six other provincial exchanges. All dealings are done through brokers (known as *agents de change*) and all securities must be traded on the Bourse.

Four types of market operate on the Bourse.

1. *Cash Market* Payment and delivery fall due immediately the bargain is complete.
2. *Forward Market* Since its introduction, has taken much of the business of the cash market. Settlement and delivery take place once a month, on the last business day of that month, although a margin of 20-40% is required immediately. The system of dealing through fixed order auctions is currently being dismantled to make way for a continuous market.
3. *Over The Counter Market* (OTC) Market for securities not on the official list, but bearing some liquidity as issue sponsors are obliged to make a market. Transactions are for immediate settlement.

342

Business hours local: 9.00am − 4.00pm
                GMT:8.00am − 3.00pm

Hong Kong

Four separate exchanges were united in 1986 to form a new single exchange for Hong Kong. This new exchange comprises a trading floor, but most transactions are carried out by telephone. Share certificates with transfer deeds must be delivered within 24 hours (at which time payment is also due). Despite computerization, registration is often a lengthy process, making selling stock immediately after its purchase impossible. To avoid this, it is common practice for stock not to be registered, making it deliverable immediately. Registration would take place if a dividend payment was due, or if a rights or bonus issue was imminent.

Business hours local: time: 9.00am − 4.00pm
                GMT:5.00pm − 12 midnight

Taxation Stamp duty of 0.3% is payable by both parties, and a transfer stamp of 0.5% is payable by the seller.

Japan

The Tokyo Stock Exchange is the largest of eight exchanges in Japan. There are two sections to the exchange: the first handles transactions in listed securities; the second handles transactions in a second tier of securities. With both sections, the main method of dealing is in open auction.

Japanese securities feature a "limit up/limit down" system, whereby each security has an allocated maximum price movement (sometimes as much as 30%) in either direction before trading in those securities is suspended for the rest of the day. It has been suggested that this system be extended to other major markets, although opinion is still divided as to its benefits.

Business hours local: 9.00am − 3.30pm
                GMT:12.00 midnight − 6.30am

Settlement Settlement and delivery is on the third business day following the transaction. The first and fourth Saturdays of each month are included as business days. Cash transactions are also possible, with delivery and cash payments usually being made on the day the bargain is struck.

Taxation Sale of securities attracts a 0.55% transfer stamp duty charge.

Netherlands

The Netherlands has three stock exchanges, but Amsterdam has the only official exchange where all Dutch securities are dealt. The majority of Dutch securities are now in bearer form, facilitating delivery, which, like settlement, is usually on a five-day basis.

Business hours local: 9.00am – 4.00pm
GMT:8.00am – 3.00pm

Taxation The exchange levies a tax of 0.12% on all transactions.

Singapore

Trading on the exchange floor is on a broker-to-broker basis, and shares are dealt in two trading "sections". The first section consists of prominent companies with a record of consistent dividend payments. All other securities fall into the second section. This distinction between the two sections is carried into permitted trading times: the first section is traded from 10.00am – 12.30pm; the second section is traded from 2.30pm – 4.00pm. Block trading away from the floor is also permitted.

When trading in first section securities, settlement and delivery can be carried out in one of two ways. First, it may be done on a "ready", which allows securities to be delivered on any business day up until the Tuesday of the week following that transaction. Second, it may be done on a "settlement" basis, on which settlement may take place on the penultimate business day of the month in which the bargain was struck. Second section securities are settled only on the "ready' basis.

Business hours local: 10.00am – 12.30pm, 2.30pm – 4.00pm
GMT:2.00am -4.30am, 6.30am – 8.00am

Taxation 0.2% stamp duty is payable by the purchaser.

United Kingdom

London boasts the world's third largest stock market, which (along with other UK markets) has been undergoing significant changes in recent years. The much-discussed "Big Bang" of October 1986, brought about by advances in technology, increased global trading and a general need for reform (highlighted by the Wilson Committee, Office of Fair Trading) abolished single capacity (the traditional divide between broker and jobber), scrapped minimum commissions, introduced SEAQ (Stock Exchange Automated Quotations) and rules to regulate the market-makers who used it, and opened up Stock Exchange membership.

The introduction of the Third Market in January 1987 was also a direct result of de-regulation. To prevent abuse of the new system, the Financial Services Act was enacted (in force from 29 April 1988), which covers all aspects of financial services. Under this Act, all companies operating in this field must be members of one of the SRO's operating under the umbrella of the SIB (Securities and Investment Board).

Members of the Stock Exchange no longer have a complete monopoly; dealers licensed by the Department of Trade and Industry may trade in equities and in securities which are not subject to the rules and regulations of the Stock Exchange (most notably in OTC shares), but must still be members of an SRO[1], probably TSA (The Securities Association).

Four markets operate in the UK:

1. *Main Market* (the full FT list)
2. *Unlisted Securities Market* (USM) Securities not on the Official List, but designated by the Stock Exchange Council as shares in which dealings are permitted.
3. *Third Market* Introduced in January 1987 for companies not eligible for USM listings, with less strict requirements – usually only one year's trading record is required.
4. *Over-the-counter Market*[2] (OTC) Essentially a telephone market, with the sponsors, who have usually underwritten the sale, placing the shares among their own clients. These securities are not subject to Stock Exchange rules and regulations, and may be highly speculative. Dealings on the OTC market on the Stock Exchange are permitted, but only in restricted sizes, and with prior permission from the SEC.

Business hours[3] 9.00am – 5.00pm

Settlement Dealing is done on account, with settlement taking place on the sixth day after the end of the account.

Notes [1] The Stock Exchange itself is a recognized SRO. [2] NASDAQ, the US OTC market is now trading in London. [3] Now, it is only options that are traded on the Stock Exchange floor (9.05am – 3.40pm), with all equity dealing taking place from offices.

United States of America

Exchanges include Boston, Mid-West (in Chicago), New York (NYSE), Pacific (the result of integrating Los Angeles and San Fransisco exchanges) and Philadelphia. There is also the US OTC market, NASDAQ[1] (founded in 1938), which has grown very quickly in recent years. NYSE's position as the largest exchange is under threat from NASDAQ at its current rate of growth; NASDAQ's 1984 volume was four times that in 1980, whereas NYSE barely doubled in the same time period. At present, NASDAQ averages over 75% of NYSE's daily volume, but has. on occasions surpassed it.

The NYSE system of trading is by auction, controlled and held together by "specialists", who are assigned about six stocks each. Specialists risk their own funds to buy and sell for accounts to satisfy supply and demand. Specialists also execute deals for brokers, for which they are paid a fee.

The NASDAQ system is essentially a telephone market, or through an electronic order execution system, introduced in 1984. Any stock to have satisfied NASDAQ's requirements for entry may be traded, and dealers are not restricted in the variety of stocks they wish to trade. NASDAQ companies are resisting becoming listed on NYSE, or any other US exchange, despite efforts by the exchanges to recruit them. By comparison, in London, the equivalent of NASDAQ, the OTC, is considered a stepping stone to full listing.

Notes: [1] NASDAQ is an acronym for National Association of Dealers in Securities Automated Quotation.

West Germany

West Germany has eight exchanges, but Frankfurt and Dusseldorf together account for over 80% of the total turnover for the West German exchanges. All exchanges are linked, and, as the rules and regulations of each exchange are almost identical, they can be thought of as separate floors of one single exchange.

Trading activity is largely dominated by banks and credit institutions, alongside independent intermediate dealers, with membership compulsory. Almost 90% of securities transactions are handled by the commercial sections of major banks. Foreign-owned banks are also eligible for membership; in Frankfurt, 20% of members are foreign-owned.

Two distinct markets are traded: the official and the unofficial. These two may, in turn, be sub-divided.

1. *The Official Market* All bonds and equities admitted to official listing by each exchange's listing committee. These may be sub-divided thus:

i. *Single Quotation* (Non-Continuous Trading) Each listed security has a single quotation price, eastablished for each trading session. There is a fixed amount of business in each equity, governed by the exchange, and this matches the maximum amount of bid and offer orders which may be cleared at that price. The Comerzbank has termed this the "principle of maximum turnover".

ii. *Continuous Quotation* Shares traded on single quotation may gain approval to be traded continuously as prices change throughout the trading session (11.30am − 1.30pm).

2. *The Unofficial Market*

i. *Regulated Unofficial Dealing* This title is something of a misnomer, "regulated free market" would make more sense. Securities may be traded if they are not suitable for listing, or if they are already listed on another Stock Exchange in West Germany. The Committee for Unlisted Securities regulates dealing. Only banks and independent intermediate dealers may trade unofficially.

ii. *Unregulated Unofficial Dealing* Securities traded under this heading are unlisted, and have not been approved for regulated unofficial dealing. Dealings may still take place in official hours, however.

Business hours local: 11.30am − 1.30pm
GMT:12.30am − 2.30pm

Settlement Securities are hardly ever physically delivered. The clearing system is computerized and centralized, and works on a credit/debit system.

347

Major Stock Indexes of the World

Australia

30 All Ordinaries Index

Known as "All Ords", it is the index most carefully watched by Australian traders and the world alike. As its name suggests, it charts 30 blue chip stocks. Other indexes for Australian markets include the 50 Leaders, 20 Leaders and the All Industrials.

Hong Kong

Hang Seng Index

The volatility of the Hong Kong market is more than adequately displayed by this index. It equates to approximately 66% of the market value of shares traded. 33 companies make up the index, with a heavy property sector bias.

Japan

Nikkei-Dow Index

Also known as the Nikkei 225. Abroad-based index, quoting 225 companies, but with a large representation from the financial sector. A 35-40% weighting in this sector means that the index moves significantly on the back of movements among the financials.

Singapore

Straits Times Index

A purely arithmetic index without capitalization weighting, made up from industrial sector shares. The Straits Times index is considered as having equal indicative value to the OCBC Index (below). It also takes into account some Malaysian stocks, and thus is also indicative of trends in the Malaysian stock market.

OCBC Index (Overseas Chinese Banking Corporation)

A traditionally weighted index consisting of industrials and financials.

United Kingdom

FT 30 (Financial Times)

Records the movements of the 30 leading blue chip industrial stocks.

FT All Share Index

As its name suggests, an index charting all listed UK shares. Its use is now diminishing somewhat, because it is considered unwieldy in size, and because of its propensity to generate "number-crunching".

FTSE 100

Commonly known as "FOOTSIE", it is considered to be the most indicative of the three London indexes, in that it gives a fairer indication of activity as well as market buoyancy. It equates approximately 70% of the value of listed shares.

United States of America

Dow Jones Industrial Average

The most widely-consulted US index, although it only lists 30 blue chip industrial stocks.

Standard and Poors 500

Shares on this index equate to approximately 80% of the market value of NYSE listed stocks, and is considered by many to have more indicative value than the Dow Jones Industrial Average.

World Standard Times

The following is a table of selected major cities, with the time difference + or − GMT. Flight times are approximate to the nearest half hour, from London. Where there is more than one figure quoted for number of stops, the lower figure is taken to calculate flight times. Times are only approximate and exact times should be checked with the relevant carrier.

Country	Time hours (+ or − GMT)	Flight times (approx.)	Stops
Amsterdam	+1	1	−
Athens	+2	2	−
Auckland	+12	28	2
Baghdad	+3	7	0/1
Bangkok	+7	15	1
Beijing	+8	16	1/2
Belgrade	+1	2	−
Bombay	+5	8	−
Bonn	+1	1	−
Brussels	+1	1	−
Cairo	+2	4	−
Calcutta	+5	17	3/4
Cape Town	+2	12	1/0
Caracas	−4	10	1
Chicago	−6	8	−
Copenhagen	+1	2	−
Dar-es-Salaam	+3	9	1
Delhi	+5	8	0/2
Dublin	GMT	1	−
Helsinki	+2	3	−
Hong Kong	+8	12	0/1
Johannesburg	+2	12	0/1
Karachi	+5	9	1/2
Kuala Lumpur	+8	14	1/2
Kuwait	+3	6	0/1

Country	Time hours (+ or − GMT)	Flight times (approx.)	Stops
Lisbon	GMT	2	–
Los Angeles	−8	11	–
Lyon	GMT	1	–
Madrid	+1	2	–
Malaga	GMT	2	–
Montreal	−5	7	–
Moscow	+3	4	–
Muscat	+4	6	0/1
Nairobi	+3	7	–
New York	−5	8	–
Paris	+1	1	–
Perth	+8	19	–
Rio de Janeiro	−3	10	–
Rome	+1	2	–
San Francisco	−8	10	0/1
Singapore	+8	12	0/1
Stockholm	+1	2	–
Sydney	+10	21	1/2
Tokyo	+9	10	0/1
Vancouver	−8	11	1
Vienna	+1	2	–
Warsaw	+1	2	–
Washington	−5	8	-

Top Twenty European Companies

Turnover figures are quoted in £m sterling, to the nearest £10m. All figures are up to date to March 1987, with no full accounts published after that date included. No preliminary or interim figures are used. For foreign companies, results for the year 1986 were used. All exchange rates are calculated on the following basis:

France (F)	9.8184	The Netherlands (NL)	3.3134
West Germany (D)	2.9427	Switzerland (CH)	2.4425
Italy (I)	2133.1400		

Note [1] Parent company only

1 **British Petroleum** (UK) Oil
Knightsbridge
London SW7
01-581-3050
Turnover: 34,250

2 **Royal Dutch Petroleum Company** (NL) Holding co., oil & gas exploration & production
PO Box 162
2501 AN The Hague
010-3170-779111
Turnover: 33,330

3 **Ente Nazionale Idrocarburi** (I) Holding co., petroleum, chemicals, mechanical construction, etc.
Piazzale Enrico Mattei
00144 Rome
010-396-5900
Turnover: 25,330

4 **Daimler-Benz AG** (D) Motor vehicle and engine manufacture
Tempel Strasse 6
Bonn
010-49-228-269090
Turnover: 22,260

5 **Shell Transport and Trading** (UK)   Oil
Shell Centre
York Road
London SE1 7NA
01-934-1234
Turnover: 22,220

6 **Instituto per la Ricostruzione Industriale** (I)
89 VV Veneto   State holding
Rome   company
010-396-47271
Turnover: 21,050

7 **Volkswagen AG** (D)   Motor vehicle
Wolfsburg   manufacture
Niedersachs 3180
010-49-536190
Turnover: 17,940

8 **Deutsche Bundespost** (D)   Postal &
2 Dreizehnmorgenweg   telecommunications
Bonn   services
010-49-228-8053
Turnover: 16,870

9 **Philips Lamp Holding** (NL)   Electrical &
NV Philips   electronic products
Gloeilampenfabrieken
Eindhoven
010-3140-791111
Turnover: 16,610

10 **Siemens AG** (D)   Electrical & general
Nonnendammallee 101   engineering,
Berlin 1000   electronics
010-4930-3861
Turnover: 15,980

11 **Nestlé SA** (CH)   Holding co.,
1800 Vevey   chocolate, milk &
01021-51-01-12   food products
Turnover: 15,580

12 **Bayer AG** (D)   Chemical products
   Bayerwerk
   Leverkusen NRW 5090
   010-49-214-301
   Turnover: 13,850

13 **BASF AG** (D)   Chemicals, plastics
   Carl-Busch Strasse 39   manufacture
   Ludwigshafen 6700
   010-496-21601
   Turnover: 13,750

14 **Fiat SpA** (I)   Holding co., motor
   Corso Agnelli 200   vehicle manufacture
   Turin
   TO 10135
   010-3911-65651
   Turnover: 13,750

15 **Veba AG** (D)   Holding co.,
   Karl-Arnold Platz 3   electricty,
   Dusseldorf   minerals, oil,
   NRW 4000   chemicals, glass,
   010-49211-45791   etc.
   Turnover: 13,640

16 **BAT Industries** (UK)   Tobacco, retailing,
   Windsor House   paper, packaging,
   Victoria Street   etc.
   London SW1
   01-222-7979
   Turnover: 13,620

17 **Electricité de France**[1] (F)   Electricity supply
   2 Rue Louis Murat
   Paris
   0101-331-42266666
   Turnover: 13,390

18   **Hoechst AG** (D)   Chemicals, dyes and
     Brueningstrasse   plastics manufacture
     Frankfurt 6230
     010-4969-3050
     Turnover: 12,920

19   **Société Nationale Elf-Aquitaine** (F)   Holding co., oil,
     La Defense 6   petroleum, natural
     Courbevoie   gas, sulphur
     Hauts-de-Seine 92400
     010-331-4744-4546
     Turnover: 12,190

20   **Renault** (F)   Motor vehicle
     8-10 Avenue Emile Zola   manufacture
     Boulogne Billancourt
     Hauts-de-Seine
     010-331-4609-9433
     Turnover: 11,340

Top Twenty UK Companies

Turnover figures are quoted in £m sterling, to the nearest £10m. All figures are up to date to March 1987, with no full accounts published after that date included. No preliminary or interim figures are used.

1 **British Petroleum Co**. Oil
  Knightsbridge
  London SW7
  01-581-3050
  Turnover: 34,250

2 **Shell Trading and Transport**[1] Oil
  Shell Centre
  York Road
  London SE1 7NA
  01-934-1234
  Turnover: 22,220

3 **BAT Industries** Tobacco, retailing,
  Windsor House paper, packaging,
  Victoria Street etc.
  London SW1
  01-222-7979
  Turnover: 13,620

4 **Central Electricity Generating Board** Electricity supply
  15 Newgate Street
  London EC1 7AU
  01-634-5111
  Turnover: 10,740

5 **Imperial Chemical Industries** Petrochemicals,
  Imperial Chemical House pharmaceuticals,
  Millbank etc.
  London SW1
  01-834-4444
  Turnover: 10,140

6 **S & W Berisford**
1 Prescot Street
London E1
01-481-9144
Turnover: 9,700

Merchanting &
commodity trading,
etc.

7 **British Telecommunications**
British Telecom Centre
81 Newgate Street
London EC1A 7AJ
01-356-5000
Turnover: 8,390

Telecommunications
services

8 **ESSO UK** [2]
Esso House
Victoria Street
London SW1
01-834-6677
Turnover: 8,380

Oil

9 **British Gas Corporation**
Rivermill House
152 Grosvenor Road
London SW1
01-821-1444
Turnover: 7,690

Gas supply

10 **Shell UK** [3]
The Strand
London WC2
01-257-3000
Turnover: 6,570

Oil

11 **Unilever**
Unilever House
Blackfriars
London EC4 4BQ
01-822-5252
Turnover: 5,950

Food products,
detergents, etc.

12 **British Coal**   Coal mining
    Hobart House
    Grosvenor Place
    London SW1X 7AE
    01-235-2020
    Turnover: 5,340

13 **Grand Metropolitan**   Hotel proprietors,
    11 Hanover Square   milk products,
    London W1   brewers
    01-629-7488
    Turnover: 5,290

14 **General Electric Company**   Heavy industrial,
    1 Stanhope Gate   electrical products,
    London W1   etc.
    01-493-8484
    Turnover: 5,250

15 **Dalgety plc**   Intenational
    19 Hanover Square   merchants
    London W1R 9DA
    01-499-7712
    Turnover: 4,900

16 **Ford Motor Company**[2]   Motor vehicle
    Eagle Way   manufacturers
    Brentwood
    Essex
    0277-253000
    Turnover: 4,370

17 **Hanson Trust**   Industrial services,
    1 Grosvenor Place   food products, etc.
    London SW1
    01-245-1245
    Turnover: 4,310

18 **Phibro Salomon**[2]   Commodity brokers,
    Victoria Plaza   etc.

111 Buckingham Palace Road
London SW1W 0SL
01-721-4000
Turnover: 4,300

19 **Marks and Spencer plc**   General store
   Michael House   proprietors
   Baker Street
   London W1A 1ON
   01-935-4422
   Turnover: 4,220

20 **BTR**   Construction
   Silvertown House   engineering
   Vincent Square
   London SW1P 2PL
   01-834-3848
   Turnover: 4,020

Notes : [1]Figures for Shell Trading and Transport are based on 40% of the Royal Dutch/Shell Group. [2]Country of control: USA. [3]Country of control: The Netherlands.

Notes

Top Twenty US Companies

Turnover figures are quoted in £m sterling, to the nearest £10m. All figures are up to date to year end 1986, with no full accounts published after that date included. No preliminary or interim figures are used. Exchange rates are calculated on the basis of £sterling = $1.60825.

1 **General Motors**
   767 5th Avenue
   New York
   NY 10153
   0101-212-418-6100
   Turnover: 63,930

   Motor vehicle
   manufacture

2 **Exxon Corporation**
   Rockerfeller Centre
   New York
   0101-212-333-1000
   Turnover: 46,630

   Crude oil & natural
   gas

3 **Ford Motor Company**
   The American Road
   Dearborn
   MI 48121
   0101-313-322-3000
   Turnover: 39,000

   Motor vehicle
   manufacture

4 **International Business Machines**
   590 Madison Avenue
   New York
   NY 10022
   0101-212-735-7000
   Turnover: 31,870

   Electronics,
   computer manufacture

5 **Mobil Corporation**   Holding Co.,
   150 E 42nd Street   integrated energy
   New York   operations
   NY 10017
   0101-212-883-4242
   Turnover: 27,900

6 **Sears, Roebuck and Company**   Retailing
   Sears Tower
   Chicago
   IL 60684
   0101-312-875-2500
   Turnover: 27,530

7 **General Electric Company**   Power system
   3135 Easton Turnpike   manufacture,
   Fairfield   consumer energy
   CT 06431
   0101-203-373-2431
   Turnover: 21,890

8 **American Telephone & Telegraph
   Company**   Telephone systems
   550 Madison Avenue
   New York
   NY 10022
   0101-212-605-5500
   Turnover: 21,200

9 **Texaco Incorporated**   Integrated oil
   2000 Westchester Avenue
   White Plains
   NY 10650
   0101-914-253-4000
   Turnover: 19,660

10 **EI Dupont de Nemours & Company**   Diversified energy
   1007 Market Street
   Wilmington
   DE 19898
   0101-302-774-1000
   Turnover: 16,900

11 **Chevron Corporation**   Integrated petroleum
   225 Bush Street
   San Francisco
   CA 94104-4289
   0101-415-894-7700
   Turnover: 16,320

12 **Philip Morris Incorporated**   Holding co.,
   120 Park Avenue   tobacco, beer, food
   New York   products
   NY 10017
   0101-212-880-5000
   Turnover: 15,800

13 **K Mart Corporation**   Discount store
   3100 W Big Beaver Road   operators
   Truy
   MI 48084
   0101-313-643-1000
   Turnover: 14,800

14 **Chrysler Corporation**   Motor vehicle
   12000 Chrysler Drive   manufacture
   Highland Park
   MI 48203
   0101-313-956-5252
   Turnover: 14,040

15 **Amoco Corporation**   Holding co., oil,
   200 E Randolph Drive   etc.
   Chicago
   IL 60601
   0101-312-856-6111
   Turnover: 11,370

16 **Kroger Corporation**   Supermarket
   1014 Vine Street   operators
   Cincinnati
   OH 45202
   0101-513-762-4000
   Turnover: 10,650

17 **Shell Oil Company**
   One Shell Plaza
   Houston
   TX 77002
   0101-713-241-4085
   Turnover: 10,470

   Holding co., oil &
   gas products

18 **Boeing Company**
   Boeing Intl Corp
   PO Box 3707
   Seattle
   WA 98124
   0101-206-655-2121
   Turnover: 10,160

   Aircraft manufacture

19 **RJR Nabisco Inc**
   RJR Worldwide HQ
   Reynolds Blvd
   Winston-Salem
   NL 27102
   0101-919-773-2000
   Turnover: 9,940

   Tobacco, food &
   beverage manufacture

20 **United Technologies Corporation**
   United Technology Building
   Hartford
   CT 06101
   0101-203-728-7000
   Turnover: 9,740

   Aircraft equipment
   manufacture

Weights and Measures

Imperial System

Basic units are the foot (ft), pound (lb) and second (sec).

Linear: 12 inches (in) = 1 foot (ft)
3 feet (ft) = 1 yard (yd)
5 yards (yd) = 1 pole
22 yards (yd) = 1 chain (= 4 poles)
220 yards(yd) = 1 furlong (= 10 chains)
1,760 yards (yd) = 1 mile (= 8 furlongs; = 5,280 feet)

Nautical: 6 feet = 1 fathom
120 fathoms = 1 cable (= 720 feet)
5,080 feet = 1 nautical mile (6,076.1 ft International and US)
3 nautical miles = 1 league (= 3.456 statute miles)
60 nautical miles = 1 degree
(a speed of 1 nautical mile per hour = 1 knot)

Square: 144 square inches (sq in) = 1 square foot (sq ft)
9 square feet (sq ft) = 1 square yard (sq yd)
30 square yards (sq yd) = 1 perch
40 perches = 1 rood
4 roods = 1 acre (= 4,840 sq yd)
640 acres = 1 square mile (sq mile)

Capacity: 4 gills = 1 pint (= 20 fluid ounces)
2 pints = 1 quart (= 40 fl oz)
4 quarts = 1 gallon (= 160 fl oz)
2 gallons = 1 peck
8 gallons = 1 bushel (= 4 pecks)
8 bushels = 1 quarter (= 64 gallons)
1 barrel (oil) = 50.4 gallons (= 42 US gallons)

Capacity (Apothecaries'):

        60 minims = 1 fluid drachm

        8 drachms = 1 fluid ounce

        16 fluid ounces = 1 pint

        8 pints = 1 gallon

Weight (Avoirdupois):

        27.344 grains = 1 dram (7,000 grains = 1 pound)

        16 drams = 1 ounce (oz)

        16 ounces (oz) = 1 pound (lb)

        14 pounds (lb) = 1 stone

        2 stones = 1 quarter (= 28 pounds)

        4 quarters = 1 hundredweight (cwt) (= 112 pounds)

Weight (Apothecaries')

        20 grains = 1 scruple

        3 scruples = 1 drachm

        8 drachms = 1 ounce

US Units (Customary Units)

As Imperial except for:

        1 pint = 16 fluid ounces (= 0.8 Imperial pints)

        2 pints = 1 quart (= 32 fluid ounces; 0.8 Imperial quarts)

        4 quarts = 1 gallon (= 128 fluid ounces; 0.8 Imperial gallons)

        1 ton = 2,000 pounds (= 0.8939 long, or Imperial, tons)

Conversion factors

Imperial to metric:

	To convert		Multiply by
Length:	inches	to millimetres	25.4
	inches	to centimetres	2.54
	inches	to metres	0.254
	feet	to centimetres	30.48
	feet	to metres	0.3048
	yards	to metres	0.9144
	miles	to kilometres	1.6093

Appendices

Area:	square inches	to square centimetres	6.4516
	square feet	to square metres	0.0929
	square yards	to square metres	0.8316
	square miles	to square kilometres	2.5898
	acres	to hectares	0.4047
	acres	to square kilometres	0.00405

Volume:	cubic inches	to cubic centimetres	16.3871
	cubic feet	to cubic metres	0.0283
	cubic yards	to cubic metres	0.7646
	cubic miles	to cubic kilometres	4.1678

Liquid:	fluid ounces	to millilitres	28.5
	pints	to millilitres	568.0 (473.32 for US pints)
	pints	to litres	0.568 (0.4733 for US pints)
	gallons	to litres	4.55 (3.785 for US gallons)

Weight	ounces	to grams	28.3495
	pounds	to grams	453.592
	pounds	to kilograms	0.4536
	pounds	to tonnes	0.0004536
	tons	to tonnes	1.0161

Metric to Imperial:

	To convert		Multiply by
Length:	millimetres	to inches	0.03937
	centimetres	to inches	0.3937
	centimetres	to feet	0.032808
	metres	to inches	39.37
	metres	to feet	3.2808
	metres	to yards	1.0936
	kilometres	to miles	0.6214
Area:	square centimetres	to square inches	0.1552
	square metres	to square feet	10.7636

	square metres	to square yards	1.196
	square kilometres	to square miles	0.3861
	square kilometres	to acres	247.1
	hectares	to acres	2.471
Volume:	cubic centimetres	to cubic inches	0.1552
	cubic metres	to cubic feet	35.315
	cubic metres	to cubic yards	1.308
	cubic kilometres	to cubic miles	0.2399
Capacity:	millilitres	to fluid ounces	0.0351
	millilitres	to pints	0.00176 (0.002114 for US pints)
	litres	to pints	1.760 (2.114 for US pints)
	litres	to gallons	0.2193 (0.2643 for US gallons)
Weight:	grams	to ounces	0.0352
	grams	to pounds	0.0022
	kilograms	to pounds	2.2046
	tonnes	to pounds	2204.59
	tonnes	to tons	0.9842 (1.1023 for US, or short, tons)

Zip Codes

The names of American states are commonly abbreviated in two ways. First there is the normal state abbreviation. Second, there is the standard abbreviation for postal purposes. This is known as the ZIP (Zoning Improvement Plan) code, and normally appears as two letters indicating the state, followed by five numerals, *e.g.* NY 10016, indicates central New York state.

State	Abbreviation	ZIP code
Alabama	Ala.	AL
Alaska	-	AK
Arizona	Ariz.	AZ
Arkansas	Ark.	AR
California	Calif.	CA
Colorado	Colo.	CO
Connecticut	Conn.	CT
Delaware	Del.	DE
Florida	Fla.	FL
Georgia	Ga.	GA
Hawaii	-	HI
Idaho	Ida.	ID
Illinois	Ill.	IL
Indiana	Ind.	IN
Iowa	Ia.	IA
Kansas	Kans.	KA
Kentucky	KY. or Ken.	KY
Louisiana	La.	LA
Maine	Me.	ME
Maryland	Md.	MD
Massachusetts	Mass.	MA
Michigan	Mich.	MI
Minnesota	Minn.	MN
Mississippi	Miss.	MS

State	Abbreviation	ZIP code
Missouri	Mo.	MO
Montana	Mont.	MT
Nebraska	Nebr. or Neb.	NE
Nevada	Nev.	NV
New Hampshire	N.H.	NH
New Jersey	N.J.	NJ
New Mexico	N. Mex. or N.M.	NM
New York	N.Y.	NY
North Carolina	N.C.	NC
North Dakota	N. Dak. or N.D.	ND
Ohio	O.	OH
Oklahoma	Okla.	OK
Oregon	Ore. or Oreg.	OR
Pennsylvania	Pa. or Penn.	PA
Rhode Island	R.I.	RI
South Carolina	S.C.	SC
South Dakota	S.D.	SD
Tennessee	Tenn.	TN
Texas	Tex.	TX
Utah	Ut.	UT
Vermont	Vt.	VT
Virginia	Va.	VA
Washington	Wash.	WA
West Virginia	W. Va.	WV
Wisconsin	Wis.	WI
Wyoming	Wyo.	WY